Swimming and Dolphins

A 42.5 Year Journey in Education

By
K. R. Miller

Strategic Book Publishing and Rights Co.

Strategic Book Publishing and Rights Co., LLC
USA | Singapore
www.sbpra.com

For information about special discounts for bulk purchases, please contact Strategic Book Publishing and Rights Co., LLC, Special Sales, at bookorder@sbpra.net.

ISBN: 978-1-68181-683-8

•

Contents

Acknowledgments

To all the students, teachers, administrators, and parents who brought a myriad of opportunities and challenges that enriched my knowledge and experience day after day.

To my parents who encouraged me to follow my dreams and gave me the moral compass to do the right thing.

Last but not least, to Maria Capella-Miller, my wife of many years, who was instrumental during the development and completion of this book. Without her assistance, counsel, determination, and hard work, this book would have not been possible.

Introduction

by Maria Capella-Miller

I know by heart the stories that you are about to read. I lived some of them when Ken and I decided to tie the knot. We internalized that, for our partnership to succeed, we had to work as a team; therefore, we became involved in each other's careers. Ken told his employers, "You are getting two for the price of one." Growing personally and professionally together is a subject for another book. This time we decided to write some of Ken's stories for the variety of subjects he portrays as a seasoned educator and the lessons he can share as a leader. Be prepared to smile when you read some of them, only because Ken was born with a sense of humor that can deescalate tense and serious situations.

I never met Ken's mother. She went to heaven before Ken and I blended our lives together, but her memory was always alive, not only because of his love and admiration for her, but also because of the many stories that Ken's siblings—Sharon, Susie, and Leff—shared. Ken was a peacemaker, a quality that he inherited from his mother. I had the pleasure of knowing Ken's father, a true artist and an intelligent man with many interests. Photography was one of them, and wherever he went, he carried his camera and developed the most amazing pictures ever. I treasure the nurturing relationship we had from the time we met to the time he departed, not only because he became part of my new family, but also due to the similarities that I saw between father and son, including kindness, gentleness, respect, and consideration for others and being a man of his word. The story of the Forbidden Planet illustrates how extraordinary Ken's dad was at keeping his promises. Mother and father both helped Ken become the man he blossomed into as an adult, which is why they are remembered in the first part of this book.

Ken protected and was an advocate for the underdog. He was bullied as a child, especially during the time he stuttered, a temporary disability that disappeared, not through the intervention of a physician, but through a thoughtful strategy implemented by his fourth-grade teacher. When he became an administrator, he was able to incorporate anti-bullying programs, including the NBA (No Bullies Allowed), in which students chosen to be School Ambassadors were trained to intervene on behalf of other students.

Some say that leaders are born. Ken's abilities as a leader began showing at an early age. When he was in eighth grade, he ran for student body president. He lost the election, but he learned a valuable lesson: You have to identify what motivates people and understand their interests and beliefs before they will step up to follow you. As a traffic boy, he took the responsibility to protect other students while they crossed the streets. The story of the giant rat tells how he encountered his own fears and learned that leaders don't leave their posts, even though that's what he did. Leaders make sure that everybody is safe before thinking about their own safety.

He began paying attention to finances and the laws of supply, demand, and opportunities when he was in eighth grade, coming back from the Santa Cruz Boardwalk, when, for the first and last time in his life, he experienced a demotion.

Due to rejections, he met Shorty Shortridge. Connecting with him confirmed the concept that "when one door closes, another one opens." This is a story of inclusion. Ken never forgot those teachers who made a difference in his life; teachers such as Mr. Mathew, who delivered his lessons using a combination of factual and fun activities. He inspired Ken to become a history teacher. Brother D. taught him the value of integrity and trust—how easy it is to lose them, and how difficult it is to regain them.

From people who demeaned others and put them down, Ken learned what not to do as a leader. "You have played your last game," were the exact words of one of his coaches, and, even though his words made a negative impact in that moment, with determination and a drive to do well, Ken made them the beginning of his sports success.

The harsh jobs he held during college made him realize that education was the key to bigger and better opportunities. Among them was the cannery job, which created awareness about manager and employee relationships and how the product can become more important than the people. The incident with the library boys taught Ken that intimidation in the workplace and fear of retaliation can prevent an employee from doing her job. It also served as a cautionary tale of resources vandalized due to idleness.

Ken comes from the generation that learned how to work hard during the summer to earn money for the purpose of attending college; planning for the future is a habit that has never left him to this day. The book *Goodbye*

Mr. Chips by James Hilton and the movie *Up the Down Staircase*, based on the novel by Bell Kaufman, inspired him not to depart from his true vocation to be an educator and to inspire others to never give up. Cody was his first exposure to this concept, and Ken helped him to find his true potential. From then on, the cases multiplied by hundreds of students that gained self-esteem and flourished under Ken's influence.

Life events happen too fast from time to time. At the age of twenty-three, Ken became a teacher of students who were only five years younger than he. He had to build credibility with them even though they seemed like peers. He made a point of letting them know that he cared about them.

During his first semester as a teacher, he became an assistant swimming coach to help the school district cover this position. Ken didn't know how to swim, but this was how he approached challenges with a positive attitude that pushed him to go further in his career. One of the students he coached won first place in swimming competitions that year. An older teacher became his mentor, and that's how Flexible Milt became an important part of his professional growth, as Milt gave Ken the right answers at the right time.

Through his career, Ken practiced and perfected many skills that can only be learned with the territory—giving opportunities for growth to those under his supervision; helping and supporting students, teachers, and staff; living life by principles; following the golden rule and the platinum rule too; paying attention to his hunches and intuition; listening and sharpening his communication for better understanding of people and situations; forgiving without forgetting, because forgiving brings peace of mind, but remembering (and learning from the situation) solidifies experience. He found in his path wonderful and positive people as well as those who played games and were negative and defiant, the ones with hidden motives, double standards, and even a few who reincarnated from the seventeenth century. He treated each of them with gentleness, and in this book, he relates some experiences that were hurtful and painful when they occurred. The title of this book represents all of them. Sharks and dolphins co-exist in the same oceans, but sharks are predators, whereas dolphins work in teams and live in harmony. Ken was able to swim with both throughout his career.

Teacher, coach, activities director, assistant principal, principal, and superintendent, Ken did it all. Throughout the journey, he dealt with pets, termites, ant infestations, swallows, gophers, lice, and the media, as well as student tardiness, smoking policies, graffiti, weapons, drugs, and the police. He had to respond to parents, the board of education, and the community and negotiate with lawyers and unions. I often compared his day-to-day performance in his career to that of a juggler who cannot drop any of the balls, or an octopus with each tentacle grasping important matters that changed from day to day, as there are no same days in the life of a school administrator. Ken's agenda was always full, not with an eight-to-five job, but with one that began at seven in the morning and ended late at night with the extra-curricular activities that even absorbed Saturdays and Sundays.

The art of delegation is a quality of a good leader, which was how writing the monthly school bulletin became one of my contributions. After defining the three main points he wanted to emphasize, my keyboard was used at a fast speed. I was part of school art committees and bilingual programs. Together, we attended fundraiser auctions, school festivals, and parades. After a phone call at two and sometimes three in the morning from the sheriff because the school alarm had gone off or vandals had started a fire at one of the facilities, just to mention a few of the incidents, Ken rushed to the school and I worried until he came back. After all, the news pictured terrible tragedies that targeted students, school personnel, and administrators. Yet, I wouldn't change anything from that life together.

I could repeat each of the stories in this book with my eyes closed, as I've heard them many times. Now they are yours too. Even though this is a non-fiction book, it would be an impossible task to reproduce the exact wording that was used forty, thirty, twenty, or ten years ago in the narration of the events. This compilation of memories fades more and more as the years pass by; they are Ken's recollection of what transpired. After his forty-two and a half years in the field of education resolving issues, making life easier for others, and inspiring them to motivate themselves, Kenny Wonder, the Dreamer, the Prince of PIGDOM, the gentle person that I respect and adore, asked me to write this introduction.

1: Molding Character

In Gratitude to All Elementary School Teachers

"Don't judge each day by the harvest you reap, but by the seeds that you plant."

--Robert Louis Stevenson

When one decides to write about his life, the beginning has immeasurable relevance, and in my case, my early years shaped the man that I would become. As a child, we are hopefully loved and cherished. One day, we are sent into a school full of strangers smiling at us and a room with twenty kids with new faces, a world for which we are supposed to be ready.

Compared to much of what you hear these days in the news, I had a good childhood and the good fortune of having two loving and dedicated parents. My father, a native of San Francisco, was a commercial photographer for Moulon Studios and master photographer for the San Francisco *Chronicle* and Richmond *Independent*. Every moment of our family life was recorded in pictures and films. If you ask my siblings, they would say their memories are rich, not because of a great sense of retention, but thanks to the treasured pictures that our father took of all of us. Birthdays, Christmas, Easter, and even buying new cars, all important occasions were recorded during times when technology barely existed.

My dad loved the smell of new cars. My mother rolled

her eyes every time he surprised us with a new car, and, to my recollection, there were many. Why did he keep doing that? Well, my father never did anything in a small way.

I remember he wanted to have a small fish tank. Guppies, I believe, were the original diminutive inhabitants of it. Before long, we had tanks in every room and began raising brine shrimp to feed the hordes. My mother put her foot down, and it worked for a while, but my father began again in a new direction.

Trains! The attic became a regular railroad station. I could hear the conductor at all hours calling the upcoming stops. Once again, my mother prevailed, and, as the trains exited, the airplanes arrived.

My father had a passion for anything that had to do with flight. He told me how, as a young boy, he remembered the historic event when Charles Lindbergh flew nonstop from America to Paris in thirty-three hours in 1927! The airplane fetish became more than a hobby. It started small just like the fish and the trains, but somehow, as usual, my father had grander plans.

Before it was over, he went from building model planes to building a full size glider on our dining room table.

My mother had to have the perfect job, that of being a saint, to deal with his indulgences. Often we needed school clothes while my father was engaging in one of the hobbies that, to our understanding, were more important to him. He even used his vacation time to go to the mountains to hike alone. I tried it once but got mountain sickness and came down the mountain lying on the back of a burro—not my father's greatest memory of my attempt to follow in his steps, nor mine.

There were many fun times growing up, too. The movies are there to keep the moments alive. Christmas at my nana's house was always a highlight. She was an amazing, well read, cultured woman who always pushed us to read and to strive to go to college. Easter was fun too. We used to collect and hide lemons because we had a lemon tree in our backyard loaded with big oval yellow balls during the months of March and April.

When I was five, I disturbed a nest of bees, and they chased me all the way home. This was almost as traumatic as the time my dad was carving a small airplane while listening to the radio in the years before television. Radio programs back then depended on dramatic music to set the suspense. He was listening to a drama called "The Whistler." It started with an eerie music track, and when the music escalated to a shocking tone, my dad lost control of the knife and stabbed his leg. Off to the hospital we flew in our new 1950 Ford with my dad sitting in the back, me sitting in the front passenger seat, and my mother driving and yelling at him: "Are you okay? Don't get any blood on the carpet of the new car!"

I was the oldest of four: two boys and two girls. The pictures tell stories of love and affection. My father, a true artist, worked painstakingly on our Christmas cards each year, creating new themes each time. Everyone loved the Miller cards!

I loved to go to the movies with my friends on Saturdays. We were too young to own a car and didn't mind taking the bus. To see two full-length movies, we paid seventy-five cents back then. I was a traffic boy at school, and one of the advantages of being a traffic boy was to enjoy a free movie ticket, popcorn, and Coke. When

I was a teenager, going to the movies was one of the biggest treats I had, especially science fiction movies.

When I was in eighth grade, I struggled with reading. My teacher asked, "Kenny, what type of reading do you like?"

"Science fiction," I said, "but the books are too long."

She brought me a book of 300 short stories, all science fiction. I read and read and read without worrying about the length of the book. I was forever hooked.

There was a much-anticipated film called *Forbidden Planet*. I was excited to see it. My dad made an unusual promise to take me to see the movie, but he got busy and forgot about it. When it came back to his mind, he kept promising. However, time passed, and so did the movie. When it left the theaters, I knew I would never see it. I was disappointed, and even though I tried to let it go, it remained in my young mind for a while as something unsettled that brought negative feelings whenever I thought about it.

Two years later my dad said we needed to go somewhere to shop. By that time, I had completely forgotten about the movie. When we arrived at the oldest theater in town, I saw on the marquee the name *Forbidden Planet*. Two years had passed, and he remembered his promise and my disappointment. He made a point to take me to see the movie! It was in an old theater with a peculiar odor far from where we lived, but to me it was the most beautiful place I had ever been in my father's company. It was also evidence of my dad's care and love. That day, I felt a stronger bond between us, for he was a man of his word, one that could deliver a promise that never aged.

My mother was one of the most wonderful women I have ever known. A native of Memphis, Tennessee, she had a beautiful smile, made us laugh, and was patient and kind. She always was concerned about others. I like to think I have been a lot like her. She worked for twenty years as an executive secretary with Mechanics Bank of Richmond. She was determined and a natural born leader. As a result, her intervention to help my father get back in touch with his real parents was instrumental.

My father developed asthma when he was young, and his parents asked his grandmother to raise him. When they tried to get him back at age thirteen, grandson and grandparents had already developed a strong bond. The matter had to be settled in court, with his having the final say: He wanted to stay with his grandparents.

This situation created hard feelings and distanced parents from grandparents for more than a decade until my dad met my mom. My mother was the stabilizer in the family. She became the catalyst, the one who reunited my dad with his real parents, and his parents with the grandparents that I knew and loved as a child.

I suffered from thumb sucking and stuttering. My elementary schooling cured me of both. When I began sucking my thumb the first day in kindergarten, the other students laughed at me. Unpleasant as it was, it helped me to finally quit sucking my thumb. My mother asked me what made me stop.

"I was embarrassed when the other kids laughed at me," I answered.

In essence, it was peer pressure at its best.

During my first three years of school, I was shy and afraid to speak in class. I never forgot how the students laughed at me in kindergarten that first day. By the time fourth grade began, I had a major problem with stuttering. When asked to speak, I had a difficult time talking without stuttering. The students' laughter made it worse despite the fact that the teachers always told them to stop.

My fourth grade teacher was my lifesaver. She pulled me aside that first week and said, "We are having a play in one month, and every student has to perform in front of the class."

I was terrified.

"Kenny, I want you to do a ventriloquist act."

She gave me a book on how to master the art of ventriloquism with a little puppet called Joey. I told her I would try hard. For one month, I practiced and practiced at home, and got pretty good at it.

On the day of the performance, I was very nervous but anxious to get started. When I appeared before the class, my first fear was that students were laughing under their breath. When I began, they became quiet. I could tell they were impressed. After the performance, the teacher asked the class to comment on my performance. I looked at her in disbelief. She smiled and winked at me. One boy said, "That was cool! The puppet Joey never stuttered like Kenny does."

"Remember, that was Kenny's voice. He doesn't stutter anymore," the teacher said.

The technique of slowing down one's speech to get the effect of being a ventriloquist had helped me. I was forever grateful to my fourth grade teacher for her wisdom and encouragement and for helping me beat my stuttering once and for all.

My mother was so happy that she went to see the teacher to express her gratitude. The teacher said, "Don't worry about Kenny. He will be just fine. He showed his internal resolve to overcome a handicap, and he was successful."

My mother never forgot what the teacher said, and every time I doubted myself, she reminded me of that kind and sweet teacher who knew how to inspire young people to reach their true potential and never give up.

2: Thoughts and Actions: The Great Earthquake of 1957

I followed rules most of the time, except one time in sixth grade. Living in the San Francisco Bay area, we always practiced for earthquakes. My grandmother often told me how unbelievable it had been to watch the great San Francisco earthquake in 1906 from across the bay.

"San Francisco was lighting up the sky with fire," she began. "Within hours, more than half of the city was destroyed. The news reported that more than three thousand people died."

She took a sip of her tea, and continued.

"I was a teenager, and was horrified by what I observed. The billows of smoke lasted for days before the fires were extinguished."

I was mesmerized. My grandmother was a great storyteller. She had the ability to engage you in the story and relive the experience with her.

Sister Mary, my sixth grade teacher, was a little nun who was so short that she needed a platform to stand on in the classroom, but she was a tiger. We were afraid of her. She always made the earthquake drills a priority. As kids, we laughed about it.

My best friend was a boy named Tom. He and I built tree forts and were always doing things together. He was also the rebel in our class. Our school was an old, two-story brick building with big cracks in it. We used to joke that if ever there were a real earthquake, the school would fall apart.

On the fateful day in 1957, we were silently reading at our desks when the whole building began to shake and rattle. It was like a swing going back and forth. We all knew it was the big one! We waited for Sister Mary to blow her gold whistle to signal us to get under our desks, but she was so flustered she couldn't blow a sound out of that whistle.

Tom suddenly yelled, "Let's get out of here before we get squished!"

I jumped out of my seat and ran out of the room and down the two flights of stairs with the building swaying back and forth the whole time. Once outside, Tom and I realized that we were the only ones who had left the building.

After the building stopped moving, the principal came outside and found us. We were in trouble. We spent many hours copying verses from the Bible as our punishment for not following the rules. Tom repeated to the principal, to me, and to whomever would listen, "If that building had crumbled, we would have been the only ones who would have gotten out alive."

The principal was not amused, but Tom was right.

My last year in elementary school was eventful for three big reasons: the election of student body officers, my final year as traffic boy, and the promotion to an all-boy Catholic high school.

The tryout for student body officers was a big deal. All

candidates ran for president, and the one with the most votes won, with the succeeding winners earning the seats of second vice president, treasurer, and secretary.

We each had a number. Mine was five. My posters read, "Rock to the jive, vote for number five." My mom helped me make posters on bright-colored, eight-and–a-half by eleven-inch paper. We stayed up most of the night making them. When I got to school and posted them, I saw that one of my competitors had wrapped the school with a sign that read, "Vote for number one and you'll get a free candy bar!" I was doomed. I was elected treasurer and had a great year balancing the books of the annual charity bazaar—good training for the future. My mother, bless her heart, said something that she had memorized in her path of doing good deeds. I found out later that the saying belonged to Edward Everett Hale: "I am only one, but I am one. I cannot do everything, but I can do something. And I will not let what I cannot do interfere with what I can do."

3: Run for Your Life

This was my final year as a traffic boy. Sixth through eighth grade students were trained to march and man traffic stops around the school and help students safely cross the intersections. All of the elementary schools in Berkeley had traffic boys. We were the original crossing guards! Each of us started as privates, and in eighth grade, we became sergeants. In sixth grade, we were all told the story of the giant rat. We were terrified every time we had duty at the corner of Mulberry Street near the church. The story was that the rat was as large as a dog. We kept our eyes on the church and had to be reminded to keep our eyes on the cars!

When I was an eighth grade sergeant, I told the same story to my unit. As we marched up the hill with our stop signs ready to do our duty, I could hear the sixth graders shaking their signs, hoping the giant rat wouldn't get them. I smiled and told them to stay focused.

When we arrived, I positioned the six boys on all the corners of the intersection surrounding the church.

I blew my whistle, which meant the privates were to take their stop signs to the street to block cars from passing while the young pedestrians crossed.

Just then, I saw a little sixth grader shaking his sign violently. He was trying to say something that sounded like "RARARARA."

He dropped his stop sign and ran away. I looked where he had been pointing and saw the largest rat I had ever seen sitting four feet from where I was standing. It was huge. The rat looked up from whatever it was chewing on, and it seemed as if we were eye to eye. I took off running, abandoning the post. It was chaos. The whole unit abandoned their posts, and I was in hot water!

The next day we all met with the chief of police in charge of the traffic boys. He told us we could have endangered the children by leaving the intersection unprotected. To this day, I am not sure they believed our story, as we were the only ones who saw the rat. However, there was that partially eaten candle that saved our jobs at least a little while.

4: Rugged Individualism, Opportunities, and Entrepreneurship

"A man who gives his children habits of industry provides for them better than by giving them fortune."

-- Richard Whately

The last saga with the traffic boys was very eventful. At the end of our eighth grade year, all of the traffic boys were given a graduation treat of going to Santa Cruz Beach for a day. All the students looked forward to the trip. We would board a train in Oakland and travel for roughly an hour and a half as it traversed through the Santa Cruz hills. All of us had worked for three years and couldn't wait to go. The trip was scheduled for the last week of the school year. This was also a rite of passage that signaled the completion of elementary school.

We saved our money month after month. I had about forty dollars to spend at the boardwalk in Santa Cruz. Most of my friends were taking about the same amount of cash. We were told to bring a backpack with food and beverages because we would be gone all day.

With great anticipation, we boarded the train for Santa Cruz at 8:00 a.m. The weather was hot, but we were told that the train was very comfortable, and we would be in Santa Cruz by 9:00 a.m. where we would have eight hours on the boardwalk. We were so excited. It was a dream becoming real.

I had survived the giant rat fiasco. Now, we were at the threshold of a fun and enjoyable closure to elementary school.

As we traveled through the Santa Cruz Mountains, I was mesmerized by the scenery—mountains, the pine trees, and different shades of green, radiant and vibrant, and far as the eye could see. I was enjoying this state of peace and relaxation when I heard the screeching of the train's brakes and a large banging sound. The train came to an abrupt stop. The time was 8:30 a.m., and we were only thirty minutes from Santa Cruz. A few minutes later, I found out that someone had pulled the emergency cord and forced a stop causing the train to uncouple. We were stuck! The news travelled fast.

"We need repairs," said the train conductor.

We became flustered with the idea that we might not get to the boardwalk after all. Everyone was hungry, thirsty, and hot, but mostly hot, as there was no air conditioning. Tempers flared as the adults tried to keep us calm.

At 2:30 p.m., the train was repaired. We limped into Santa Cruz at 4:00 p.m. and were told that we had one hour to go on rides before boarding the train at 5:00 p.m. We all ran to the boardwalk rides and took one look before a feeling of doom settled over us. The lines were long.

I sat down next to my best friend Tom. "I won't be able to ride one rollercoaster before we have to board the train for home," I said, utterly dejected. He didn't look too upset.

"Aren't you mad?" I asked Tom.

"Remember the lesson our teacher told us when we were studying California history—the one about the four big railroad guys?"

"Who cares," I mumbled.

"Remember all that stuff about rugged individualism and seizing the moment?"

"Yeah, so what? What does that have to do with any of this?"

"Look at all those crazy kids trying to go on rides, and we have to get back on that train in fifteen minutes."

"So what?" I was exasperated now.

"How much money do you have?" Tom asked.

"Almost forty dollars," I answered, thinking that I had not been able to spend any of it.

"These kids have a lot of money that they will not be able to spend. They already ate all of their food on the train. When they get back on, they will be hungry. Let's be rugged individualists and seize the moment."

I still didn't get it.

"Look," Tom said, "if we pool our resources, we can buy eighty dollars' worth of food, Coke, and candy, and resell them on the train for a profit."

"Isn't that wrong?" I asked.

"No," he said, "we are simply being good entrepreneurs."

So off we went and bought eighty dollars' worth of food.

"Are you joking?" the lady at the concessionary store asked when we told her how many hamburgers, Cokes, and boxes of candy we wanted to buy.

"We are buying supplies for the trip home," I said to her.

When we boarded the train, all the kids were upset because they didn't get to do very much before they had to get on the train to go home. Ten minutes into our trip home, our private enterprise venture took wings.

"We have hamburgers, Cokes, and candy for sale," my business partner and I began shouting.

Once the kids realized we had the only food available, they dug in their pockets for money. When we arrived back in Oakland, we had earned more than two hundred dollars on our eighty-dollar investment. The last hamburger sold for two dollars a bite and fifty cents for a sip of a warm Coke.

We were elated when we got off the train. When my parents asked me how it went, I summarized the events that took place. They said we shouldn't have taken advantage of the situation.

"But Tom said we were only providing goods and services to those in need," I replied.

The next day we had another meeting with officer O' Reilly, the man in charge of the traffic boys.

"Well, Kenny, we meet again," he said sarcastically. "What were you guys thinking when you charged so much for food? I heard you even charged some kids five dollars a bite!"

"No, sir, we only charged two dollars a bite," I answered self-righteously.

"We were just practicing supply and demand," Tom said. "We learned about it in our history class."

"Never mind," Officer O'Reilly said. "You have to give

your profit to the church for charity. Also, you are no longer sergeants but privates."

In other words, we had been demoted. We spent the last week of elementary school carrying a stop sign, but it was worth it for the lifetime memories and the innocent risks we took thinking that they were the right thing to do.

5: Craving Acceptance

Throughout my elementary school years and into high school, I was the underdog. Small in stature, skinny, and wearing horn-rimmed glasses, I had been given a variety of nicknames: Skinny Kenny, Four Eyes, Little Guy, and the list went on.

I had a loving family that nurtured me. My mother was my best coach ever. She said to me repeatedly, "Each life experience teaches us something either good or bad. Adversity is a way of life. Those who overcome it become successful. Never forget what Sister Mary said: 'Kenny will be okay. Don't worry about him.'"

Armed with my mother's encouragement, I began my high school career in the fall of 1958. I weighed only ninety pounds, was five feet four inches tall, and eager to face the challenges of high school.

My first day as a freshman was a memorable one. My mother had asked if there was anything special I wanted for the first day of high school.

"Yes," I said, "two things."

"What are they?"

It wasn't like me to say that I needed something special. After reflecting for a few minutes, I said, "I want to take the bus and go by myself."

"Okay," she said. "I know you want to show me that you don't need your mother to take you to school on the first day anymore," she added with a grain of sadness that I was not able to define back then. "If you think you can handle it, no problem."

Next came the hard one. I cleared my throat and said, "Mom, I really want new shoes, and not just any shoes, but the popular ones."

Up until then, I had always gotten the trendy shoes two years after they came out. When I got my first white buck shoes, they were out of style, and kids constantly teased me about them. I wanted to make a good impression on that first day. Mom melted and said, "Let's go shopping. You can choose whatever shoes you want."

We went to the nearest shoe store together, and I said to the clerk, "Show me the hottest shoe that you carry, the big hit. This is my chance to wear the newest thing on the market on the first day of high school. No more white bucks for me."

The clerk took me back where the new shoe arrivals were located. He opened a box of Hush Puppies. I had heard about them on TV. I was so excited to see them. Even before the box was completely open, I could see the color. They were bright red. They glowed in the dark.

"First pair of its kind," said the clerk.

"I am not so sure they are the best choice, Kenny," my mom said.

Her love for me overruled her fears and my best judgment. We left the store with the box of bright red shoes under my arm.

The first day of high school was traumatic. On the solo bus ride from El Cerrito to Berkeley, everyone laughed at my shoes, even the bus driver.

"How far did you chase him to get those shoes?" she shouted laughing.

I shrunk in my seat.

Maybe they are just kidding, I told myself. *Maybe no one else will tease me about my shoes.*

It was the longest twenty-five miles of my life. When I reached the school steps, the roar of laughter was deafening. I wanted to flee, but my name was called, and I sheepishly went forward. Brother Bernard walked me to my classroom.

"The teasing will pass," he said. "Everything will be okay."

Brother Bernard turned out to be one of the best teachers I ever had. He was caring, nurturing, and a great friend throughout my high school years. He took it upon himself to help students who were shy, withdrawn, insecure, and self-conscious about their disadvantages.

My three newest friends that first day of high school were much like me: short and unnoticeable. The freshmen had been classified into groups A, B, and C. We were in the B group class. The day continued to be painful at lunch recess with people teasing me about my shoes. I kept my mouth shut and decided to tough it out. If I had had a cell phone in those days, I would have called my mother to bring me my old pair of shoes.

On the bus ride home, I took off my shoes and kept them in my backpack. When I got home, I went upstairs and threw those bright red shoes into the deepest part of the attic. Thirty years later, when my parents were emptying the house to move to a new home, I saw those shoes in the far corner of the attic, now a dull red from layers of dust, and the events of that first day of high school flashed back. I remembered the story fondly as a time of youthful innocence, of a kid who was merely seeking acceptance.

6: Gains and Losses, and Never Giving Up

"Blessed is the influence of one true, loving human soul on another."

-- George Eliot

Within the first few weeks, I had settled in. I really liked sports. I tried out for football, basketball, and baseball, and never made it past the weight machine.

"Sorry, ninety pounds! You have to weigh one hundred pounds to try out," I heard many times.

What a stupid rule, I thought.

Finally, I made the Debate Team. I never won a debate. Little did I know that it wasn't going to be the last team I was on, or that lessons learned about teamwork would play a big role in my future career as a leader.

The freshman year gave me a chance to get closer to my father. My Dad loved building model planes and had gotten me interested in building a scale model of the "Spirit of St Louis." Using his photography skills, my father took a picture of the plans for the plane and made a scale version of it. The wingspan was fifty inches. I had started it when I was in fifth grade and had lost interest. Since I wasn't making any teams, one day my mother suggested, "Why don't you finish the plane with your dad's help?"

My father was happy that I wanted us to complete a

project together. For me, it was a good diversion from school. He never made any of the parts or did any of the work on the plane, but he guided me and showed me how. I had to put it together piece by piece, a principle that he wanted to make sure I learned from him. I can't count how many times he stood behind me and said, "Kenny, there is an old saying that I have heard many times, but I want you to hear it first from me: 'If you give a man a fish, he will have food for a day; teach him how to fish, and he will have food for life.' This is where you are." He pointed to a specific place on the plan. "And here is where you need to be. I am not doing it for you."

I finished the model around January of that year, and entered the model airplane contests as a junior contestant. The judges did not believe that I had made the plane. I had to undergo a three-hour interrogation using the plans to describe how I made each piece. Finally, the panel was convinced. I won the California state championship of model airplanes in my division that year. Completing this project to the final stage of winning a prize helped me gain confidence and self -respect, not to mention the admiration of my father.

I tried out again to make the freshman baseball team. The one hundred-pound rule prevailed, and I weighed ninety pounds. As I walked out of the gym totally depressed, head and shoulders down, I met a classmate who had the same misfortune. Shorty Shortridge was his name. He wore a baseball hat most of the time.

"No big deal," he said. "How would you like to join my league? We play every Saturday at the school field, three on three. I do all the stats and keep the records."

Shortridge was amazing. We had teams of three that

played on half of the field. Left field, shortstop, and pitcher were the three position we used. The opposing team provided the catcher. We all pitched, hit, and played the field. It was the best summer of my life thus far, not to mention I was learning how to play baseball. We even had our own version of a world series—best two out of three games—and we had an all-star team. We all made it! I was the only left-handed player and had to master the art of hitting to left field. This constant practice paid big dividends later in my career in baseball.

My sophomore year began the same as my freshman year. Regardless of my eating habits to gain weight, I stayed at ninety pounds; therefore, joining school sports teams was nothing but a dream.

It was during this year that three terrific teachers had a profound impact on my future.

Mr. Mathew, my world history teacher, was a character. Every day he entered the room wearing his very thick glasses on the end of his nose. He looked like a big fish with those thick glasses. He proceeded to his desk without saying a word.

"Are you ready for the most wonderful adventure in your life?" He asked with a deep voice that echoed throughout the whole room.

We were spellbound as he engaged us in the world of ancient history. He was a natural born storyteller, and we couldn't wait for his class to begin so that we could listen to his lectures. They always involved some kind of action or response from every student. Each could end up being a warrior in an ancient battle or the enemy of the king. Often we were aboard a time machine that took us back in history. One time we were learning about Hannibal and the crossing of the Alps, which Mr. Mathew described as being difficult and very dangerous. A student asked the teacher why it was so dangerous.

"Everyone out of your chairs," he said. "Now, pile the chairs on top of one another."

There was noise, movement, desks scrambling to touch each other and to keep balance as the pile went up more than five feet high.

"Okay, now try climbing over them."

As teen boys in an all-boys school, we had a blast. Chairs were falling as students dropped on top of each other and off the pile only to charge up again and again until the principal arrived to see what had happened. We didn't revisit Hannibal crossing the Alps again, but we learned the dangers Hannibal must have encountered with elephants falling over the cliff much like Tommy in our class who was rather heavy; he lost his footing and crashed to the floor.

The year in Mr. Mathew's class culminated in the great goldfish caper. We knew the teacher could not break character when he entered the room. We wanted to see if we could get him to flinch, so we plotted for each one of us to bring a goldfish to class in a small glass. The day came, and before he entered, we placed thirty-two glasses of water on his desk with a goldfish in each one. When he entered the room, we were all holding our breath. True to form, looking like a big fish with thick glasses on the tip of his nose, he intoned, "Open your book to chapter eight. Read silently."

He managed to smile at our tomfoolery, but he never

commented on the prank. Fortunately for us, he didn't overreact. In our teenage minds, this little prank was a way to convey our respect for him. He may not have seen it that way, but he never brought it up, and handled it with grace and humility.

Mr. Mathew was so much fun and created such a desire to learn. Unfortunately, the administration did not appreciate his teaching methods as much as we boys did, and he left the following year. He was able to ignite our imagination, which was an inspiration for me, as I hoped someday to be a history teacher just like him. This interest grew as the years progressed, and, yes, I taught history for eight years. I never forgot him.

The second teacher who had a profound impact on my life was my Spanish instructor, Brother D. He was not only my Spanish teacher but the advisor to the yearbook, a committee for which I had volunteered as a freshman, working closely with him. He was energetic, fun, and full of life.

I did quite well in Spanish class and maintained a high B average. When the final exam came, I was worried about my grade. I had written a list of words and their correct spellings in Spanish on a sheet of paper. On the bus, I kept going over the vocabulary, trying to memorize all the words for the exam.

I entered the classroom, put all my papers under the desk, and positioned the list of words in a way that I could lean over slightly and read them if I needed to.

Halfway through the test, Brother D. came over and stood by my desk. He asked me to bring the exam to the front desk. When I approached, he accused me of cheating. He took my exam and told me to return to my desk. I was embarrassed.

When I received my test back, a big F covered the whole paper. My grade for the semester was a D.

"It was only a help sheet," I told him. "I never looked at the list once the test began, and I didn't cheat."

"The worst of it is that I lost trust in you. It will take a lot for me to regain my trust," he answered in a soft voice that went through my ears as a sword directed toward my heart.

The following semester, I changed classes and quit the yearbook committee. I blamed him for how I was treated. Even though my intention was to look at the paper if I needed it, I never used it. I believed that he had treated me unfairly.

Many years later, at my twenty-fifth high school reunion, I saw Brother D. again. Several of my classmates were talking to him. He was a retired brother, and had come to the reunion as a curiosity more than anything. Everyone kept asking him if he remembered them. When my turn came, he said, "I don't remember your name, but I remember the help sheet."

A student interrupted and said, "I never used Spanish. Why was it so important for us to take a language class that we would never use?"

I turned to him and said for all around to hear: "It has been twenty-five years since the help sheet incident, and I want to apologize for my behavior. You were right, Brother D." I paused then continued. "The help sheet was a cheat sheet, and you taught me a very valuable lesson. It is better to lose a battle (a test) than to lose a war (the final grade). In my case, I not only received a lower grade in your class, but I also lost your trust. Besides just teaching a language, you taught us principles and integrity. Embarrassment and humiliation were the natural consequences I had to endure for violating your trust in me."

The old retired teacher smiled nodding. What I had said made his visit to the reunion a validation of his life work. I was grateful to have the opportunity to make amends.

This lesson provided me years later with the necessary tools to instill the same importance of principles and integrity in the many students I taught throughout the years.

The third teacher who had a profound impact on me was Brother Bernard, whom I briefly mentioned before. He was the teacher who rescued me from total shock my first day as a freshman, and all the students liked him. He was in his early sixties when I met him. He was the father of four grown children. When his wife died, he chose to enter the brotherhood and teach in a Catholic high school.

Brother Bernard was always on the playing field sitting in his comfortable chair. Every day after school, a group of my friends and I used to play flag football. As a teacher, he offered encouragement and told us we could make the high school teams once we got a bit bigger. We smiled and kept playing. His positive approach made us feel valued. I had many conversations with him standing by that rusty old chair where he sat. He was a good counselor and a friend. Throughout my high school years, as I tried out for teams and eventually was selected, he just smiled and said, "I told you so. Never give up."

A pattern was emerging that if I wanted anything bad enough, I would go the extra mile. These early struggles to achieve against all odds built a strong foundation for the challenges to come and the accomplishments gained in the journey.

In the spring of my sophomore year, I was taller, and I weighed one hundred and five pounds, so I tried out for the baseball team. I made the junior varsity team after hitting a ball over the fence in tryouts, and my career as an athlete began. Not only did I make the team, but so did Shortridge, to whom I gave credit for the wealth of knowledge acquired while playing in the summer league. I became the hitter who always hit to left field. I was so proud when I brought my uniform home to show my mom and dad. My mom reiterated, "Dreams come true if you never stop trying."

As a junior, I wanted to play football. I now weighed about one hundred fifty pounds. I asked if a junior could try out for the junior varsity team. I was told I could, but I didn't stand much of a chance. On a cold and chilly afternoon, the coach took the last four people who didn't have a spot on the team and said the fastest runner in the group would be the last player chosen. I never ran so hard in my life. I came in first and was the last player to get a uniform! I was so excited when I dressed in my uniform that I put the hip pads on backward, which caused me to waddle like a duck! I had a new nickname: Quacker!

One day, in the closing weeks of the season, the varsity coach came up to Robert, the tight end and field-goal kicker, and asked him to join the varsity team.

Wow, what an honor, I thought.

The coach looked at me and said, "That goes for you too, Kenny."

The last two weeks of varsity were a treat. They threw Robert and me to the wolves. I had never been tackled so hard in my life. We were able to practice with the first unit. I never forgot the first pass route. I caught the ball and immediately was tackled. It was the hardest tackle ever. I got up slowly, and the players applauded. I had passed the test. Next play, a bomb was thrown long and deep. I caught the ball, and a new phase of my life began: being accepted by the in-group, the jocks, the big men on campus. It was an eye opener.

7: Determination Matters

"Always seek out the seed of triumph in every adversity."

-- Og Mandino

The rest of my junior year was amazing. The in-group had accepted me. I was asked to join the Block SM Society, an athletic honor society comprised of players who had earned their block letter based on their performance at the varsity level. It was a big deal for a young man like me. Unfortunately, it was tarnished when one of the jocks said, "You need to associate with us more than with the friends you have had until now."

It was clear in my mind that I was not going to disown my close friends just to be accepted by the jocks. Later on, my decision not to participate in the Block SM Society caused problems with the in-group.

Spring came, and with it, the baseball season approached. I tried out for the varsity baseball team and was the last one picked, a pattern that was all too familiar by now, but I had learned that all I ever needed was a chance, and from there I would make it work. As the seventeenth player selected, I was directed to sit on the bench to learn from the seniors. I was happy just to be part of the team.

The first game was unreal. In the sixth inning, the score was 1 to 1, a tight game. The coach called me to sit next to him. He said, "Kenny, you will bat next."

I almost fell over. The senior that I was going to bat for was called the Grizzly Man. He had a beard and hair all over his body. I remember saying to him politely, "Sir, I will be batting for you."

He looked at me with disdain and laughed.

"Kenny will be batting for you," the coach told him, and that settled it.

When I stepped up to the plate, I was shaking like a leaf. We had the go-ahead runner on second base. The first two pitches were swinging strikes. I could hear the seniors snickering on the bench. I stepped out of the batters' box to collect my thoughts. As I looked around the field, I remembered the many times I had hit the ball to left field during the summer playing in Shortridge's league. I stepped back in the box more relaxed and hit the next pitch into left field. We scored the winning run. From that day forward, I was the new right fielder, replacing the Grizzly Man, and producing hits and contributing to the varsity team.

By mid-season, we were locked in a battle for the championship. It was the sixth inning, and a ball was hit to me. I ran to pick it up, but it bounced by me. I retrieved it and threw it home. The throw was on target, but the first baseman cut off the throw and the runner scored. I was taken out of the game and replaced. I sat on the bench for the remaining two weeks, a tough decision to swallow. However, we won the league in the playoffs.

My senior year was a mixed bag of athletic successes and adversities. I had a good year on the football team, but as a whole, we had a tough season and lost the majority of our games. The first varsity game was memorable. I was the starting wide receiver. We were playing a large high-school team from East Oakland. The game was a defensive struggle. We were behind in the fourth quarter and needed a touchdown to win. The first time the ball was thrown to me in the first quarter of the game, I was so nervous I dropped the ball.

When the coach sent a player in to tell the quarterback to throw the ball to me again, the quarterback refused to call the play and changed it in the huddle. The next play, another player came into the huddle and told the quarterback to throw the ball to me or he would be taken out of the game. He looked at me with arrogance and an air of superiority, and shouted, "You better not drop this one, or you will never get another pass!"

I didn't have enough pressure on me, did I? It was third down, and we needed seventeen yards for a first down. As I went to the line of scrimmage, I told myself, *I need to catch the ball and run as fast as I can to make the first down.*

The play was perfect. I caught the ball and ran eighteen yards before I was tackled on the four-yard line. I made the first down with one yard to spare. Two plays later, we scored the winning touchdown.

Our starting quarterback was injured three games after we began the season. Our losses piled up as we suffered injury after injury. By the time we reached the halfway point of the season, every one of the starters had been injured but me, and that was what the newspaper mentioned: that I was the only one who hadn't been injured. *I have a target on my back,* I thought.

The next game was against Bellarmine, a major

football powerhouse. They were undefeated in thirty-three straight games. It was our homecoming game scheduled for 2:00 p.m. on Saturday. All the players received a telephone call at 8:00 a.m. from the coach.

"Report to the locker room at ten, because we have to resolve an issue before we play," he said.

As we filed into the locker room, we whispered and mumbled among ourselves, wondering what was up.

In those days, we shared our facilities with the Oakland Raiders. It was their first year in existence. We thought that sharing the facilities with them was cool. We were able to meet the players as we came for practice every day. The Raiders had just installed a special locker facility to house their game jerseys.

When we arrived, the coach told us, "Someone has stolen four Raiders jerseys. You have two hours to return the jerseys, or you have to forfeit the game."

After the coach left, a few of our players admitted to stealing the jerseys. One had already tried to remove the player's name from the back of one jersey. They agreed to get the jerseys back to the Raiders. The jerseys were going to be flown to Buffalo, New York, for the Sunday Raiders game.

After the incident was resolved, we were able to play the game. The bad news was that we were crushed thirty-three to zero!

After the events of the previous week, the whole team seemed beaten, both physically and emotionally. We had embarrassed our school on the field and off. The coach told us that we would practice in full gear all week in preparation for the next game.

For the first time, I dreaded practice. *Just get through it . . . Just get through it*, I repeated to myself. When Monday's practice began, the coach caught me doing my pushups halfheartedly, and it got worse from there. Three times during practice I was off sides when the quarterback called the play. The coach was infuriated with me.

"What's wrong with you?" he yelled. "Miller, one more time and I'll personally come over there and throw you off the field!"

It was the first time he had ever addressed me with that tone of voice. As I returned to the huddle, I was still thinking about what he said.

Get it together, Miller, I said to myself.

The next thing I knew, we were breaking the huddle and heading for the line of scrimmage. I looked at the right tackle and asked, "What is the count?"

"Two," he said.

"You are not kidding me, are you?"

"Oh, no," he said.

Well, the joke was on me. I blasted off the line of scrimmage on two. Everyone laughed watching me, except the head coach. He was usually a soft-spoken man, but when he was angry, he was scary. He came over, grabbed me by the shoulder pads, and threw me about ten feet in the air.

"Don't come back unless you are ready to play!" he yelled.

Heading to the locker room in dismay, I wondered what had just happened.

As I showered and dressed in silence, I became more and more upset with my behavior. As I road home on the bus, I thought, *I will arrive home at 4:30 in the afternoon. What should I do to let off some of this steam?*

There was a park close by where a lot of guys played basketball. I headed in that direction to play some ball. When I arrived, I saw a lot of my neighborhood buddies playing.

"What are you doing here?" they asked. "Aren't you on the football team at St. Mary's?"

"I took the day off," I said, as if that would have been all right. I didn't want to tell them what really happened.

Just then, I recognized a player I knew well. He had antagonized me for many years, a real bully named Gene, almost two hundred twenty pounds, six feet four, strong, and aggressive. People knew who he was because he was always bullying someone. Gene was on the football team of another school.

"I took the day off too," he said.

Everyone laughed. I didn't laugh because I was in a weird, foul mood, still upset about the events at football practice. I often ran into Gene because he attended the same church I went to and was a member of the church teen club where I was the president. He always interrupted and made jokes to get attention from the girls. Whenever I asked him to be quiet, he would say, "Are you going to make me?"

"Oh, Gene, come on," I would laugh nervously, but he would laugh and ignore me.

So the scene was set for the basketball game. Gene made sure that we were on different teams.

"I'm guarding you, which should be very easy," he said, laughing.

The game started, and Gene began pushing me out of the way. The third time he did that, I became angry and did the unthinkable. I stood up to him.

"Stop pushing me!" I shouted with determination.

You could hear a pin drop. No one said a word.

"Excuse me, what did you say?"

"You heard me," I said.

"Are you going to make me?"

Everybody else laughed.

This was normal behavior for him. All the players knew it was suicide to mess with Gene.

At that moment, I flashed to the coach throwing me off the field telling me not to come back until I was ready to play. I'd had enough of the bullies of the world pushing me around, and I was ready and willing to stand up for myself and take the consequences no matter what happened.

Without flinching, I looked right in his eyes and said, "YES!"

Gene clenched his fist and hit me in my right eye. My glasses hit the ground flying, but my body hit the pavement first. I was down on the ground, stunned and groggy, and trying to clear my head. I stood up and staggered backward blocking his punches. They didn't really hurt. I was in good shape from football and got a few good punches in. Gene was getting tired right about when my head began to clear. He threw a wild punch that grazed my chin. At this point, everyone thought that I was going down again.

I saw that he had dropped his guard for a moment. I reached way down into my inner being and launched a fist into the air, a direct hit. The blow stunned him as my fist caught him on the nose and his left eye. He went down and hit his head on the cement. He was nearly out.

I stood over him and said, "Get up."

He was done. He didn't want any more of me and left the court limping. Everyone was congratulating me for doing the impossible: beating up Gene!

I arrived home with a huge black eye. I had to explain the day in detail to my dad, culminating with the fight, and then repeated it to my mom minutes later. Just then, the telephone rang. My dad answered it. I was in the kitchen holding a steak over my right eye, an old prescription that was supposed to reduce swelling.

"It is Gene's father," my dad said. "He wants to talk to you."

What does he want with me? I thought. *Doesn't he know that his kid is a bully?*

I was prepared for the worst and ready to defend myself.

"Thank you for teaching my son a valuable lesson." Those were Gene's father's first words.

I was shocked.

"I have told him that one of these days someone was going to stand up to him. I am grateful that he was not more seriously injured."

He said that Gene was sporting a huge black eye, and he informed me that I would never have a problem with his son again.

What a day! My father told me, "I understand your actions in this case. However, when confronted with the need to defend yourself against those who try to hurt you mentally or physically, use your brain, not your fists. Use words and intelligence."

My father knew about emotional intelligence years before it was theorized and applied at schools and corporations.

When I returned to school the next day, the news had traveled fast. Even my coach knew about it. He looked at my black eye and said, "Well, it looks like you came back to play."

All seemed to have been forgiven, and my renewed focus guided me to practice the way I needed to, giving 100 percent of my effort for the rest of the season. As a team, we committed to regaining the respect of our school, our coach, and one another.

There were times later in my life when I felt the need to defend myself against all odds, and my father's words would resurface: "Use your brain, not your fists."

One of my fondest memories of that magical season is of the games on Saturdays. We played on fields surrounded by eucalyptus trees. The wind made the leaves wave from side to side, producing a peculiar soothing sound: the voice of nature at its best. We filled our lungs with the rich minty, pine scent of the trees. Often, on a cool winter morning, the smell of eucalyptus trees brings back the sweetest memories of times when our young minds, full of energy and dreams, felt undefeated, and we tried again and again with big hopes to become like one of the famous sports players we had admired for years and years.

My family was the highlight of those games, with my father taking movies during a time when digital videography was nonexistent and cellular phones were only in James Bond's hands. My father was a photography genius in his time. My mom in those days screamed encouragement from the stands, and my two sisters, Sharon and Sue, and my brother, Leff, cheered with each pass. It is a truly warm feeling every time I think of those days.

On one occasion, I had just caught a pass and made a dash for the end zone. The play covered sixty yards. As I approached the end zone, I looked over my right shoulder and saw that the closest player was at least ten yards behind me. I coasted into the end zone. Just then, on my left side, I was hit. I had forgotten to check that side, and I fumbled. The player picked it up and ran it back eighty-nine yards for a touchdown! My teammates thought I had scored and were coming off the field as the other team player was going the other way. It turned out to be the longest fumble recovery return in high school football that year.

As I hung my head in shock, I could hear my dear mother yelling, "That's my boy! THAT'S MY BOY!"

After the game, I told my mom that I had fumbled and it had cost us the game. She didn't care.

"You looked so graceful running with the ball. I'm proud of you no matter what happened," she said. My dear mother, my shining light!

The name of the player from the other team that ran it back was called Shu-Shu. Only after this game did I realize why he had gained that nickname: He was so fast that when he ran by you, all you could hear was *shu-shu-shu!*

During the break from fall to spring sports, we had assemblies in our gymnasium. Little did we know that these entertainers—the Fogerty Brothers of Credence Clearwater, and Carlos Santana, just to mention a few of our own classmates—would go on to become big stars. Back then, they rocked our gym.

The spring baseball season came again. I lost my starting job to a younger player. I spent the majority of the season on the bench. For the first time in my life, I wanted to quit something. I faced a true test of my will, because when I told my father that I had had enough and wanted out, he sat me down and spoke to me about the importance of not quitting.

"There is much more to learn about life in not giving up when things are not going our way," he said.

The last game of the season, the coach started all of the seniors. I finished the season by getting four hits in the last game.

"Coach, if you had only given me a chance, I could have proved you wrong about my baseball skills," I said.

This was probably the first time I had stood up to any authority figure in my life. My coach was upset at my audacity. "You have played your last competitive baseball," he said.

He had issued a challenge, and I relished it. What he didn't know was that I had been successful against all odds and circumstances my whole life up to that point, and a fire of wanting to beat the odds burned inside me every time someone put me down or told me that I couldn't do something.

8: Education Is First

"An investment in knowledge pays the best interest."

-- Benjamin Franklin

The Salt and Sugar Caper, the cannery and a trip to the pound, the Library Boys, the Frozen Food Adventure, and the Peach Orchards. Ah, life is an adventure!

Graduation approached. My father, taking his eyes away from the Sunday newspaper, told me as I was coming down the stairs, "Kenny, I have to talk to you about something."

"What is it, Dad?"

"I want to discuss with you what is next in your life. You have three possible options: go to college, join the military, or get a job, even if it is a part-time job. You need to begin the world of work. Think about it and let me know."

My first job was a short one. I worked as a bus boy at a local diner. Truckers came for breakfast, and I had to handle many tasks at once: taking orders, cleaning dishes, clearing tables, and filling the salt and sugar containers at the end of my shift. It was a lot for a young person used to having Mom around doing basic chores.

The third day of work I heard one of the truckers gasping for air.

"Yuck!" He made a sound of disgust.

Mixing words that I choose not to mention, he said, "Someone put salt in the sugar shakers!"

The coffee was ruined, and accusatory eyes turned in the direction of the new employee. Simple as it was, my mistake affected other employees who had to pitch in during a busy time for everyone; furthermore, it could have affected the business, as clients may have walked out. The owner apologized to his patrons and gave the lucky client a free breakfast and a gift certificate. For me, the third day was my last day.

As I left the diner, I passed a used car lot, and sitting right in the middle of it was a beautiful sports car. I vowed that soon I would be able to get a sports car. Well-motivated, and with a target in mind, my search for another job intensified.

My uncle worked at the Del Monte Cannery, and I asked my mother if he could get me a job for the summer. He said he would, but he also told her that it was hard work, and I would receive no special favors just because I was his nephew.

I was hired and excited. I would have to take the bus to downtown Emeryville, as the cannery was close to San Francisco.

When I arrived, I was introduced to the foreman of the cannery. He said, "The main thing here is to be safe. A lot of people get injured by not paying attention."

He assigned me to one of the toughest positions: the assembly line—it was where the boxes came off the conveyor belt after they were glued and ready for transport. We had to stack them six feet high on pallets.

There were eight lines of boxes to be stacked. Each line

had a different kind of fruit, with the fastest line being fruit cocktail. When boxes came off the assembly line, you could hear the tick of the counter as each one passed. The fruit cocktail line was so fast that it didn't click; it hummed!

At the end of the first day on the line, I was exhausted. We each had a partner. I was partnered with an African-American guy named Will, a strong virile guy about my age. He taught me how to stack the boxes by swinging them and not lifting them. This technique saved me. I still only weighed one hundred fifty pounds, and the eight-hour job was a tough one physically. I dreaded fruit cocktail day because the boxes never stopped coming. Will and I became close friends, and he called me the Lone Gray, as I was the only white person working the line.

I guess no one expected me to survive the job, but I liked the challenge. One day, Will and I were working the peaches line right next to the fruit cocktail line. As usual, the boxes were screaming off the assembly line. I noticed that another employee was working the line alone.

"Where is your partner?" I asked him.

"I think he quit. It was too hard for him," he answered.

"They wouldn't stop these machines even if you dropped dead," I said, noticing he looked beaten.

"Yes." He smiled and nodded.

Ten minutes later, I heard the boxes crashing to the ground. My first thought was, *I bet that guy quit too.*

Just then, Will began screaming, "Man down! Man down!"

The noise level in the cannery was so high that people couldn't hear the screams. The forklift operator ran to assist the downed worker. Within minutes, ambulances appeared. Will and I were told to get back to work immediately to take over the fruit cocktail line. I was shaking, trying to be calm, and also ready to quit. Many workers walked off the job that day.

The cannery kept going even though one of its workers had just died of a heart attack. I thought about this the whole rest of the day

We were all stunned, but we kept working. We had to. I will never forget that crucial moment because it was then that I realized that my education was the ticket out of this kind of manual labor.

The bond between Will and me grew. We helped each other and talked about everything, including race relations, differences between blacks and whites, and the need for tolerance on both sides.

One day I was more tired than ever, and Will offered me a ride home. Usually, I took the bus, but this day I was really tired, so I accepted his offer. When our shift ended, we walked outside. I was ready to jump in Will's car and take a quick nap while he drove me home.

Will said, "My sister is picking us up. She will take you home."

Will's sister arrived with a car full of girls.

"Where should I sit?" I asked.

"Just let Susie sit on your lap," he said laughing.

I was so nervous.

"It will be okay," Will said. "You girls can take Ken to the Pound!"

"Are you going to take me to the dog pound?" I asked.

There were more laughs. We arrived at a burger joint called The Dog Pound, and once again I was the only lone gray! Will introduced me to everyone, and we had so much fun laughing and cutting up. A long-lasting friendship continued for the remainder of the summer.

The cannery had multiple accidents that year. Not only did a person die, but a man had his arm cut off while working on a machine. The season ended a week before the beginning of my first semester in college, and I was mentally, emotionally, and financially ready to embrace it, more sure than ever that I was not going to depart from the educational path.

9: Resources Are Everyone's Responsibility

"My fellow Americans, ask not what your country can do for you.

Ask what you can do for your country."

-- President John F. Kennedy

While in line to register for classes for the fall of 1962, I recognized one of the students who lived near my house. He had just graduated from El Cerrito High School. Students had nicknamed him Mr. Clean. (I don't remember his name, but I remember his nickname.) He looked like the genie on the Mr. Clean bottle—six feet six, very muscular, and bald. He smiled at me, and we began sharing our summer experiences.

"I work for the public library," he said. "It is a good experience. You should check it out. A lot of guys in our neighborhood work there. They mostly check in books and shelve them. I'll hook you up with the person in charge of the hiring."

After registering for classes, I immediately arranged an interview for the library position and was hired. I was so excited! Starting college with a part-time job was awesome. Now I would be able to afford that sports car I had been dreaming about for so long. By next summer, after saving my money for a year, I would be able to fulfill that dream.

Long gone was the three-day job I had at the restaurant

with its craziness and commotion, where I was on my feet all the time. The dangers of the summer assembly job were also a distant memory. I was beginning my third job at the El Cerrito Library, a quiet, air-conditioned environment where peace and serenity were valued.

The first few weeks went very smoothly. The library personnel were nice, and the workload was easy. Retired people as well as college and high school students visited often. The head librarian, however, warned me: "The high school students are scary. We need to keep an eye on them."

"What kind of problems do they cause?" I asked.

"You'll see," she said.

It seemed odd that she was so mysterious about what to expect from them, but they became a true challenge. First, they recognized me as the new hire and teased me relentlessly. When I was shelving books, they made inappropriate noises and yelled out catcalls. "Hey, library boy, want a kiss?"

The teasing started gradually, but over time it became a problem.

"Please stop," I said over and over.

Catcalls and noises were every night's drill.

"These high school students are really rude and obnoxious," I told the librarian.

"Ignore them," she responded.

When I told my library friends about the situation, Mr. Clean suggested that a visit from the library boys was in order. The plan was set. On the next Monday, they appeared and sat in various places, waiting for the high school students to begin their bullying. They showed up as expected. When the head high school bully named Butch started his "Hey, library boy" routine, Mr. Clean stood up and said, "I am the library boy today. Do you have a problem with that?"

"We're library boys too. Have you got a problem with library boys?" said one of the boys that Mr. Clean had brought with him.

The other adults and students in the library seemed relieved that someone had confronted the bullies and held them accountable for their actions.

Mr. Clean said, "I better not hear of any more abuses toward library boys, or we'll be back."

"Yes, sir," Butch answered timidly in a soft voice I had never heard him use before.

The next six months were heaven on earth. The high school students behaved for the most part. During the last week of the school year, the library was mostly empty with the exception of a few retired people reading. I was shelving books when I saw Butch and three of his buddies enter the library. They passed by me and sat in the study section where couches and small tables were located. At about 8:45 p.m., one of the adults approached me and said, "I smell smoke in the study section."

Sure enough, as I approached, I saw Butch smoking a cigarette.

"There is no smoking in the library," I told him, motioning for him to put it out.

He took the cigarette and tapped it out of the window to knock off the ashes and brought it back into the library.

He took another drag from his cigarette. His three buddies were laughing.

"No, the whole cigarette," I said.

He got up, and the four of them went into the men's bathroom. I went to the librarian and told her what had happened.

"Let it go," she said. "Nothing will happen."

After the boys left the bathroom, I immediately went inside to see if anything had happened. They had broken all of the door handles and had carved "Library Boys Suck" in the mirror.

I reported the damage to the librarian and told her to call the police. She said that she was afraid of these students and feared them coming after her. She refused to call the police, stating, "Our insurance will cover the damages."

I went after the boys and found them near the checkout counter. "Stop," I told them. "I need your names, addresses, and phone numbers to contact your parents to pay for vandalizing the men's bathroom. If you refuse, I will turn the situation over to the police."

Two of the boys complied with my request. Butch and the third boy refused.

"Come on, Butch, let's go," said one of the boys who complied. "We don't want to get in trouble with the police. Put your name down."

Butch ignored them. He looked right at me, and with his finger pointing at me in a menacing way, he said, "I'll see you outside in ten minutes, and you won't have your library boys to protect you this time."

Ten minutes? I thought. *If I wait ten minutes, I'll get fearful like the librarian.*

I jumped over the small checkout stand, grabbed Butch from behind, and physically steered him out of the library. He turned to hit me, and his hand accidentally hit the wall. I think he broke it—his hand.

After the police interviewed all the witnesses who explained what transpired and the damages the boys had caused to the library bathrooms, I was let go. The bullies' parents came to their children's defense stating that they were good boys who came to the library every day to study. They were shocked by the statements they heard from witnesses about their young angels.

The incident at the library could have had a worse outcome. I learned at an early age that taking a problem into my own hands was not the best approach, regardless of whether or not I was right. I lost my temper for the second time in my life, but now it was at a job, not on the playground. My father's advice flashed through my mind: "Use your words, not your fists."

For me, it not only meant the loss of a job, but also a lesson in the importance of effective leadership on the part of supervisors, managers, and decision makers to take action in a timely manner to solve problems before they get out of hand in order to provide their employees with a safe working environment.

10: Preparation Meets Opportunity

"The gem cannot be polished without friction,

nor man perfected without trials."

-- Chinese proverb

I worked the following summer in the peach orchards of California and inside a frozen foods building with a temperature in the low twenties. These two jobs were a means to an end: saving money for my final two years of college. In addition, I had to take two remaining college classes during the summer to be able to transfer to the university. I attended classes from 8:00 a.m. to 12:00 noon each day for six weeks. At my supermarket frozen foods warehouse job, I worked from 5:00 p.m. to 1:00 a.m. This work schedule left me with about four hours to sleep.

My grandmother had instilled in me a love of history. She used to buy history books for all of her grandchildren at a time when we were more interested in receiving toys. She shared exciting stories about her youth and talked about events in the past that I found fascinating. She planted the seed that grew and became my direction years later.

When I interviewed with my college advisor, he helped me to select a path that included an emphasis on social sciences. The first class I had during the summer was a history class that began at 8:00 a.m. After working night hours, waking up early was not easy. I was very tired the first day of class, and fell asleep during the last fifteen minutes. The teacher informed me that if that happened again, I would be dropped from the class. From that day on, I sat in the front row. When I began nodding off, I hit my face to wake up. I tried hard throughout the class not to fall asleep. The day before the last class, the teacher said, "Mr. Miller, you have earned an A so far on the tests. Your class participation was vague to say the least. To reward you for your efforts, I give you permission to go to sleep in class today so the other students can hear my instructions for the test without your having to slap your face to stay awake."

I took him seriously, thanked him, and fell fast asleep within minutes.

My two jobs that summer were very different. As a dispatcher for one of the fifty Camby Family Stores, I worked at a huge warehouse full of products, both frozen and dry goods. I took the lists, organized them, and gave them to the attendants. All the employees drove small battery-operated vehicles that towed a cart to put the orders in a sequence, then they drove the carts to the delivery trucks where they were loaded. Once the orders were filled, the drivers filled the trucks with the supplies organized by the store stops they had the following day.

Each driver had on winter clothes, gloves, boots, and goggles to withstand the cold in the huge freezer. The first day I drove the vehicle, my glasses split in half and broke when I came out of the freezer into the summer heat. No one had taught me that I couldn't use my glasses when I entered the freezer. I had to buy a new pair of glasses with my first paycheck.

After a month working at the warehouse, I was promoted to replace one of the attendants who had fallen ill. The money was good, and I liked the added responsibilities. It was a union job. The shop steward was nicknamed Rat. He had a reputation for not liking the college students who worked in the warehouse.

"You need to join the union and pay initiation fees," he kept telling me.

"I am doing this job only until school starts in the fall," I said.

"You have no choice," he replied.

The initiation cost was five hundred dollars, a huge amount that would affect my college funds. Feeling cornered by his insistence, I accepted.

"You will feel the bite of the union dues," he said sarcastically, and he laughed.

When I arrived at the union office, the secretary asked, "Have you ever been in a union?"

"Yes," I said, "when I worked in the cannery last year."

Joining only cost me a five dollar transfer fee. I received my buttons and forms. I never told the steward what I had paid until I left the job for school. He was mortified.

I had to complete the second summer class, which was public speaking, before I headed to my second job in the peach orchards. Every speech I gave I received a grade of B. The instructor said I always had a humorous take on the assignments and needed to have more substance.

"You are missing the *wow* factor," he said.

I felt that regardless of my efforts, the outcome was

not going to change. The final assignment was worth 50 percent of our grade. It was supposed to be a thirty-minute speech on the following topic: The Role of the American College Student in Today's Society.

"Mr. Miller, here is your challenge: You will give the last speech on this topic on the last day of the class. It better have depth and a *wow* factor!"

What a challenge! After twenty-five speeches on the topic, everything had been said. My day finally arrived. I walked to the podium knowing that after my speech the class would be over for everyone. The students and the teacher all had smug grins on their faces.

As I stood before them, I took a deep breath and said with emphasis and great eye contact, "The role of the American college student in today's society is to find himself or herself, and that is where I am going right now!"

I picked up my books and left the room. I heard the students cheering and laughing.

"He nailed it," one of the students said. "He had the *wow* factor, was inspirational, and showed depth in a speech that lasted less than a minute. Wow!"

I kept walking to avoid being confronted by the teacher, but I needn't have worried. I had an accumulation of good grades, and I passed the class.

I didn't have time to waste. I was packed and ready to work for six weeks in the peach orchards before attending California State University, Chico. The hours were long and hard. One day, a farm worker asked me to drive a load of fruit up to the weigh station while he went to the bathroom. I pushed the button to go forward but didn't know how to stop the vehicle. I hit a platform and fruit went everywhere. Luckily, no one was hurt, just a few bruised pieces of fruit and my understanding that I was not ready to endure the science of manual labor, as it was not as easy as it seemed.

A highlight of that summer was working with my cousin Richard and sharing the same apartment. We heard music together and had long talks. We worked twelve to fourteen hour shifts. The money was great, enabling me to pay for my college expenses for the year to come. The last workday, I loaded my little sports car to the brim with peaches, clothes, and excitement. I had just gotten my summer grades: B+ in history and B+ in Speech.

Chico State, here I come!

11: Blast from the Past

"Peace is a journey of a thousand miles, and it must be taken one step at a time."

-- Lyndon B. Johnson

To say that I was excited to attend California State University would be an understatement. The drive would take more than five hours. I turned off the radio and immersed myself in the panorama and the horizon. The freeway full of drivers going and coming, all in a hurry, kept my senses alert to the route that I needed to follow back when paper maps were the only way to navigate unfamiliar streets.

Little by little, the drive became monotonous, and I began reflecting on the two years that had passed since my high school graduation. Jobs, college, friends, and family—all intrinsically connected in the journey toward completing bigger and better goals.

The world around me had been changing. One of the first major developments was the Cuban missile crisis. The tension between the United States, Cuba, and Russia escalated after President Kennedy announced to the world that Russian missiles had been delivered to Cuba and were being deployed. My father called an emergency meeting of the family the night before the Russian ships were supposed to arrive at the United States blockade of Cuba. The president had warned Russia that the missiles had to be removed "or else."

I remembered my father telling the whole family that in the event of a potential nuclear war with Russia, we were to come home to be together. He said it would be pointless to try to escape the Bay Area. We prayed and prepared for the worst-case scenario. The critical day arrived, and we all hugged and kissed each other, and I went to college. I was in my history class when the loudspeaker came on informing all of us that classes were canceled due to the crisis. That day, we were released thirty minutes before the Russian ships were supposedly due to reach the blockade.

As I left the class, many students headed to the cafeteria where a large speaker was broadcasting events as they unfolded in real time. I sat with a group of my friends as we wondered if the Russian ships would attack the blockade and discussed possible repercussions for all of us if that happened. I heard a male college student consoling a female college student who, weeping inconsolably, kept saying to him, "I'm still a virgin. I have never had sex in my life, and now the world is going to end!"

The male student sitting next to her offered to provide that outlet for her. He convinced her to follow him just as the Russian ships were approaching the blockade. I'll never forget what happened next. The announcer began screaming: "The Russians have stopped short of the blockade. They have stopped dead in the water."

We all jumped and let out a huge cheer! The only person who seemed disappointed was the male student who almost deflowered the young female with whom he was talking. She yelled, "Now I don't have to give up my virginity!"

Everyone who heard her cheered. Those were two victories in one moment in time.

I looked at my watch. A whole hour had passed on my journey toward Chico. For a second, I focused on the variety of things typically happening during the California summers. The roads are full of trucks carrying tomatoes, melons, watermelons, kiwis, persimmons, peaches, and all kinds of vegetables and fruit. Once Highway 99 is reached, rice fields can be seen flooded with water. Agriculture regains a life of its own. Old bi-planes roaring in the air fumigate and fertilize the fields. From time to time, driving is slow because cars have to share the one-way lanes with tractors. Whether you take Highway 99 or Interstate 5, the trip from the Bay Area to Chico feels long.

I began reflecting again, and the next major event came to mind. That one happened during my second year of college: the assassination of President John F. Kennedy. I was in class that day when the loudspeaker came on announcing that our president had been shot. We were all stunned, and classes were released. The next three days were very dismal and dark. Our country was in shock and sorrow. Roger Mudd, a CBS Washington correspondent, stated in one of his reports, "It was a death that touched everyone instantly and directly; rare was the person who did not cry that long weekend."

Healing after such a huge loss took a long time for all. Young, charismatic, energetic, and a father of small children, John F. Kennedy portrayed everything that the country wanted for a president, and it was all gone in a matter of minutes. We mourned. Sadness and anger filled our hearts as we wondered, *Why?*

As I drew closer to my destination, the memory of

Kennedy's assassination brought the same feelings of sadness, anger, and frustration.

The next major development was the war in Vietnam. I was not sure yet how it would affect me. The fear of having to stop my education to join the war had me worried for the next thirty miles, as this type of event had the power to change people's lives drastically. As Americans, we learn at an early age that we have to be ready to serve when called, to preserve freedom, and I was not an exception.

I finally arrived at the university and drove into the dormitory parking lot, welcoming my new challenge. The excitement came back, and my fears were forgotten. I looked around and saw beautiful brick buildings surrounded by ancient trees that made everything look green and attractive. A squirrel looked at me and moved its long tail as if waving to me and saying, "You made it."

12: A Sergeant in Women's Clothes

"Let's be what we say we are: a fraternity, not a club, run by men

and not boys, and based on ideals, not expediency."

-- Ralph Daniel

For the first time in my life, I was struck by the fact that I was embarking on a life away from home. The place that I called home for the next five months was a majestic new building known as Craig Hall. I had applied for and been accepted to another dorm on campus, but when I heard that the first co-ed dorm was opening and that I could switch, I jumped at the chance. Upon arriving to my room, I was surprised to see a familiar face. It was Dave, a co-worker of mine from the cannery. We got along fine, but my first reaction was negative, as I was hoping to disconnect from the past and start completely fresh in a new place with new friends. Dave had found out that I was in room 204 and asked to be transferred to my room. Attitudes are tricks of the mind, and we ended up being good friends. There were four of us sharing a totally awesome, large clean space with brand new bathrooms.

The girls lived in the other side of Craig Hall. We had a very stern housemother who indoctrinated us about strict rules to follow. With two hundred fifty boys and one hundred girls, she made it clear that we were not allowed in the girls' wing.

Thus began the amazing ninety days of dorm life: meeting at 1:00 p.m. the first day. The housemother introduced herself and told us the first rule of business.

"I am Mrs. T. The first thing you need to do is select a president of the dorm to represent the interests of the students," she said with a determined voice. "It has to be someone with sixty credits or an upper division student. Who has sixty units?"

I was one of two who raised his hand.

"I will flip a coin," she said.

I had picked heads hoping not to win, but I did and became the dorm president. It was my first leadership role in college dorms.

The first week was hectic: signing up for classes, creating a workable schedule, and having daily meetings with Mrs. T. going over specific instructions about my new role. She had installed a two-way speaker in our dorm room. Any time she called, I had to be ready to respond and fulfill her requests. One night, she called all frantic.

"Come quick," she said. "We have a disaster here!"

I jumped up from my bed and put on some shorts in a hurry. As I approached the girls' wing of the dorm, I saw Mrs. T. running toward me.

"Birds, birds!" she yelled. "Birds are everywhere!"

There were hundreds of finches flying inside the girls' dorm. The girls, dressed in a variety of colorful pajamas, were screaming and trying to get the birds away from them and out of their hair. It was amusing and confusing at the same time.

"Get to the bottom of it," Mrs. T. told me. "There will be a high price for this prank."

As president, I had become in the eyes of the students someone they had to keep out of the loop, particularly when it came to pranks, and this one was the first of many. I found out that some unnamed students had just seen the movie *Birdman of Alcatraz*, bought finches for two dollars from several local pet stores, and released twenty-five of them in the girls' dorm.

I relayed the info to Mrs. T. and told her that no one had admitted to being involved. As a result, we were given a curfew. We had to be in our rooms for bed checks by 11:00 p.m.

A week later, the pranksters struck again. At 2:00 a.m., Mrs. T. interrupted my sleep.

"Come to my suite immediately," she commanded.

"I will be there in a minute," I replied.

When I arrived, the front door of the lobby was blocked by what seemed to be a huge dead cow. I managed to open the door and was greeted by Mrs. T.

"What do you think about this?" she asked, her eyes almost popping out of their sockets.

"That's a strange place for a cow to die," I said looking stupid.

"Are you kidding me? It's another prank! Solve this case or your job as president is in jeopardy."

Her threat sounded appealing to me. The actions of others were taking a toll on me, preventing me from having a good night's sleep. Also, I disliked the fact that I was perceived as somehow responsible for the vandalism by not catching the perpetrators.

I had been invited to pledge a fraternity in an effort to meet new people. This was my outlet from the predicament of being dorm president. Pledge week was a lot of fun. Every fraternity had a party with music, food, and beautiful ladies. I hoped I would be chosen to pledge with one of the fraternities. As it turned out, I was asked to pledge two of the best. During pledge week, I hung out with a group of guys from Vallejo.

"We're pledging Delta Sigma," they said.

When I dropped my acceptance in the box located in the Student Union, I choose Delta Sigma, to find out later that they all had gone with another fraternity.

The fraternity events gave me the perfect excuse to resign as dorm president. I was not proud of being appointed by a coin toss, and Mrs. T.'s frequent demands were getting old. She accepted my resignation and announced that a real election for president was coming. This time, I didn't put my name on the ballot. Surprisingly, I received the bulk of the votes. I graciously declined, and was, at last, free from Mrs. T.!

Pledging the fraternity was a good and a bad choice. Socially, I was enjoying every minute of it. Academically, I struggled with a full academic load, and had difficulty completing my assignments. Fraternity life could be a book in itself. I will share just a few highlights, as my heart still honors the secret codes of conduct.

13: Embracing Group Values and Diversity

"Unselfish and noble actions are the radiant pages in the biography of souls."

-- David Thomas

Teamwork is not always pleasurable, but it is necessary in order to succeed at school, work, and family. In my life, all the rhetoric about "being in this together" and "all for one and one for all," has never stopped. I have experienced it again and again, including my membership in a fraternity.

In the fall of 1964, I began my journey of the pledge class of Delta Sigma. We had thirty pledges, an unusually large group compared to other fraternities. We had chores to do and workouts to complete in the basement, and we were at the beck and call of the established members.

Hell Week was at the end of the semester, and that was when decisions were made as to whether a pledge was worthy to be a Delta Sigma member. Even though my pledge class came in all shapes, sizes, athletic abilities, and political persuasions, we all had one singular purpose: membership.

The name Hell Week was an understatement. First, we had to spend the week living in the fraternity house where we were kept awake, yelled at repeatedly with commands of all kinds, shouted at constantly that we were unworthy, and exercised until we dropped. The last night was the worst. After four days without sleep, our minds were frazzled.

I know I can make it if I can sleep for a couple of hours, I thought.

At about 10:00 p.m. on that historical last night, hell reached its zenith! We were blindfolded and taken to the kitchen in loincloths where the temperature was around 150 degrees.

"You are going to be branded," they told us.

I believed that they were not going to hurt us, but the mere idea of being branded made me uneasy.

Two guys grabbed me and restrained my arms.

"You are branded with the fraternity logo Delta Sigma," they said ceremoniously as they led me out. (Later, I found out that they had used dry ice in the branding iron, which sounded like the skin was being burned when it made contact with the body.)

If that is the worst of it, I will be okay, I thought.

"Now, you are going to sail the Nile," I was told. "When you reach the other side, you are going to find out if you made it or not."

What happened next was frightening, but at that point I was ready to do anything to belong. Still blindfolded, two frat brothers told me to lie in a box that seemed very much like a coffin. They threw a cold steel chain across my chest. The top of the coffin was closed, and I was submerged under water for a few minutes, gasping for air, a time that seemed like an eternity. I was taken out of the coffin when

I reached the other side. All thirty of us were still blindfolded, dripping wet, but we had made it "across the Nile."

"If you feel a slap on your back, you passed the tests," they said.

I heard a lot of slaps but not on my back, which made me nervous.

What didn't I do right? I gave it all I had, I thought, with a dash of frustration. And then my back was slapped.

Never before had I welcomed a slap on the back as I did that day. What a feeling! I was one of the newest members of the Delta Sigma Fraternity.

The memory of Hell Week was unforgettable. It surprised me how some of the members seemed to enjoy the punishment phase. I was raised in a family where kindness prevailed, and now I was worried that someone eventually was going be seriously hurt—physically, mentally, or both.

Twenty-five of the thirty new members—including myself—moved into the fraternity house, a three-story, beautiful, old southern mansion. We occupied bunk beds on the third floor. There were balconies with verandas that looked out on a street full of oak trees. A Catholic church was only eighty feet from our doorstep, and bells serenaded us every morning and evening. It was a university requirement that all fraternities had to have a housemother, and ours happened to be hard of hearing. We were not allowed to consume alcoholic beverages in the house except when we had a party.

As we settled in at the fraternity house as new members, we became accustomed to a number of pranks perpetrated by the new pledges trying to become members. They kept stealing the front door of the house. When they returned it, they faced stiff workouts.

"Don't you pledges have any creative ways of pranking us?" we asked.

One night, when we all were sleeping in our bunk beds, I felt something warm. The pledges were going around putting our hands in warm water as we slept. When we woke up, we rubbed our eyes, combed our hair with our hands, scratched our necks, and went through all the movements a person does when he wakes up. Shaving cream was leaving its trace all over our faces and everywhere. It was just another mundane prank, nothing special. They repeated this one so many times that we became used to it; we were able to wake up without getting shaving cream on our bodies and faces.

One memorable night, we all woke up to the sound of chickens clucking. As we descended the stairs, we saw about fifty sick-looking chickens running all over the house. Then, one of our members came down the stairs with an axe in one hand and his other bare hand ready for action. Calling himself Farmer John and dressed in overalls, he killed the chickens one by one. It was horrifying watching some of the chickens still moving with their heads cut off, while other chickens ran everywhere trying to escape their fate. I saw one scurry to the veranda to escape; it was looking back at Farmer John when it ran off the third deck to its demise.

When this mess was over, we were all in shock. This was the prank of all pranks. Our poor housemother left shaking her head, saying that she was not returning until the mess was cleaned up.

"You have to feed yourselves breakfast," I recall her saying as she closed the door behind her.

I went into the kitchen for a bowl of cereal. Upon pulling out a chair to sit, I saw a chicken that had survived the massacre. When he saw me, he let out a gasp and dropped dead in fear.

To this day, the memory of that event still sickens me. We made a pact that day to never again use cruelty toward animals, as it was not going to be tolerated. The subject brought the conversation to the topic of Hell Week as a way to accept new members, and some of us discussed options to tone it down.

We always had a meeting to decide whether or not to accept all or some in the group of pledges. This year the group was particularly not interested in one candidate. Discussions went back and forth on his merits. Chris (I cannot remember his real name), one of the recently accepted pledge brothers, raised his hand to make a point. He was a soft-spoken person and very respected by all of us.

"The reason you don't want him has nothing to do with his personality or character," he said. "Basically, he is unattractive. Some of you think that if he wears our logo, it may hurt our image."

You could hear a pin drop. Chris had in one succinct sentence clarified what no one had been able to spell out. His honesty and courage led us to do the right thing, and we agreed to accept the whole pledge class. The person in question turned out to be one of the most productive and dedicated members of our fraternity. Chris hit home with his message: "It is more important to value who you are and the potential you have to become a worthy member than to focus on your looks and possessions."

This truth resonated throughout my entire life. Philosopher Dan Bennett once wrote, "How monotonous the sounds of the forest would be if the music came only from the top ten birds." Inclusion means doing whatever it takes to give all the inhabitants of the forest the same opportunities.

The spring of 1966 brought the beginning of a long-running tradition at the college. To honor the pioneer spirit of California, the college dedicated a week to its heritage, appropriately called Pioneer Week. Each fraternity would select a sheriff candidate and the sororities chose Little Nell candidates. Little Nell represented a heroine rescued by the sheriff, according to a legend created over time by the students at Chico State University. It was a recurrent theme each year.

Each group would compete in five categories: theme, presentations, float decoration, quad projects, and selecting a sheriff and a Little Nell.

The overall theme for the year was "Waterways in California." We had decided to use keelboats as our theme, and we chose one of our strongest candidates as our sheriff. He was Keelboat Wayne.

Each year we built a pioneer town on campus for one week. Lumber mills, gold rush, honky-tonk hotels, and our keelboat were among the entries. A large part of the week's activities included presentations in the auditorium. Each group had ten minutes to put on some sort of performance to introduce their candidate. Singing and dancing were the norm. As we prepared, we selected our cast of characters.

Our director had come up with the theme of Keelboat Wayne coming to the rescue of Little Nell. I was Chief of the Indian tribe Heckaya (where the heck are you). Heckaya was the recurring chant. It was a comedy. Our fraternity had never won presentations. Our rival always won.

The night of the performances was magical. The auditorium was packed with five thousand screaming, crazy students. As we prepared to take the stage, I was shaking with nerves, dressed in a loincloth and a beautiful Indian headdress. When it was my turn to speak, I said my two hundred lines perfectly. The audience roared with laughter. Our skit culminated with a slow-motion fight scene mimicking the old time movies as lights flickered in the backdrop.

At the end, we received a standing ovation. We won first place in presentations. We had started the most fantastic week, culminating in Keelboat Wayne winning sheriff.

14: The Prize behind the Path

"Teaching creates all other professions."

-- Author Unknown

Senior year was getting closer. Members of my fraternity encouraged me to try out for the Head Yell Leader at the college. I had become popular after the success in the recent spring sweepstakes competition among the fraternities on campus. Two of my best friends were gymnastic specialists eager to show their skills. They talked me into it.

On the day tryouts took place, we were a surprise entry. The fraternity that had always won had become comfortable winning and didn't anticipate the challenge brought by new competitors excited to win. It was an easy victory for us. The next day the incumbent fraternity filed a complaint stating that the advertisements were faulty and blamed their failure on poor college communications. We had to do it over again.

"What is meant to be will be. If winning is our destiny, it will happen again in the redo," I answered, taking a deep breath.

To our delight but not our surprise, we won a second time.

My senior year was my best. Not only was I Head Yell Leader of the college, but also I received my highest grade-point average ever.

Soon, the graduation ceremony was approaching. Hundreds of students gathered at the commencement ceremony. The school administrators and teachers lined up with their special doctorate gowns to shake our hands, give us our diplomas, and congratulate us as new graduates. The students were walking, one by one, in their black caps and gowns to receive their diplomas. A story from my childhood came to mind. I was around eight years old. My favorite treat was a box of Cracker Jacks. My father always came from work with a box of Cracker Jacks in his hands for me. Anxiously, I looked for the prize before devouring the delicious caramel popcorn and peanuts. One day, when I opened one of the boxes, I saw that there was no prize inside. I was upset and threw it on the ground in anger.

"Why did you do that?" my father asked.

"Because there was no prize," I said crossing my arms in front of me, eyes on the ground.

"Son, don't be confused. The prize is really the Cracker Jacks," he said.

My dad took the opportunity to teach me a valuable lesson.

Walking on the stage to receive my diploma, I reflected on the many ups and downs and the pathway to this moment, and I recognized that the true prize was not the bumps and stops during the journey, but the completion of a life goal against countless odds—the Cracker Jacks.

Choosing a lifetime career was next. Of the many books that my grandmother gave me, one made a difference in my life: *Goodbye Mr. Chips*, by James Hilton. I didn't read the book right away. I don't really remember when I decided to read it, but once I opened it, I was unable to put it down. Mr. Chips's students revered him, and he inspired me. I knew then that I wanted to be a teacher who made a difference in students' lives.

One day, I visited a career fair with one of my friends. I didn't plan on doing any interviewing. I was just waiting for him to finish his interviews. A gentleman in a new suit asked, "Do you want to be interviewed?"

"I want to be a teacher, sir," I answered, declining his invitation.

"Well, the practice will be helpful for you," he insisted.

I agreed and followed him to his office. His first question was, "Have you done anything in college, besides attend classes?"

"I belonged to a fraternity and held various offices in the fraternity," I answered. "I was Head Yell Leader for the college during my senior year."

He looked at my highest grade point average and noticed that it occurred while I was Head Yell Leader. I mentioned that I realized that in order to be successful, I really had to get serious. He laughed out loud.

"Well," he said, "I will offer you a job right now."

I was shocked. He was serious.

"You stood out in a leadership role and were able to balance school and social life," he said. "Remember that there is only one Head Yell Leader in a college."

He offered me a job on the spot. The starting pay would be twice a starting teacher's salary. I graciously declined. I knew exactly the path that I was going to take: Teaching.

After earning your bachelor's degree, in California you became eligible to student teach. As I entered the threshold of my student teaching career, I never dreamed that in forty-two and a half years, I would be teacher, coach, activities director, assistant principal, principal, superintendent, and a motivational speaker. Teaching was the beginning of a path that challenged my perseverance and rewarded me beyond my wildest expectations.

15: Unfolding Your True Potential

"Life's most urgent question is: What are you doing for others?"

-- Martin Luther King Jr.

My student teaching experience began in 1967 at the local high school. I was given two classes to teach: Drama and US History. I was qualified to teach the history class. The drama class was a surprise and a challenge that I accepted as a new learning experience.

Exactly a week before I began my student teaching, I saw a movie titled *Up the Down Staircase*, based on the novel by Bell Kaufman about her experiences teaching in an inner city school. As a new teacher, Bell was idealistic and full of energy. Upon encountering the realities of an overflowing classroom, she became so overwhelmed that she signed students out of her class without even trying to convince them to stay in school. As I left the movie theater, I made a promise to myself not to give up on any student. A few weeks later in my United States history class, a boy I'll call Cody arrived to class ten minutes early and wanted to talk with me.

"I'm an F student," he informed me, matter of factly. "I am okay with it. I just wanted to let you know."

True to form, Cody did not put any effort into his first exam and received an F.

"Why didn't you write anything in your test?" I asked him.

"I am just saving you some time in correcting my paper," he answered.

"I expect you to write something next time," I told him.

"I can't spell," he said.

"Explain your thoughts in your own words, and do your best," I said.

He wrote three pages on the next test. I could barely decipher his writing, but he did get the gist of the question. I gave him an A. When I passed out the papers, he raised his hand.

"Mr. Miller," he said, "somebody got my F. I received someone else's A."

"You earned that A, Cody."

Turning to the class, I announced that Cody had understood the question and knew the answer.

"Cody, explain to the class why King George's decision to put a severe tax on tea led to the Boston tea party," I said.

He stood up, and before his astonished classmates, he clearly described the feeling of the colonists. He didn't feel unnoticed anymore, and he blossomed. His interest for history increased, and his academic success extended to other subject areas and other teachers.

A group of juniors challenged us student teachers to play a football game with them on any Saturday we chose. The challenge was too enticing to ignore. Six new student teachers took on the juniors one Saturday in the fall of

1967. It had rained the day before, and the field was a muddy mess. Over thirty juniors showed up to play in the game. It was supposed to be flag football, but it turned into a tackle game within a few plays. It was fun, and the muddy conditions made it safe to play. The juniors were in better shape and younger, and they enjoyed beating the student teachers. Thirty minutes later, we were exhausted and looking for reinforcements. I saw Cody in the distance. He was watching the game through the fence. I called out to him and asked him to join us. He declined my invitation.

"Hey, Cody," one of his classmates yelled. "We need you to help out the old student teachers!"

"Okay, I'll play on the teacher's team," Cody said, and took off running toward the game.

"What position are you going to play?" I asked.

"I always play center," he replied.

"Not today," I told him. "You're our running back."

From the moment he took the ball, he was unstoppable. It took three of his classmates to bring him down. Needless to say, Cody was the talk of the school on Monday morning. From that moment on, his social life changed. He made the varsity football team as a senior and became an honor roll student. In a way, Cody was my first success story. He received positive encouragement. I learned early in my career how powerful it is to never give up on my students.

My master teacher had handed me the keys to the classroom my first day of student teaching and said, "Good Luck."

I was shocked and excited at the same time. I was

completely in charge. On the other hand, my drama master teacher expected detailed lesson plans with a word-by-word dialogue so he could follow along. When I strayed from the script, he interrupted me. These two experiences were on either end of the spectrum.

One day in the drama class, I decided to use my script as a guide to enable me to be more animated in teaching the skills of acting. It was a huge gamble that paid off.

"You don't need to follow your script word by word," he said. "You have proven that you are prepared."

While working as a student teacher that fall, I found a part-time job selling life insurance. Within a month, I was making over two thousand dollars a month. The company had been trying to convince me to accept a position in the state of Washington running a program tailored toward college students. The offer was tempting: excellent salary, benefits, and incentives based on performance. As I pondered the possibilities, for the second time I came back to the realization that teaching was definitively my vocation. I loved working with young people, and I was thoroughly enjoying my student-teaching experience. About three weeks before the end of the semester, the principal stopped me in the hall.

"I have heard great things about your teaching and the rapport that you build with your students," he said. "Are you interested in a job opening in the social science department starting immediately after you complete your student teaching at the end of January?"

After much soul searching, I accepted the offer. Teaching was always my passion and my first choice because it offered excitement, challenges, and plenty of opportunities to make a difference in children's lives.

Three weeks later, after a whirlwind student-teaching experience, I said goodbye to my two classes and began my career as a full-time social science teacher.

Teachers are usually hired to begin the school year in August, not mid-year in January. I found out through the grapevine that I was replacing a teacher who was fed up with the public school system after teaching for many years. He had just failed sixty-five percent of his seniors in a US government class. Before he left, as he finished cleaning his drawer, he handed me a list of one hundred thirty-five students that he said were "problem kids," and, as if he was doing me a big favor, he added, "Watch out for them!"

As that first day came closer, I kept looking at the list. Of the one hundred eighty students I would have in my classes, at least three quarters of them were trouble-makers. I was a twenty-three-year-old rookie, and many of these students were eighteen years old.

When I entered my first-period class, you could have heard a pin drop. A student yelled out, "We got rid of the last one. Are you next?" I paused and asked the student to step outside for a moment. When he left the room, he was ready for a verbal and perhaps physical fight.

"You need to give me a chance," I told him. "Respect is earned both ways. Return to class with me."

He looked shocked.

"You mean you are not going to kick me out?"

"You need to pass government in order to graduate in June, so we need to get started," I replied.

He followed me into the classroom and sat down without a word.

I looked at the faces before me. The one thing that struck me was their sense of anger. They were still mad that the other teacher had given them failing grades, thus requiring them to take government again. They were waiting to hear my first words. Slowly I pulled out the list of names from my folder and said, "Your previous teacher gave me a list of all the troublemakers in my classes."

I held up the list in both hands and tore it into pieces.

"I will make up my own mind about who the troublemakers are," I told them. "This is a new beginning, and together we will all pass the class."

I spent the rest of the day writing fake lists for each of the remaining classes because I had torn the original in first period. The same effect occurred as I went from class to class: hope and relief.

16: Learning, Demonstrating, and Inspiring

"Life doesn't require that we be the best, only that we try our best."

-- H. Jackson Brown Jr.

The first lesson I learned after my first day of teaching was to pace myself. I began my day with a lot of energy and after lunch, I was dragging. I asked a veteran teacher to advise me on how to pace myself.

"Always keep a little something extra for the afternoon classes," he said. "The students are tired too, so you need to preserve your energy for the last two periods."

I eventually got in the swing of keeping the right balance while distributing my time and activities with the students. The second week, the school added another teacher with the same last name as mine. I overheard a group of students talking about their teachers.

"I have the new Mr. Miller," one of the students said.

I've been teaching for only one week, and already I'm the old teacher! I said to myself.

George, one of the teachers that began at the same time as I did, was very popular with students. However, he was not good at record keeping.

"I lost the records for all of the books I checked out. The book lady is on my case," he told me frantically.

At the end of the year, he had lost thirty-nine books. Hearing him bemoaning his fate made me more conscientious about keeping good records.

The halls of the school were always crowded. As students and staff scurried from one class to another, I noticed one student who looked shy and, day after day, walked so close to the wall that he almost touched it. He usually looked down and out. I always wanted to help the underdog and for that reason, I decided to get his attention. I found out that his name was Richard. As he passed my classroom door, I said, "Good morning, Rick."

He looked up and hurried off without saying a word. I made it a point to always say hi to him, hoping to get a response. Finally, after a week, he stopped and looked at me.

"My name is not Rick! My name is Richard!"

From then on, I called him Richard. One Friday night I was assigned to work in the booth at the high school football game keeping statistics. I needed someone to give me a hand. I saw Richard in the cafeteria.

"Are you going to the game?" I asked him.

"I hate sports," he answered roughly. "No, I am not going."

"I need a spotter to help me identify the players," I said.

"No," he said. "Not me!"

"Well, if you change your mind, I will be in the press box."

He showed up! The game was great, and he was a good spotter. Four years later, he was our high school announcer. He had found his niche. A little encouragement goes a long way. Sometimes students need just a little push to reach their potential and realize that they have value.

About two weeks into the spring semester, the principal stopped me in the walkway.

"I need to talk to you after school," he said. "I need to ask you a favor."

"Sure," I said.

When school was over for the day, I hurried to his office, puzzled.

"What do you need?"

"I need an assistant swimming coach," he replied.

"I don't swim very well," I told him.

"It doesn't matter," he said. "I need a credentialed teacher. The head coach is qualified, and the college assistants will do most of the coaching."

Aiming to please, I accepted. The first day we showed up to the pool and all of the swimmers were eager to begin, with one exception: the senior long-distance swimmer. When he arrived ten minutes late, he had two young ladies hugging him, one under each arm. He was tall, handsome, and confident.

"Is the pool ready?" That was his first remark to me.

"Yes, but not for you," I said. "You are late. We start at three o'clock sharp."

"It's your loss," he laughed and left.

Three days in a row, he tested us. Finally, he agreed to our rules and joined the squad. He was an excellent swimmer, but he was lazy. The head coach asked me to be his coach and try to get the most out of him. Each day I yelled encouragement and made him do his required laps. I wasn't a good swimmer, but I could yell.

"Stroke! Stroke!"

Each time he came up for air, he was swearing. I acted like I didn't hear it.

"What did you say?" I asked each time.

By the end of practice, he had been forced to really work on his stroke and endurance. He took first place at the state meet at the end of the year. At the awards ceremony, he looked at me and thanked me for pushing him.

"You know, Mr. Miller is not a good swimmer, but he is the reason I won the championship," he said during the awards ceremony. "Without him forcing me to give my best every day, I wouldn't have been successful. He brought me back to do what I needed to do to get this medal."

In my government class, I wanted to have lessons that would engage the students in role-playing. We were studying the branches of the federal government, and I had created a lesson called Ground Zero.

In the lesson, I told the students that a bomb had gone off, and we were forced to stay in the room for one full year. I told them that I had all the provisions needed to survive stashed beneath the classroom floor. I had thought of everything.

"Accommodations for men and women are ready, including restrooms, food supply, and water. There is one rule: No one can leave. You are in charge of forming a government."

That was my introduction and the assignment.

The students really got into it. First, they voted who would stand by the door. The biggest student was selected. The students were very engaged in the activity. Just then, the door opened, and the principal brought two nuns dressed in full nuns' habits into the room.

The class yelled, "Contamination, contamination!"

The nuns ran out of the room. Needless to say, I had to explain to these visiting nuns from Ireland that it was a lesson and not a reflection on them. The nuns were very forgiving.

"Next time you plan something like this, let me know," the principal said over his glasses.

The lesson was a success. The students created a government that had checks and balances to protect the rights of the citizens. A month later, I received a letter from the nuns in Ireland asking for a copy of the lesson plan.

As the year came to a close, I had so much for which to be thankful, including a job that I loved. I was a coach, a teacher, and I never lost any textbooks!

17: Mantras, Subjects, Classes, and Themes

"If you cannot see where you are going, ask someone who has been there before."

-- J. Loren Norris

Spring mornings open the sky with new colors in the horizon. The weather is mild, and flowers bloom all over. The school year ends sometime in June. Summers are a welcome break filled with all kinds of family activities. The mind rests, clears up, and resets. In a predictable cycle, the school year begins each August. Students are excited to return to school in their new clothes, starting at a new level in their educational journey, meeting new teachers, and seeing old friends again. As the year began, I saw George with a stack of books and book cards.

"No lost books this year," he said winking an eye.

"That's good," I said.

I entered the staff room and smelled the smoke permeating the room. Looking back, it seems odd that we didn't allow students to smoke, but the teachers sneaked into the staff room every period to have their smoke. When the door opened, the smoke exited with the teachers, in their breath and on their clothes. Most of the staff never went in there except to get their mail and papers for the day. Spirited conversations on politics, both local and national, and gossip about the school in general took place in there, and that was why eight relatively new teachers loved the staff room. We had all learned that the older teachers had their own special seats. We never sat in them because we didn't want to be told to move.

The third day of class, the principal called me to his office.

"I hired a swimming coach," he informed me. "I want to thank you for your service. Do you have any other interests in coaching?"

"I would love to coach baseball," I answered after thinking for a moment.

"Great. You are the new junior varsity head baseball coach," he said.

I was thrilled. I had played baseball in high school and college, so this was a dream come true. The news traveled fast. I didn't know that one of my colleagues wanted the job, and was upset. I approached him and said, "Let's work together and share the role and the salary."

He agreed, and a long partnership ensued. He was strict and I was easy, but we learned to use each other's strengths, which made us a good team.

The next day, I saw the head track coach.

"Congratulations," he said. "In order to be successful in baseball, you need to know three things."

"What are they?" I asked eager to hear his words.

"Hum baby, atta batter, and spit in the glove!"

I coached with that mantra for over twenty years.

As the years passed, my skills as a teacher improved.

However, I still found myself in mid-sentence when the bell rang to change classes. I went to my favorite seasoned teacher and asked him if he could give me some advice to avoid this problem.

"Have you heard of the acronym ROME?" he asked.

"No," I answered. "I have not heard of it."

"It stands for Review, Objective, Meaning, and Ending," he said. "You need to review at the beginning of each class, set objectives clearly with the students, clarify the meaning and purpose of the lesson, and finally, have a good ending to wrap up what they just learned."

"Can I bring you one of my lesson plans for suggestions?" I asked.

"Sure," he said.

He was a champ in my eyes.

"You have a good relationship with your students, but they need more structure and focus. I am sharing with you a plan that will give you both." He gave me a pat on my shoulder and said as he walked away, "In teaching, you need to always be prepared and stay flexible."

After that, I always referred to him as Flexible Milt.

The teacher whose class was next to mine was a real trickster. He was funny, loved practical jokes, and loved to show movies in his class. Sometimes the noise was deafening. He would turn it up just to get my goat. One day, my students and I had enough.

"All of my movies have a purpose," he said. "The one that I am showing on Friday is about Pearl Harbor."

As a class, we decided to get back at him. We organized

ourselves into three rows. Some of the students got on their knees in the first row, the next group of students crouched in the second row, and a third group of students stood in the last row. We all made paper airplanes, and when the movie was playing the attack, we turned off the lights, opened the sliding door that separated the two classrooms, and fired off more than four hundred airplanes into the bewildered students in his class.

We reached an agreement not to play any more pranks on each other and not to jack up the volume of the movies to the point of disrupting the neighboring class. We referred to it as the peace treaty at the end of the Second World War.

One of the other social science teachers wanted my collaboration. We were both teaching world history, and he suggested a lesson on dictatorships. Dressed like Cossacks and wearing Russian hats, old clothes, and fake beards, we took pictures of ourselves and showed them to the students, telling them that we were dictators. We challenged the students to come up with a plan to overthrow us. The students really got into it, and it turned out to be a highlight of the classes for both of us. Students loved situations where they were able to engage in their own learning as opposed to straight lecturing.

The following year I was asked to teach a speech class. In this class, I had two students I will never forget: a young lady who had a burning desire to overcome her self-consciousness, and the starting quarterback for the varsity football team. The young lady worked very hard and became one of my best students, self-assured and confident in speaking before large groups. The quarterback gave some of the most heart-warming speeches as he shared how it felt to be expected to be the best.

"I have felt lonely," he shared. "People just want to befriend me because I'm the football star. I just want to be accepted for who I am, not for my athletic accomplishments."

Years later, the young lady became a successful speech therapist, and I hired the quarterback as one of my teachers when I became a principal.

Another opportunity for more learning came when I was asked to teach a social science class—marriage and family. We covered many issues that face young people. We planned a mock marriage where students learned about the costs of furnishing a house, paying for food and gas and utilities, balancing checkbooks, opening and maintaining bank accounts, and planning a budget. The first time we did it, the class chose a couple to marry. They had to share similarities and differences that could make their marriage happy or dysfunctional. When the date of the wedding arrived, the real boyfriend of the girl chosen wanted to beat up the pretend husband-to-be. I adjusted the lesson plan and brought in a real couple already married to play the part.

We had a rule in the class: There was no such thing as a dumb answer or question, and no laughing either, because that would stifle questions and answers. One day I asked if anyone knew of a difficult first date.

"My cousin had a rough first date," a girl said. "The guy cut her head off."

We all gasped. We had forgotten that the murder investigation had been broadcast in the news recently. It was tough not to have a reaction from the class, but we all kept our cool.

"Well," I said, "I am sorry to hear that. Fortunately, most dates don't end up that way."

After that, we focused on the awkwardness of first dates, and choosing a place to go, like a movie or a restaurant.

For many students this was the first time they were able to discuss issues regarding puberty and coming of age. It required tact on my part, and often I had to defer to their parents for more details than I was able to share. All in all, it was a beginning course in Relationships 101.

18: Inspire Others to Motivate Themselves

"Try to be a rainbow in someone's cloud."

-- Maya Angelou.

In my fourth year of teaching, I was assigned five classes of senior government. It was a magical year, and when it ended, I was surprised to find out that the senior class had dedicated the yearbook to me. Usually, it is given to an older teacher near to or beginning retirement. I was shocked.

I jokingly thought that I was too young to receive this honor. I was quickly brought back to reality by one of my students—a boy who always tried to get extra attention and had complimented me while he was my student, but I always had the hunch that his words were forced. When he received his final grade, he immediately started yelling at me as he left the room. "You are the worst teacher I have ever had, and you don't deserve the honor of having the yearbook dedicated to you!" he shouted.

I was shocked and shaken. It was the first time I had experienced the angry reaction of an unhappy student. It caused me to doubt myself. I went to my mentor, Flexible Milt, with my dismay.

"We can't be liked by everyone, Ken," he said. "You need to toughen up. We have to be honest with ourselves and look at ways to become better. Use this incident as a way to be self-reflective on how you can be a better teacher. In my opinion, you already are successful, but there is always room for improvement."

I reflected on his words. An episode came to mind from my first year of teaching: the Fur Post Caper. The class was United States history targeted to a group of juniors. I loved to give essay tests, which were easy to create but labor intensive to grade. In one of the classes, I gave a test that covered the early settlers in the new Americas. One of the questions asked the students to describe life on one of the fur posts in the wilderness.

Neil was a very bright young man who always wrote volumes and had gained the reputation of being a straight A student. When I returned the tests, I asked for volunteers to read their answers aloud if they had answered the question correctly. Neil raised his hand eagerly.

"Go ahead, Neil," I said.

He began. "The fur post was a very strange pole that miraculously grew fur," he said. "Everyone from far and wide came to see the miracle of the post where fur grew!"

His description went on and on. The students thought he was making it up just for a joke. I knew that he was just summarizing what he had written on his paper. Neil's response was a valuable lesson for me. From then on, as tedious as the task could become from time to time, I read every word written by my students. For the rest of the year, they tested me to see if I was really reading their work. Ever since that day, I made sure to read all the work the students turned in, whether a test or homework. I owed it to them.

My conversation with Milt left footprints in my soul.

Being soft spoken and kind by nature, I had to learn to toughen up, as he advised. Ironically, I met the unhappy student years later at a class reunion. He apologized for his behavior, saying that he was just mad about his grade.

"I learned from your words," I said to him. "They challenged me to be a better teacher."

Coaching furthered my growth as a teacher. I was asked to be an assistant JV football coach. I had played football in high school and was overjoyed to be chosen. I was going to be the line coach. I studied so hard, read all the plays, and put them down on three by five cards. The players knew I was a new football coach and joked about my three by five cards.

"Our last coach didn't have note cards," they remarked.

The first game was a home game played at the university stadium. We were playing a large school from Sacramento. My neighbors came to cheer me on. After the first quarter, the score was thirty-five to zero. We were getting killed.

"It's your fault," the neighbors yelled jokingly.

I had a headset on and was in communication with the press box where the varsity coaches were watching the game and relaying advice.

"What can you tell me?" I asked one of the coaches.

"Your boys are not blocking or tackling," he said.

"Are you kidding me?" I responded. "I can see that."

After the game, I walked off the field totally crushed. I had worked so hard and with such intensity to prepare the players, and I felt like I had let them down. The old coach saw me and sought me out. He put his arm around me and said, "Your boys did the best they could do. The team you faced was just that much better."

"As coaches we do everything we can to motivate the players," I said.

"No. Your job is to inspire the players to do their best to reach their potential. They are the ones who must motivate themselves."

His words had a profound impact on the rest of my life. The mantra "Inspire to motivate" was born and was the very foundation of my future teaching, whether it was coaching, teaching in the classroom, or managing personnel.

At the end of the season, we had won only one game. It was difficult to accept that we had not done better.

"Go to the football coaches' convention in San Francisco to learn more about game strategies," the head varsity coach told me.

Little did I know that once again I would be moved by the words of another coach. As I looked at the agenda for the conference, I noticed that Grant Teoff, the coach at Baylor University, would be speaking. I had heard a lot about him and was excited to hear him speak. He began sharing a story about one of his players who was injured in his junior year. The way I remember the story is that the big tackle became increasingly depressed. He had high hopes of being drafted in the NFL, and to be able to provide for his family. His daughter had been a regular at the practices.

When Coach Teoff heard how his player was doing, he went to him and told him that he needed to stomp on it and rise above it. He challenged him to return to his discipline, and with that, he could return to football and play in at least five or six games his senior year.

With the help of Grant Teoff's encouragement, he returned to his core values and began in earnest to get in shape. All along, his coach was there for him. When the senior year came, he was able to play enough games to qualify for the senior bowl. Grant was one of the coaches, and he selected his tackle. He had earned it. As a result, he was drafted by the NFL in the spring of that year.

A few months later, the coach received a phone call that brought him to his knees. It was that big strong tackle telling Grant that his little girl had died in a terrible accident. Grant didn't know what to say. In his speech, he described to the audience a dialogue that, in essence, was close to the following:

"I need you," the tackle said.

"I will be there on the next flight," Grant said, wondering what he could offer him and how he could help.

As Grant walked up the pathway, he saw him sitting on the steps with his head in his hands. They embraced, and Grant said, "I don't know what to say."

"I am going to stomp on it and rise above it," the big tackle said with resolve, looking him in the eyes.

The coach had made that kind of connection with him. The player knew that Grant cared about him as a person.

Grant closed his speech with a strong message: Invest in people, and they will know that you care. They will exceed your expectations. Inspiring to motivate cannot come without a true connection, a sense that you really care about them.

I learned a lot about football strategy at that conference, but the words of Grant Teoff affected my teaching and, later, my years in administration in a positive way. Never lose sight of your true purpose. It is not about winning. It is about being the best you can be. Play at your highest level. Winning will take care of itself.

19: Following Rules and Learning from Mistakes

"I follow three rules: Do the right thing, do the best you can, and always show people you care."

-- Lou Holtz

There were two assistant principals: one in charge of curriculum and the other in charge of discipline. A very good friend of mine was promoted from activities director to the role of assistant principal in charge of curriculum. With this promotion, his teaching position was vacant. The schedule included teaching student government and three prep periods in the afternoon. Coordinating dances, athletics, and rallies were part of the school's activities program. The principal called me to his office.

"I want you to be the new activities director," he offered.

"I need a day to think about it," I told him.

I went to the friend who had held the job for two years and asked his advice.

"You can accept if the principal grants you these twenty-six, non-negotiable demands."

"I know this list is going to make it hard for the principal to swallow."

"You asked my advice," he said.

I went to my mentor, Flexible Milt. "What do you think about this job?" I asked him.

"It is a good fit for you," he said. "You are outgoing, funny, and playful. You will be a natural. Go for it. We need your enthusiasm and energy. Just make sure you have an escape clause such as going back to teaching full time if it doesn't work out."

Armed with his encouragement and the list of demands, I went into the principal's office.

"What is your decision?" he asked.

"I will accept the job only if this list of non-negotiable demands is met," I said sheepishly, not feeling as confident as I sounded.

"When can you start?" he said after looking at it. "I figured you'd do your homework."

I was shocked.

He added, "Remember to keep your sense of humor. You are now in a quasi-administrative role. You will attend my cabinet meetings with my assistant principals each week. You will see a slippage in connectivity with your colleagues. They will see you as an administrator. Be strong, and don't take everything as a personal affront."

The first case that I encountered in my new job as activities director was the Chocolate Chip Cookie Caper. Little did I know it would happen my first week on the job. The high school football game was Friday night. I was in charge of concessions and all the logistics. The senior class was running the concession that week, and I met with the parent representatives. All was a go. When I arrived at the stadium, there seemed to be a big argument between some of the parents and one of the teachers. A US history teacher was trying to sell chocolate chip cookies to raise funds for his classroom. The parents were upset because they were told the profits from the concessions went to their senior prom fundraising. I listened to both sides, and then I informed the teacher, "You can sell the cookies at the next football game, but you have to go through the correct procedures to sell anything at a game."

"This is not over," he replied furiously.

The following week he had gotten a number of his parents riled up, and they requested a meeting with me. I heard their concerns.

"I just took the job, and I am following the rules that are in place," I said to them. "I apologize for the misunderstanding about the proper protocols to sell anything at football games. I want to personally contribute to the class fund for the cost of preparing the cookies."

The parents seemed pleased, but the teacher wanted blood. He kept bringing it up in the staff room and trying to discredit my leadership. I wrote a formal apology and included it in the school newsletter. After that, the worm turned. As the teacher continued to talk about it, the staff made fun of him and kept sending chocolate chip cookies to his office. Finally, he relented.

Supervision of pep rallies was part of my new role as activities director. Every Friday during the football season and throughout the calendar year, we had a pep rally to build the school's spirit and support the teams. During my tenure as activities director, there were many highlights.

Two special students with an uncanny wit performed the Russ and Randy Show at the rallies. They were very entertaining and made everyone laugh. They dressed like the Blues Brothers and performed as an air band using kazoos to play music from the movie *Shaft*. They stopped mid-sentence and said, "What they do!"

The crowd went nuts. They became folk heroes on campus.

That same year, the principal came to one of my student government meetings.

"A football team from Kauai, Hawaii, is coming to our school to play a football game. We need to put together a special assembly to welcome them," he said.

Russ and Randy put their heads together and created an elaborate welcome for our guests. They dressed as Hawaiian royalty and came into the gathering to music and an entourage of warriors. We found out later that our guests were not pleased. From then on, I learned that the buck stopped with me and that I had to be more aware of the possible implications of the attempts at humor by the students. I apologized to our guests, and we were able to get past the incident.

I was sad to see Russ and Randy graduate, as they were truly a great team. Later in life, they made small independent films and had their own gala openings and the like. They were very special.

20: The Best Christmas Present Ever

"Life is a series of thousands of miracles."

-- Elena Brower

As the fall holiday season approached, it was time to create the annual holiday assembly. During those first three years as activities director, it was always a challenge to do something different and unique. I had talked an older teacher into being Santa for a skit, and he loved it. Actually, it helped him gain some popularity with his students, and he became an advocate for student activities. He had gone from skeptic to supporter.

With the fourth year approaching, we were all wondering what we could do different. As we sat around talking about the assembly in our student government class, one of the more soft-spoken students raised his hand. Vince rarely said anything in class. He was a junior always willing to volunteer. If we needed somebody to get paper, supplies, or to go to the office, Vince was our guy.

"I have an idea," he said.

We all were surprised. He was usually silent.

"I have written a story called Never Say Never."

"Give us more details," I prompted him.

"It is about all of the toys that are left behind when Santa leaves for Christmas Eve," he said. "I have learned how to speak like the Muppets. I can do the voices of Kermit the Frog, Animal, and Miss Piggy. I have the puppets, and I have created roles for each student, such as Princess Lea, Yoda, and Luke Skywalker."

You could hear a pin drop. Everyone asked him to demonstrate. He began singing the song "The Rainbow Connection" from the Muppet movie. We were all shocked. Everyone was excited. We only had three days to prepare, and Vince said he would bring the scripts the next day. We all agreed to keep it a secret.

We were hosting a student government meeting for our region, and forty schools were going to be our guests at the holiday assembly. I was crossing my fingers that Vince's performance was for real.

The next day he showed up with puppets, scripts, costumes—everything we needed. Vince said he needed someone to play the piano while he sang the song. One of the girls in the class was a skilled piano player. Together they were magical. The climax of the skit finished with Santa leaving without all the toys. Then Kermit the frog told all the other toys to "never say never," and he sang "The Rainbow Connection." As he finished the song, Santa returned to get all the toys.

I couldn't wait for the day to arrive. It was going to be so special. Our last practice was after school the day before the assembly. After practice, I told Vince how proud of him I was.

"Your parents need to be here to see it," I said.

"If you tell my parents, I won't do it," he said abruptly.

"Why?"

"My father makes fun of me when he sees me playing with puppets and practicing various voices. He thinks it is a waste of time. He wishes I was an athlete." The sadness in his eyes spoke volumes.

I promised him I was not going to tell. As I walked back to my office, I saw the principal.

"Is the assembly going to be any good, especially with forty schools visiting?" he asked me.

"It is going to be very special," I said, and told him the story about Vince. "I feel bad that his family is not coming, but I promised not to tell his parents."

The principal listened and said that he wanted to attend the assembly. The pressure was on!

The next day, all the preparations were set for the performance of "Never Say Never." It was scheduled to be the concluding part of the assembly. I worried about the students' reaction to the story with puppets and singing.

The skit began in Santa's workshop with a Christmas tree, a piano, and a giant sleigh filled with toys. The gym was packed. Everyone was anticipating the final performance as word had leaked out that something special was going to happen.

The story unfolded. Santa leaves a number of toys behind because he doesn't have room in his sleigh. The toys have a funny dialogue that keeps the interest of the audience. I was sitting in the stands next to a group of visitors who were unaware of what was going to happen. I eagerly awaited Vince's performance; he was hidden behind the piano and not visible to the crowd. After Santa departed, all the toys began crying and asking why they'd been left behind. How could this happen? Just then, the voice of Kermit the frog called out from where he was sitting on the edge of the piano.

"Don't cry!" he said. "You should never say never when things don't go your way. There is a reason for everything." Then, the piano played the introduction to the song. Kermit, in all his glory, sang "The Rainbow Connection."

Somebody in the crowd yelled, "It's the record! The puppet is just lip syncing!"

At the end of the song, Vince stood up and sang the final words of the song. The place went nuts as Santa arrived on cue to pick up the other toys! The audience was chanting, "Never say never! Never say never!"

The assembly ended with a rousing shout of Merry Christmas to all, and the audience rushed to Vince. He and Kermit had become instant celebrities.

I approached him to congratulate him. He was surrounded by his new fans. It was then that I noticed a middle-aged gentleman walking toward Vince with tears in his eyes. He gave Vince a hug and said, "Son, I am proud of you. I will never make fun of you again."

I had tears in my eyes as father and son embraced. Miracles are everywhere. This was the best Christmas present ever for them and for me. I asked the father who had told him about the assembly.

"The principal called me and told me that my son was performing at the assembly, and that I shouldn't miss it."

I never forgot this caring act by the principal. He took the time to do something special for one student. He took the time to care.

As for Vince and Kermit, they graduated together,

mortarboard and gown. Kermit even sang hard rock songs at the rallies, including Jimmy Hendrix's "Purple Haze"—and why not!

As I relive the story of father and son embracing, I remember my own three children—two girls and a boy— and the beautiful life that we had together during their childhood. They became a reason for me to excel and grow professionally, as I still had one foot in the teacher realm and one foot in the administration world. My drive intensified, as I wanted to be a good provider. They began growing and living the life of children of an educator, a person who worked many nights, as school activities required my presence. I remember my youngest asking me one day, "Daddy, where do you live at night?" These were among the unrecognized sacrifices that teachers and administrators make because of their dedication to students.

Christmas was very special, and a time of joy. As a young boy, my own memories of Christmas were rich in family experiences. My children also loved our own unique ways of celebrating Christmas morning. We taped a piece of Christmas wrapping paper across the doorway for the children to break through when they received the green light to see the Christmas presents that Santa had left for them.

As young children, they loved life, participated in plays and sports, and had access to all the opportunities available: scouts, music lessons, science camps, soccer, baseball, field hockey, cheerleading, student government, and football, just to mention a few of the many interests they explored.

I was getting closer to a new frontier, a job that would

tax my resolve and challenge me beyond my wildest dreams, a job that would provide immeasurable joy and sadness. Two of my children were attending the high school where I would soon be the youngest assistant principal ever hired. They lived the experience of their dad wearing two hats at their school: assistant principal and father. It wouldn't be until much later that a tragedy of unimaginable pain marked our lives forever.

21: A Gym Rocks with Life

"A good teacher, like a good entertainer, first must hold his

audience's attention, then he can teach his lesson."

-- John Henrik Clarke

Not all assemblies went as well as that special holiday event where Vince's creativity moved everyone in the audience. Some events failed. The events that I pursued were educational and with a dual objective: to provide entertainment and to have substance. One November, I received a call from the National Champion Highway Program asking if we were interested in a free assembly led by a champion Indianapolis driver. I said yes, and he sent a letter confirming his engagement to speak at our school on December 12.

When that date arrived, the students piled into the gym. It was a full house. We waited and waited, but no one showed up. Besides being frustrating and a little embarrassing, this altered the whole school schedule. We had to let the students go to lunch early, and I was called to the principal's office. He was very upset about the fiasco. I told him I had the paperwork to prove the driver had confirmed. I rushed to my file and brought the letter.

"It says December twelfth," he read, "but it is for NEXT YEAR!"

I missed it by a year. I never thought that someone would schedule anything a whole year in advance.

"It will never happen again," I vowed.

After that, I was teased constantly. I had to be a good sport. However, it was not my last embarrassment.

One day, I received a call from a magician name Mr. Mike. The flyers that he sent described him as a wonderful magician with a performance that was worth the time. So, I scheduled the assembly. I faithfully called the night before, something I had learned to do to make sure it was a go. When I called, Mr. Mike assured me that he was going to be there.

"Have my check ready," he said.

"No problem. We are looking forward to your performance," I told him.

You guessed it. He didn't show up. Twelve hundred students sitting in the stands waiting, and no magician. Needless to say, I became the brunt of many more jokes.

"Nice assembly, Mr. Miller. The magician disappeared!"

"That's it," I said jokingly, "that was his best act. He came, but no one saw him."

I never found out what happened to him. At the next rally, the students introduced a boy about eight years old and said he was Mr. Mike. He did a few tricks, everyone laughed, and I always wondered if the whole thing was another set-up to put additional emphasis on Mr. Mike's disappearance.

Rallies, dances, basketball games, donkey basketball games—the gym was constantly packed with students, parents, and visitors.

During one of my favorite rallies ever, the students created two unforgettable skits. The first was the pump house. On the field was an old pump house. When the players needed to be disciplined, they had to crab walk all the way to the pump house and back. This entailed putting their hands on the ground and running sideways like a crab, which was very hard to do. At the rally, the students brought out a paper mâché pump house and set it on the gym floor.

All the coaches were asked to participate in a crab walk around the make-believe pump house. They all agreed, and the race was ready to begin. The pump house was only ten feet from the starting line. The whistle blew, and the coaches took off. When they approached the pump house, it moved. A student was inside the pump house moving it away from the coaches while they chased it. It was hilarious.

After school, all teams took part in a crab walk to the real pump house. The students said it had been worth it to watch the coaches crab walking as they chased the moving pump house!

The second all-time best was a skit that portrayed the cafeteria lady. She regularly closed the snack bar window too early. To dramatize this, the students created a snack bar window.

"Snack bar open!" the student representing the cafeteria lady shouted.

Students ran to it. As they approached the window, the cafeteria lady shouted, "Snack bar closed!"

The whole thing repeated again and again. Never had I seen so many students laughing uncontrollably.

As a result of this skit, the rules for the real snack bar were clarified and changed.

One of the most interesting events occurred on a stormy and rainy day. I was in my office when the principal summoned me to his office. I could tell from the sound of his voice that he was worried and concerned about something.

"I just received a call about a bomb threat," he said when I arrived.

"What do you want me to do?" I asked.

"I want you to immediately take the students to the gym while we check out the school," he replied.

I thought for a minute. "But Bill—"

"No buts," he said. "Just do it."

"Yeah, but—"

"No buts. Take the students to the gym!"

I left his office. An announcement over the PA system requested all students to report to the gym. We had a mock rally and entertained the students for over an hour. When the all-clear bell rang and the students returned to class, the principal approached me.

"Why did you keep interrupting me instead of immediately doing what I said?"

"I was trying to ask whether you had checked the gym yet. Maybe the bomb was in there."

He turned white. "Wow, you are right! I didn't even think of that. From now on, I will definitively let you complete your sentences."

We had many fond memories working together and often recalled the "But Bill" story.

Fortunately, nothing happened as a result of the bomb scare, but it made us implement formal procedures if faced with more threats.

22: The Courage to Do What Is Right

"Supervision is an opportunity to bring someone back to their own mind, to show them how good they can be."

-- Nancy Kline

For thirteen years I was the number one dance chaperone. I have always loved music, even though I can't carry a tune. As I traversed the thirteen years of dance supervision, my favorite time was the Bee Gees era, smooth melodies, and love songs. The era of hard rock was rough on my ears. To this day, I believe that my hearing loss is a result of those 156 dances that I supervised.

Scheduling dances as an activities director was one thing. Supervising them once per month throughout the school year, including the junior and senior proms, was another.

I never forgot the Trike Incident. One Friday night after a football game, the cafeteria was packed with students enjoying the music. A boy on a trike entered the back entrance. Everyone was laughing, but it was crazy trying to get him to stop, as students jumped fast to get out of his way. When I asked him to get off his trike, he refused. We had police supervision on the perimeter of the school, and I called them to help out.

"You are kidding me," the officer remarked. "You can't get a boy off a tricycle?"

"I wouldn't be asking for your help if I was able to do it without physically restraining him," I answered through my walkie-talkie.

It was obvious to everyone at the dance that the person on the trike was under the influence of something. When a police officer came, he commanded, "Please stop!"

The teenage rider gestured with his hand in an uncomplimentary way, which prompted the officer to take down the trike bandit. The boy was taken to the police department and turned over to his parents. There was no trike riding for him for a while without supervision.

The police officer apologized to me later for questioning how I had handled the situation. It would not be the last time I would be questioned by the police about problem behavior in certain students. Repetitively, after each incident, they gained a respect for what I had or had not done once they confronted the facts themselves.

The Drunk Guy situation happened from time to time. It was always a different case with a different student. Making sure that students were not under the influence of alcohol or drugs when they entered the dance was one of my responsibilities. At every dance, three staff members helped with the supervision. I usually stayed near the door looking for any hint of students who had been drinking.

One evening at about 10:30 p.m., I was told by one of my teachers that there was a disturbance outside. The teacher outside was a big strong male very capable of providing a physical presence around unruly students. When I went outside, the student was yelling, and when he saw me, he used foul language to invite me to fight him.

It was evident that he was under the influence of alcohol. As he came closer, he tried to hit me with a punch. I grabbed him and swung him around so he couldn't hurt me or himself. However, I was getting fatigued trying to avoid being hit by him.

"Come and help me," I asked the teacher who was standing close by just watching the episode.

"You are doing fine by yourself," he said, chuckling.

I shook my head in disbelief. I needed him to give me a hand, and he just laughed it off. Fortunately, a patrol car was passing by, and the police officers stopped and took over. I never forgot the teacher's pleasure at watching me struggle with the student. Walking back to the dance, I said to him, "Thanks for your help!"

"No problem," he said laughing. "Glad to help."

The Bad Oysters case was one that opened my eyes to the different behaviors adopted by students when parents were present versus when they were not around.

I generally liked the proms the best because students tended to behave better when they were all dressed up. Most students went out to dinner at a nice restaurant before attending the dance. Many parents hosted dinners in their own homes before the prom.

At this particular junior prom, I was told that a girl was throwing up in the restroom. "Go into the restroom and attend to the student," I asked one of my female supervisors.

"I was drinking prior to attending the prom," the student confessed to me as soon as she saw me. She was cleaning her face with a wet towel that the female supervisor had handed to her, dried her teary eyes with it, tried to pull together her disorderly hairdo, and kept moving one hand up and down to get the wrinkles out of her stained new dress.

As a result of her admission, she was due to be suspended for attending the dance under the influence. Her parents argued later that she had not been drinking.

"She had just had some bad oysters," they said.

Instead of the parents thanking the school for holding their daughter accountable for her actions, they protected her from the consequences of her decision. I found that high school students usually tell the truth, but when lawyers and parents show up, they lie with the hope of getting out of trouble. I faced many such cases in my career as an assistant principal. These are the best opportunities to instill in young people's minds the sense of ethics, accepting responsibility for their own actions, and, simply put, telling the truth. Instead, covering up and protecting behaviors that had to do with breaking written, known rules were the norm in these cases. Shiv Khera wrote, "If a child goes the wrong way, it is not the child who is to blame; it is the parents who are responsible." Even though I understand that this is not always the case, parents are the very first teachers in children's lives.

The last dance was always music to my ears, and the last dance, Casual Possession episode, was one of the countless incidents during that season of my life.

Usually, I was ready to collapse after working all day and supervising the football games and dances. The last song was always "Stairway to Heaven" by Led Zeppelin. I knew the words by heart after years and years of listening to it. It was also one of the longest songs ever recorded. At one of the proms, I took the chance to go to the bathroom before "Stairway to Heaven" was played.

It has been a good night, and nothing is going to happen in the last ten minutes, I told myself confidently.

When I entered the bathroom, a strong smell of marijuana permeated the facility. I immediately saw four boys passing what looked like a marijuana joint. They threw it in the toilet and flushed it when they saw me.

"Have you been smoking marijuana?" I asked each of the boys.

"Yes," said the first one.

"I did it, too," said the second one timidly.

"Guilty!" said the third one raising one hand.

"I can't deny it," said the fourth one.

Individually, they all admitted to doing it, and I reported it to the administrators. The parents were called, and one by one, the boys were given their punishment. One of the boys was the star of the track team. When faced with being removed from the track team, his parents appealed the suspension. It went all the way to the board of education. A hearing was held. After cross-examination, their attorney argued that the young track star only had "casual possession." He was just passing it but didn't smoke it. At that point, it was my word against his.

"Why would I make up his confession?" I kept saying.

"I was afraid not to admit it," the boy answered firmly.

I could not believe what was happening! We took a break, and I went to the bathroom. One of the teachers I had respected for years was also a strong advocate for the young track star. As he entered the bathroom behind me, he looked at me and said, "Don't take it so hard. It's just a game."

"My integrity is in question. I would never lie!" I said.

"Relax," he said. "It's not a big deal."

"You have always been a role model to me," I said. "Why are you on his side?"

He shrugged his shoulders without answering my question, and left. I had the worst taste in my mouth and felt that my principles and sense of ethics had been violated. The track star won his case. However, he was never the same after that incident. He never looked at me in the face again, nor was he ever as good a runner. There is a powerful and untouchable tool inside the human body called the conscience. It compliments us when we do the right thing, but it is our worst prosecutor when we don't. The teacher who minimized the fact that the student was lying and lied with him taught me not only who he was, but what his values were. I saw him as a chameleon—he could change his color to his advantage depending on the issue. It was not the last time I would be on the opposite side of him.

23: A Lapse in Judgment

"It is almost always the cover-up rather than the event that causes trouble."

-- Howard Baker

As an activities director, I was advisor to student council, prepared for rallies, and supervised dances, games at all the sporting events, and the cheerleaders. The last of these responsibilities was fraught with peril. The girls were always having some sort of drama. Part of my responsibility was to help them select their advisor for each year. It was always tough because the pay was minimal and the responsibility huge.

Cheerleaders were expected to cheer at all home and away games in football and basketball with overnight stays during away tournaments. One particular year, we had a difficult time finding an advisor. Finally, one of the staff—a teacher with more than thirty years' tenure—stepped up to assume the role.

As usual, it was a relief to finally find someone, but at the same time, the advisor was a man. This was viewed with skepticism. All went well during football season, and he settled in as the cheerleaders' official advisor. At the beginning of December, the annual basketball tournament held out of town signaled the beginning of the basketball season.

Our team did well in the tournament. The Sunday

paper highlighted their efforts. The team didn't win but played well according to the news.

Each Monday morning we had administrative council meetings in the principal's office with the two assistant principals. An activity director was a quasi-administrator; therefore, I was always present. Our meetings began at 7:30 a.m. before the beginning of classes. At about 7:45 a.m., the advisor to the cheerleaders opened the door to the principal's office.

"Everything went well this past weekend," he said. "There were no problems."

It seemed odd that he interrupted the meeting, but I figured it was no big deal.

At 2:50 p.m., I was getting ready to leave the staff room to coach the baseball team. Just then, the cheerleader advisor entered the room and asked me to sit down because he had something important to tell me. The dialogue, as I recall, went something like this:

"It happened at the basketball game, and it was not good," he said.

"What are you talking about?" I asked.

"Well," he explained nervously, "after the game, back at the hotel, the cheerleaders told me that they were planning on going to a party hosted by the players from the other school. I told them they could not go. They told me they were going unless I bought them beer.

"You didn't, did you?" I asked.

"Yes I did," he said. "I can't believe I did that, but it was the only way to keep them from going out."

"Are you kidding me?" I exclaimed in disbelief. "You

need to go right away to the principal's office and explain what really happened in detail."

"I'm afraid I will lose my job for my decision."

"Do you want the principal to find out through the newspapers when the word gets out?" I said. "You have to go to his office right now to make him aware of the situation."

"No, I can't. No one will say anything," he argued.

"The baseball team is waiting for me, and I have to leave now for practice. You need to go to the principal immediately. These things don't stay quiet. If you don't tell him by tomorrow morning, I will tell him."

All during baseball practice I kept thinking about what he had told me, and I was mortified all over again. After practice, I headed to the principal's office and asked to speak with him.

"He left for the day," his secretary said.

"Did the cheerleader advisor stop by to talk to the principal?" I asked.

"No, I don't think so," she answered.

Back at home, the whole evening and throughout the night I was tempted to contact the principal. I had knowledge of a behavior that was inappropriate, and I didn't want to wait until the next day to discuss the situation, but I didn't call. After a restless night, I went to work the next morning earlier than usual. When I arrived at the school, the cheerleader advisor was already there, waiting for me, pleading with me not to say anything.

"I am heading right now to the principal's office. You can join me if you want."

When we entered the principal's office, I told his secretary that I needed to speak with him.

"He is very busy," she said.

"What I need to discuss with him is very important. It is something that can't wait."

"He said he will see you within a few minutes."

While waiting, the cheerleader advisor kept saying that he had been a teacher for over thirty years, and that he had never been in trouble for anything before.

"I was frightened for the girls and was actually trying to protect them," he said, trying to justify the episode.

"I knew I had to turn you in yesterday," I said, "but I tried to give you a chance to do it yourself. I should have followed my instincts and told the principal immediately after you told me."

Meanwhile, the news had traveled fast. Within a day, what had happened was common knowledge among the students. The girls had already leaked the information. I found out later that other staff members were aware of the episode, but had not come forward to the administration.

Throughout the conversation, the principal couldn't believe what he was hearing. He shook his head back and forth for almost fifteen minutes as the teacher provided a detailed report that included a justification for his actions.

"I will take this to the district office," the principal said.

The teacher was suspended, and an investigation began. Teachers were called to the district office to declare what they knew about the situation. Once a person heard about it and maintained silence, he or she became part of the problem, or part of the cover-up as the district called it.

To my recollection, we all received letters of reprimand. Even though I was the one who brought him in, I was held to the same standard.

At the end, the teacher's past record was in his favor. He had been without any negative incidents throughout his entire career, and that saved his teaching job.

Time off during evenings and nights doesn't exist in an administrator's life. When situations related to young students' involvement in alcohol consumption arise, the nature of the events not only can be detrimental to the students, but also to the school in general. That's why they have to be resolved promptly. Knowledge creates responsibility, and timing to make corrections is crucial. When it comes to upholding moral and ethical principles in schools, there is no such thing as "I'm telling you something in confidence."

24: Teamwork Means Together

I coached junior varsity baseball for over ten years. After teaching all day, I transformed into a coach after school. Coaching was still teaching but with a different dynamic. When I began coaching, my old sage teacher told me, "Remember, the students will listen to you because you have the ball. You decide who makes the team and who plays."

This was a basic thought, but very true. Students who struggled to stay motivated in class made an extra effort to improve because they wanted to play. They would go the extra mile to make the team.

JV baseball was the best of both worlds. I was coaching a sport I loved, and the pressure to win from parents and fans was minimal. When I became a varsity coach, the stakes increased dramatically.

One JV season in particular comes to mind. I had two pitchers with a unique ability. They were extremely talented. On one occasion, they pitched back-to-back no-hitters. I am referring to a season that was special in many ways. The team was strong in all positions with one exception: the right fielder was new to the game and had trouble catching the ball. Of the fourteen boys on the team, he was the best available for that positon.

One day, we were in a very tight game, and our best pitcher had only given up one hit. The runner had advanced to second base and represented the tying run. It was the bottom of the seventh and two were out. We only needed one more out to win the game. The batter hit a high fly to right field, and we all prayed the right fielder would catch it. Well, he lost the ball in the sunlight, and it hit him on the head. You could hear the impact like two cars colliding. The ball fell to the ground, and the runner scored from second base, tying the game. The player was out cold, and by the time the ball was picked up and thrown to the infielders, the winning run had scored. All of this took place as I ran to my player who was unconscious.

As I tried to wake him up, my pitcher stood over him yelling, "You cost me the game!"

I looked at him in utter disbelief.

"He cost you the game? We are a team here. You should be more concerned about his health than about the game. He tried his best to catch the ball. When he wakes up, you need to tell him that he did a good job."

Within seconds, the pitcher regained his composure. When the right fielder woke up, he asked, "Did I catch the ball?"

"It was a nice try," the pitcher said to my amazement. "That ball was hard to catch in the sunlight. You'll get that one next time."

I was glad to hear his words as it seemed to soften the blow of losing our first game. From that point on, we never lost a game. The most improved player was the right fielder. At the end-of-the-year celebration, he received the most improved player awarded by his teammates. When he accepted the award, he said he wanted to thank someone special. I thought he was going to mention his coach, me!

"When the pitcher encouraged me after I missed that ball in our only loss," he said, "his words made me relax and challenged me to do better because, as he said, we're a team."

The championship for the league was settled on the last game of the season versus the team that had beaten us twice. The game was a classic. The lead changed five times. We managed to pull it out in the last inning winning by a score of 20-19. Unbelievable! Both teams were exhausted!

When we arrived back at the gym, the players asked for a few moments alone, so my assistant coach and I left them alone for a few minutes wondering what they were talking about.

"The team has one more duty to perform," the pitcher told us.

"You just won the championship," we said. "The season is over!"

"We decided we would not have won the championship without you coaches," the pitcher said. "Our rule was one lap for every unearned run. We always ran those laps. We gave up fourteen unearned runs today. As true champions, we will run them together now!"

"That's not necessary," my assistant and I told them as they headed to the track.

We both had silent tears of joy. They had won more than a championship. They were all winners on a team that put each other first for the common good.

25: Do-Overs Don't Always Work

When in Doubt, Pay Attention to Your First Hunch

After thirteen years as a JV baseball coach, I was ready for a change. The varsity coach was an institution, and I never thought he would retire from coaching baseball. I dropped by to see him while he was in his office one day and announced that I was resigning as JV coach.

"Guess what?" he said. "This is my last year. Do you want the varsity coaching job? It's yours if you want it."

I could not believe my ears. We had just won another JV championship, and I was about to inherit a very talented group of players. For me, it was a dream come true.

"Yes, I will do it," I said. It was hard to contain my excitement.

The team was comprised of juniors and seniors that I had coached at the JV level. The starting catcher was a senior who had been voted All League Catcher as a junior. Two of my pitchers were juniors and outstanding players, and I had a strong nucleus of supporting players. One of the best players from the JV team was a catcher. He was a backup to my all-star catcher, and a good hitter. I used him at first base. Within the first few games of pre-season play, it was obvious to everyone that we needed a shortstop.

One day after practice, the catcher came to me and

said, "Coach, I'm willing to play shortstop, and then the other catcher can take the job behind the plate."

"But you have earned the right to be our catcher," I said.

"Well, it is for the good of the team," he answered.

"I have to admit you're right."

From that moment on, we came together as a team. The shortstop and new catcher were doing great. I received a ballot for all league candidates early in the season. Usually, you recommended seniors by position for consideration. I was limited to four players. I selected the seniors by position. At the time, the all-league catcher was playing that position. I forgot about the ballot until the end of the season. The new catcher had established himself both on the field and at the bat. The new shortstop was outstanding, and played exceptionally well.

As we approached the last game, we needed a win to have first place outright. If we lost, we would finish in a tie. Our best pitcher had just thrown seven innings, and I couldn't use him for a full game. I needed someone to cover the first few innings. One of the players was a senior and the brother of the new catcher. I had used him in pre-season, but his success had been limited. I decided to have him start the game, and planned to use our star pitcher as a backup.

"Give me three good innings," I told him. "Keep the ball down and don't throw any curve balls. Just throw strikes."

He was a great kid. He had accepted his role as a pinch hitter and runner, and was a pleasure to coach. After two innings, he hadn't walked anyone, and no one had gotten a hit. He was throwing strikes low, and his brother was framing every pitch perfectly.

One more inning ... one more inning, I kept thinking.

In the bottom of the fifth inning, he still had not allowed a hit or walk. He was pitching a no-hitter! We were ahead by one run, and the other team seemed like they didn't care. However, in the fifth inning they realized they were in danger, and they began to take each at-bat more seriously. I wanted to change pitchers but couldn't do it. Had the pitcher given up a hit, I was prepared to make the change.

As we approached the bottom of the seventh, I knew we had to support this unbelievable effort, and I challenged the players to get it done. The first hitter hit a long fly to center, but our player was able to catch up to it; now we had only two more batters to face. The next player hit a shot down the third baseline, and the third baseman jumped in the air and made an amazing throw to first to get the batter. One out to go, and the next batter would walk. Still the no-hitter was intact. The next batter hit a shot to right of shortstop. I was sure it was going to be a base hit, but the shortstop made the play of the season and threw the runner out. In his attempt, he injured his ankle and was done for the season. We were champs, but we had lost our best player for the playoffs. At that moment, this fact was far from anyone's mind. The only thing that mattered was that we were the champions. The team of brothers had done the unthinkable. It was so special. Many began saying that I should have played the senior pitcher more. In my mind, what had just transpired was very big. He had earned the right to start the playoff game with his brother.

The next day, the newspaper headlines highlighted the magical ending to the season. It was the feel-good story of the year. Below the article was the announcement of all-league selections. As expected, the converted shortstop had been elected again along with another one of the senior players. I was happy for them, but was focused on preparing for the playoffs without a shortstop.

Monday morning I was in my office before practice when my catcher came in and said he was upset.

"What's the matter?" I asked.

"You didn't recommend me for all-league," he shouted.

"When the ballot came out, you were not playing catcher," I said. "Usually, seniors are recommended. You were definitively playing like an all-star the second half of the season. The process is flawed."

"I'm quitting the team," he said.

"What?" I exclaimed. "You will be letting your teammates down!"

He walked out of my office. At practice, I informed the team that he had quit, and I explained why. His brother was there but remained silent.

"We need to make adjustments," I said.

"I could do it," my second baseman said, "but I can't make the throw to second base."

"That's fine," I said. "They will think that you're our regular catcher, and won't test your arm."

It was a long shot, but we needed to make the adjustment. We moved players around to cover shortstop, and began practicing for the coming game. Four days later, the catcher came to my office and began crying.

"I was wrong. I shouldn't have done what I did," he said.

"I will have to talk it over with the team," I told him.

Upon discussing it with the team, some of the members expressed their disappointment and resentment toward him.

"It's up to you, Coach," they finally said in consensus.

I met with him, and said he could suit up but probably wouldn't play. He agreed with my terms. When it was game time, we were facing a pitcher who had scouts from the major leagues watching him. He was averaging more than fifteen strikeouts a game. I started the senior pitcher, and within the first two innings, he had given up two runs. They were hitting his pitches. I made the change for our star pitcher. We scored two runs on walks, bunts, and a suicide squeeze play. We had tied the score in the fifth inning.

The catcher on the bench had been cheering for his teammates from the dugout. As we approached the extra innings still tied, my makeshift catcher said, "Coach, I haven't got anything left."

In the tenth inning, I approached the catcher sitting on the bench with the comment, "Did you learn your lesson?"

"Yes," he said looking at me.

I put him in the game. He got the winning hit in the bottom of the inning. As he approached me, I went from being excited to sad when I heard his comment, which was loud enough for all to hear.

"I told you that you couldn't win without me."

You could feel the wind being sucked out of the team. Instead of celebrating a great team win, everyone was focused on his behavior. Needless to say, we didn't play well in the ensuing game, and we were eliminated.

On the ride home, I wondered whether I had made a mistake by playing him. In the end, I still believe I did the right thing. He chose a behavior that affected the whole team. As it turned out, in his senior year, he continued to make choices that kept him from achieving positive results.

As the new season approached, I met with him and explained how I felt about the previous year. "You need to be a positive leader," I told him. "Don't just focus on your own accomplishments."

"Yes, Coach. I am sorry about last year. I will be different."

Once again, I believed him.

The year started out well, but the players kept missing signs, such as taking a pitch, bunting, stealing a base, throwing bats in disgust, and cussing a lot.

"What's up?" I asked. "Why are you making so many mistakes?"

I had led most of the players on this team to two straight championships. As we approached our sixth regular-season game, we needed to win to stay in the race for the championship, but we played terribly. I had never experienced this on any team I had ever coached. At the conclusion of the game, I took the team to the outfield and gave it to them.

"We have three games left," I said. "We need to pull it together and play with pride. No more missed signs, bats thrown in disgust, and negativity. I am giving you Friday off from practice. Rest and reflect on how you can be part of a cohesive team. I will see you on Monday. Be ready to finish the season with class."

When I returned to school on Monday, I was told that three players had cut school on Friday and gone to the lake to party. I called the first two players into my office.

"We cut school, but we weren't drinking," they said.

"You are not going to play in Tuesday's game, but you need to be at practice," I told them.

Neither player seemed fazed. When the catcher showed up, he was defiant. "You said we could have the day off," he said.

"I said a day off from practice. I didn't tell you to cut school," I said.

He was evasive about what had transpired, and seemed unwilling to take responsibility for his actions.

After lunch, one of the players that I trusted came to talk with me. "The catcher has been behind all the things that are going wrong," he said. "I heard him telling the others not to do what you say anymore because you told him that you hated everyone on the team."

I couldn't believe my ears. "We have won two championships! Do you believe him?"

"No, I don't," he said, "but he shouts down anyone who questions him."

As I went to practice, I wasn't sure what would happen. When I got to the field, I told the team to begin exercises. Not one of them got up to begin.

"I have been told that you are not going to do what I say, and that you were told that I hated each one of you. That's not true," I said.

"You're lying," the catcher shouted leaping to his feet. "You said that you hate us!"

148

I kept my calm and said, "You are finished as part of this team. Go to the gym and turn in your gear. The rest of you need to go down the line for exercises. If you choose not to, please go to the gym and turn your gear in."

Slowly, each player headed down the line as the catcher kept yelling. I turned to walk down the line. Just then, he pushed me from behind. Not expecting that move, I fell to the ground. My first response was to defend myself, but my assistant coaches intervened. I left the field with him following me, yelling, cussing, and inviting me to fight with him.

"Calm down," I told him. "You just assaulted me. The authorities are going to be involved."

I went directly to the principal's office and described what happened. After I almost knocked the principal down showing how hard the catcher had pushed me, events unfolded quickly. In the investigation, we learned that an adult volunteer on the track team had accused me of yelling at the player and sided with him saying that I had provoked him. He said he was not able to hear the words that allegedly provoked me to raise my voice.

Each one of the players was interviewed, and they all gave an accurate account of what really happened, including the low morale they were experiencing due to the catcher's demeanor and threats.

The player was removed from school and sent to the continuation school. His parents hired a lawyer, and the school district entered into negotiations. They came to me and to my lawyer with a compromise. I knew the player like a book.

"He probably wants to go to the prom and graduate with his class," I told my lawyer.

"Are you kidding me? No way," he said.

Twenty minutes later, the lawyer came in and said, "You were right!"

"I agree to the terms of the settlement," I said, "but I refuse to chaperone the dance and graduation."

It was the only year that I did not supervise a graduation or a prom in forty-two and a half years working as an educator.

The following day I met with each player. They aired their grievances, and I listened. We agreed to finish the season with class. We won our last few games and played inspired baseball once again.

Ten years later, I received a call from the existing varsity baseball coach. "I received a request from the player who was removed from school that fateful year of the pushing incident," he said. "He wants to meet with you. I could be present as a mediator of the meeting if you accept to see him."

"Yes, but what are his expectations? What kind of outcome could be drawn from that meeting?"

"He wants to apologize," the coach said, "but he also hopes that you will let him play in the alumni game."

Frankly, I felt it might help him if we met, so we agreed to meet at a local pub. It was awkward for both of us. He apologized for his behavior. I said I was sorry that things had to end the way they did. He still tried to stick with his old story.

"Look," I said, "it's been ten years. I still really don't know why you rebelled in the first place."

He started to blame me for his misfortunes of the past ten years because he was kicked off the team.

"The choices you made are to be blamed. Every decision you make in life has consequences, positive or negative. I am not responsible for the last ten years of your life. You made the college baseball team and continued with sports. I heard that you want to play in the alumni baseball game. I have a proposition: You catch, and I will pitch."

"Are you serious?" he asked looking shocked.

"Sure," I said. "It may help with the healing."

Believe it or not, on a beautiful Saturday morning, the alumni team played in the game with the catcher and the ex-coach as battery mates. The gesture brought some uplifting closure to one of the most unfortunate occurrences from many years ago. I have taken pride in helping others to be successful, and a degree of sadness invaded me when I saw that, in spite of many efforts and opportunities, individual students ultimately ignored the advice and second chances that were given to them. Once they made this decision, the path they chose took them in a counterproductive direction.

26: Resort to Your Principles

"A people that values its privileges above its principles soon loses both."

-- Dwight D. Eisenhower

During my last season as head varsity baseball coach, a few key players had injuries. However, I decided to make the best of the season with the players I had and not promote new junior varsity players. The players were mostly seniors. The team was full of high achievers, unselfish players who always tried their best. Even though we were not winning, they never gave up.

Once again, we were playing out of town at the school where we had won the championship two years before. They were beating us 7-0 in the sixth inning. The other team's coach told his players to take the bats up to the gym. It was a long walk up the hill. My players looked dejected as they saw the bats being removed from the opponent's dugout even before the game was over.

"Do you see those bats going up the hill?" I said. "They think that you are defeated. We are going to tie this game now!"

The miracles began with a base hit, an error, and a dropped fly ball by the opposing team. I knew their coach. He had never taught his players how to handle bunts, so we kept bunting. It was almost dark when my fastest player reached third base with the tying run. There were two outs. All they needed was the final out. We had practiced stealing home with the player at third base many times but never had the occasion to try it out in a real game. He was the fastest player I ever coached. I gave the "steal home" sign. The batter got as deep in the box and as far away from the plate as possible so the player would have a chance to score. The pitcher ignored the runner because all he needed was to get the final out. As the player headed for home, no one from either team said anything. The umpire, the catcher, and the other team were in a state of shock as the player's hand slid across the plate. We had just tied the game!

The runner that scored dusted himself off and said as loud as he could, "Go get the bats!"

It took thirty minutes to bring the bats back to the field. We played until it was so dark that the ball couldn't be seen. The game was suspended due to darkness. We felt as if it had been our greatest victory. We made up the game two weeks later and lost, but no one could take away the moral victory.

The last three weeks of the season began. We were playing our crosstown rivals, who had not lost a game. We had played six games in a row, and we had lost each one of them. We were in every game but couldn't close the deal. With a 0-6 record, we were facing a ferocious team with a star pitcher. We knew baseball scouts were going to be in the stands watching every second of his performance.

I told my team, "We can win this game. Play with emotion!"

Well, our fastest player drove in two runs, and we were

leading 2-1 in the last inning. My pitcher got nervous and walked the bases loaded. I knew if they tied it up, we would probably lose. I called time out and walked out to the pitcher.

"Are you taking me out?" he asked.

"No, I came out here to say that you need to relax. You have pitched a terrific game. You are the best we have, so strike out the next two batters. They will try to get a walk. The third batter always tries to hit home runs. Throw him high pitches. He will pop out, and we will win the game."

I turned and walked back to the dugout. I could hear the chants from our fans: "Fire the coach! Fire the coach! It's his fault." You learn that if you lose at the varsity level, it isn't long before you hear the naysayers.

Miracle number two occurred: two strike-outs and a pop fly to win the game! It was just as I said it would be. The team mobbed each other as if we had won the championship.

The sportswriter from the local newspaper ran up to me. "How do you explain that?" he asked, breathless. "Your team was 0-6 and they were 6-0. You beat the best pitcher in the area. He's going to the majors!"

I looked at him and said, "He's not going to the majors today."

The headlines quoted me: "He's Not Going to the Majors Today."

With morale sky high, we won the next two games easily, and if we won our last game, we would finish 4-6. We were all excited with the winning streak and anxious to finish the job.

I had decided it was time to resign as varsity coach. The events of the past two years were a distraction. You usually know inside when it is time to move on. I was at peace about my decision. I had not told the players yet because I wanted to wait until the season was over.

We were playing against a team with a coach who had a reputation for being a tough guy. I had played against him many times in softball games. He was a fierce competitor whether playing or coaching. When I walked over to him before the game, he said, "This is my last game as coach. I'm fed up."

I was shocked. "It's my last one too," I said.

"I'm going to win," he said.

"Why is your best player in tennis shoes?" I asked.

"Oh, he got caught cutting school. He won't play. I'm a man of principles," he continued. "By the way, I'm going to bat in this game."

"What did you say?"

"I'm going to bat," he repeated.

"You can't do that. This is a high school game."

"You can bat too," he said.

"No way," I replied.

The umpire was listening. He said, "I don't care. The game is meaningless .You are both fighting for a 4-6 record. Good luck. Play ball!"

The game was magical. Both sides fought with intensity to win. I had told the players as we started the game that it was going to be my last one. They were surprised, but a few of them said, "Don't worry coach. We'll win this one for you."

In the sixth inning, we were tied 1-1. They had the go-ahead run at second base. It was then that their coach walked up to bat. Everyone in the stands was shocked. I called time out and protested. He said he would bat, but refused to wear a helmet. He finally came to his senses and returned to his dugout without batting. I went out to the pitcher after things settled down and called the infielders in. I told them that their coach would try to bunt the guy over from second base so he could score on a fly ball. We had a play in mind that we had practiced many times.

"Remember," I said to the third baseman, "you need to yell 'Bunt, bunt!' and charge toward the plate."

I told the shortstop to run toward third base. I told the pitcher to count to three then quickly turn to throw the ball to the second baseman, who would pick off the runner. "This will work. We practiced it many times," I said, and I left the field.

Sure enough, we tricked them and picked the runner off. Their coach was furious. He got caught in our trap. In the last inning, we got a lead-off hit. Their coach called time out and told his pitcher, the one wearing tennis shoes, "Get your glove."

He put him in as their pitcher. Our players saw him and mumbled, "We're doomed!"

I yelled to the coach, "I thought you were a man of principle!"

"I'm going to win this game," he yelled back, laughing.

I learned from Stephen Covey, one of my favorite authors, that "there are constants in life ... change, choice, and principles," and if ever you're in doubt, if you resort to your principles, you will never go wrong.

I called the first batter and whispered, "I want you to bunt. The pitcher is wearing tennis shoes, not cleats. He wasn't supposed to play. He will fall and throw the ball away."

Sure enough, we bunted the next three times, and each time he threw the ball into right field. We scored three runs and won the game. It was a satisfying win and a great way to complete my high school career as a coach. A man of principles won that day, but it wasn't the other coach!

27: Trust Your Own Approval

"Try not to become a man of success but rather try to become a man of value."

-- Albert Einstein

My final season as a baseball coach was nearly over. I was looking forward to welcoming new challenges with a ready-to-begin attitude. I had just been selected as the summer school principal.

As soon as I finished baseball practice, I returned to my office to work on the details of initiating a comprehensive K-12 summer school program. I was enhancing the core class structure of reading, writing, and mathematics with enrichment courses. The mission statement of summer school was to provide enrichment classes not offered during the regular school year.

I was motivated by the administration to be creative. I asked staff throughout the district to make suggestions for possible courses and to attach a synopsis of the potential offering. It was a successful endeavor as I received many worthwhile suggestions such as bicycle safety, sewing for fun, hiking and exploring, and swimming safety.

I selected ten new courses to enhance the summer school curriculum and prepared the necessary documents to submit to the board of education for approval. I met with the district administrator and submitted the ten-course synopsis two weeks in advance. It was mandatory that the board of education received them one week prior to the board meeting. When I left the assistant superintendent's office, I had a feeling of accomplishment and was proud of the work that I had done.

The educational climate in the state of California was changing drastically, and things began to unravel. A grassroots initiative was put on the ballot to end the annual increase in property taxes on existing homes.

The new law was called Proposition 13. Property taxes were frozen at their current rate. This action severely affected current school funding and future funding because property taxes made up the largest part of funding for local schools. As a result, the rumor was that no money would be allocated for summer school. Furthermore, if summer school was offered, it would probably only include the basics, such as remedial reading, writing, and mathematics.

To better understand the issue, I went to see the assistant superintendent. As I recall, the conversation unfolded like this:

"I think I should pull the enrichment classes before the board meeting."

"It's too late," he replied. "It won't be a problem."

"I'm concerned," I continued. "I could explain why we should pull those offerings because of the passage of Prop 13 and the uncertain funding issues that arose for the state of public education going forward."

"Don't worry about it," he said. "The board probably won't even ask any questions."

I was told to be early for the board meeting and to

report to the assistant superintendent's office. When I arrived, he told me, "If anyone says anything about your enrichment classes, just stick with the mantra, 'I followed the mission statement.' Don't even mention that you suggested we pull the enrichment classes."

"I'll look foolish if I say I didn't think about the impact on summer school after Prop 13 passed," I said to him.

"Don't worry, it will be all right," he answered.

When I stood up to present my summer school program, I was drilled by the board of education.

"Didn't you think that a comprehensive summer school program with all of these enrichment classes was a bad idea?" one of the board members asked. "Do you expect us to accept this proposal? It's a boondoggle summer school program and a waste of taxpayers' money."

I wanted to explain, but I caught the eye of the assistant superintendent, and he motioned for me to stay the course. I kept referring to the mission statement and the process I had taken to create a rich and comprehensive summer-school program to no avail.

The summer school was cancelled due to uncertain funding. I walked out stunned by what had just happened. The assistant superintendent smiled at me.

"Good job," he said.

Yeah, I was your fall guy, I thought. I had protected him and taken the heat.

The next day, the newspaper editorial referred to the summer school proposals as a boondoggle program initiated by an inexperienced young administrator. I was mortified.

I had to call the hired staff to lay them off. They all joined the unemployment lines, as they qualified for unemployment benefits. On the other hand, initially the district refused to pay me for over sixty hours of summer school preparation because I had "failed to complete the contract." I was able to resolve the issue without much fanfare, and I received compensation for the work I had already done.

With respect to taking one for the team, as I did for the assistant superintendent, I resolved that never again would I compromise my integrity by not being totally truthful. Mario Cuomo once said, "Every time I've done something that doesn't feel right, it's ended up not being right," and I believe this statement. I could have saved face by telling the school board the truth. I knew in my heart that it was the right thing to do. I was young and new, and the first taste of temporary administrative employment ended with a lesson learned.

28: Oh, for Goodness Sake!

"For all of its uncertainty, we cannot flee the future."

-- Barbara Jordan

After the dust settled, the entire summer was in front of me to regroup and figure out what was next. Free of my responsibilities in coaching, time opened up, which allowed me to focus on a part-time job that I had been involved with as a coordinator of an extended, day educational program through a college in Los Angeles. I had created and managed a teacher in-service program that focused on educational topics on all the current research in public schools K-12 for the past five years. The program was very successful and consisted of fifteen different educators who shared their particular expertise over a full semester. In the beginning, I was only working one night a week. With the increased free time, I could possibly enhance the program by expanding it to nearby cities.

I was developing the next round of course offerings and hiring guest lecturers. I decided to ask my mentor, Flexible Milt, to be one of my presenters. We met for coffee to discuss the possibilities. He had the same twinkle in his eye that I had seen since the time I first met him. His thirty-five years of experience teaching had given him a wealth of knowledge. He was always lively, funny, serious, and reflective. I could spend hours listening to him. He had a positive spin on everything. If he couldn't be a guest lecturer, coffee with him was still fun, as I always gained from his insights and advice.

He graciously turned down my invitation, but then he asked, "How is it going? What are your plans?"

I was pleased he asked. It gave me a chance to share my thoughts. "I'm considering becoming an administrator. The role of activities director provided me with over nine years of experience attending weekly administrative meetings with three different principals and assorted assistant principals. I'm ready for a new challenge."

I shared with him my disappointment with the way summer school ended abruptly. I told him the story and said I was a little disillusioned by the whole thing, including my staying quiet at a critical moment in the deliberations, because I was following specific instructions from my superior.

"I remember when you were first hired," he said. "You were full of enthusiasm and had boundless energy. You have not lost that spark. You continue making a difference in students' lives."

I was eager to hear his positive input.

"I remember one day in particular in your first year of teaching," he continued. "A group of teachers were in the staff room complaining about the status of negotiations. You questioned the teacher who was representing the teachers at negotiations. I'll never forget her response to us all. She said looking at you, 'If you really want to make a difference, get involved. We need lots of help, not criticism.' The reason I remember that day is because out of the ten or so participants in that discussion, you were the only one who stepped up to the plate and became part of the solution, not a part of the problem."

I had forgotten about that day, but he was right. I did get involved, and had been a member of the current teacher negotiating team for the past six years.

"If you are thinking about becoming an administrator full time, I have some suggestions," he said, and I scribbled notes to keep up with the suggestions that poured forth.

"Number One: Visit some administrators that you respect and know in the neighboring districts. They can give you a true perspective of the role of administration personally and professionally.

"Number Two: You need to remember three critical things: you need a good memory, a good forgivery, and a good forgettery.

"Number Three: You need to stay regular! Administrators never take bathroom breaks. I suggest prunes!

"Number Four: Create an exclamation phrase that is not antagonistic.

"A good memory is required for this job because you need to remember people's names, events, facts, and all sorts of other details. Always take good notes and keep accurate records.

"With a good forgivery, even though a word like this one doesn't exist in the dictionary, it is important to follow the rhyme, but you need to be able to forgive those who hurt you in thoughts, words, and deeds. You cannot take things personally, even when the criticism is directed toward you.

"You need a good forgettery, another made-up word, because, in addition to forgiving others, some things require being totally forgotten. They are negative and not that important or worth worrying about. Do a gut-check to see if what is bothering you is serious enough to require action on your part.

"Eat prunes, and I'm not joking. You need to stay healthy. Eat right, take a lunch break, and make sure you are regular. People will notice if you are not.

"Non-antagonistic phrases will help you when dealing with difficult situations. You will need a good response to people who upset you and make you want to react, who try to take you off track and make you defensive. A non-antagonistic response phrase is an important coping mechanism that all administrators must have in their bag of skills. Let me tell you the story of the phrase 'Oh, for goodness sakes'."

Milt paused to give me time to flip to a new page in my yellow notepad.

"Two elderly seniors at a rest home were sitting on a porch in their rocking chairs. One of the seniors was brand new to the home. As he sat quietly, for three days straight the other senior kept bragging about himself on and on, never once asking the other person about himself or his life. The new person said after each story, "Oh, for goodness sakes," but he wanted a chance to say diplomatically what he really thought of the bragger.

"On the third day, the gentleman who had been speaking straight for three days asked the new person why he always said 'Oh, for goodness sakes!' The other gentleman said, 'Often in the past, I would tell people exactly what I was thinking. It got me in a lot of arguments. My wife sent me to a counselor, and there I learned that I needed a response to help me when I was getting upset, angry, or when I wanted to overreact to something that was said in front of me that I felt was inappropriate . So now, instead of reacting by saying what I think all of the time, I just say "Oh, for goodness sakes." It has gotten me out of trouble and helped me to focus on being a better listener. By the way, it was about time you asked something about me.'

"You will need something like this to help you when you are attacked, threatened, challenged, or need time to reflect," Milt emphasized.

I knew that this was the meeting of my life. Milt was wise. As if I was a sponge, I absorbed each word.

"Finally, I want you to read this small book on the fine art of sailing. It is a short book, but if you read between the lines, I think it will help you understand the challenges of administration."

I put down my pen and said, "I don't have enough words to thank you, Milt. I will take your advice. I feel more empowered to make the right plans for the future."

I typed up Milt's suggestions and kept them in a secure place. His advice would prove critical to my future success as time passed. I did read the book on the fine art of sailing but failed to realize one of its deeper meanings until later.

Following Milt's advice, I visited a successful administrator who lived in a neighboring district. He agreed to meet me for lunch. It was a very interesting afternoon. He had risen through the chairs in his district from teacher, coach, activities director, and assistant principal of students.

He shared with me how difficult it was to move within one's own district. When he became assistant principal of students, the transition was challenging because the staff still saw him in the role of activities director. It was difficult going from good guy to tough guy, and his fellow teachers questioned his ability to make the adjustment.

"Once you cross the bridge to a full-time administrative position, you will lose many of the close friends you have on the staff. It doesn't mean that they don't like you. That's just the way it has to be. You may have to evaluate them or reprimand them. Therefore, they cannot be your buddies anymore. It comes with the job."

"I had not thought about that, but it makes sense," I said.

"This is a job that demands long days," he continued. "It is hard to take time for a break or to be able to have a restful lunch."

"With all the negatives, why do you stay in the position?" I asked.

"Because I know that I'm making a difference in the lives of the teachers and the students. I feel fulfilled and valued by both. Someday, I hope to be a principal," he replied.

As I left our lunch, he looked up at me with a smile and said, "Remember, if you choose to stay at your same school, you can't avoid the assistant principal job. It is in that chair where you will be tested the most. Good luck!"

I thanked him for taking the time to meet with me and left with renewed hope that I would eventually be given another chance to apply for an administrative opening in the district. Little did I know that my summer preparation and outreach would help me prepare for the challenge of being an assistant principal of students at my own school when surprising events occurred within three months of the opening of that school year.

29: A Leap from Fear

"A man cannot discover new oceans unless he has the courage to lose sight of the shore."

-- Andre Gide

The fall marks the beginning of a brand new school year. From there, the year flies by. Each fall, I was excited to meet my new students, and I began the year refreshed and ready. I had enjoyed my summer meetings with my old friend Milt and the administrator from the neighboring school district. Their advice was a treasure, and I was carrying a golden bag full of skills to practice.

After the first three weeks of school, we were told that the assistant principal of students had been selected to be the new assistant principal of curriculum at another school, effective two months hence. His last day was scheduled for the first of November. There was an attempt to interview candidates for that position. I chose not to apply. It seemed that the timing was not great, and I had already connected with the students in my classes. Probably my insecurities created doubt about my readiness for the position. I felt comfortable in my current role.

The first interview cycle ended without the district finding the appropriate candidate. I was called into a meeting with the district staff.

"Are you interested in assuming the position for the

remainder of the year?" the principal asked me. It was the end of October, and already a lot of issues were unresolved.

"Your title will be temporary terminal assistant principal," I was told. "At the end of the school year, you can apply for the permanent position if you are still interested. We guarantee that you will be able to return to your old position of activities director and social science teacher next year if you choose not to apply for the permanent opening in the fall."

"I thank you for your confidence in me," I said. "I just need a day to consider your offer."

I tried to sleep that night but couldn't. I tossed from side to side, used relaxation techniques, and counted sheep by the hundreds, but the proposal and doubts raced in my mind like a film without an ending. After much soul searching, I decided to take the leap. Up until then, I had been the jokester on the staff, the one making everybody laugh, as I needed everybody's support for student activities. Laughing at staff meetings after my comments was usual. The assistant principal of curriculum said that I was "a tough act to follow" because he had serious stuff to cover.

I was going to jump into the fire with a big role reversal. The best part of the offer was the escape clause. It was time to see if I could make that change and still be successful. Here was my chance to address issues that the staff had been complaining about. I would now be able to help teachers so they could focus on teaching without worrying about discipline issues or student attendance.

I am one of them, and together we can make a difference, I told myself.

The sage advice from the administrator who had offered me a position in the bay area came to mind.

"I understand why you are electing to stay in your current position," he said, "but my advice is when doors open, take them. You will always be better for having made the leap of faith!"

I knew that I was chosen because it would cause the least disruption to the school. I was the activities director, and only taught two classes.

I began working in my new position on a Friday. Challenges began the first day.

"I am still doing the job of activities director, and we have a rally with over forty schools visiting our campus," I told my secretary. "Please do not interrupt me today."

Here is an example of how communication can go in a different direction. After the rally, I returned to my office to find that my new secretary had told a district administrator that I was too busy to return his call. She also repeated the same message to an upset parent.

Needless to say, my first official duty as assistant principal was to call both the angry parent and the district administrator to apologize for not being available. I made them aware of what was going on, they understood the circumstances, and all was forgiven. I learned that day that taking the time to be clear and specific when giving instructions was crucial. Also, the situation gave me an opportunity to assess what my new secretary needed in terms of training on handling upset callers, a lesson I never forgot. Be clear in your expectations from your staff from day one.

As I tried to catch my breath at the end of the day, a

veteran science teacher came into my office and said, "Boy, they screwed up when they selected you for the job. You're not man enough for this position. We have serious issues here. I believe that you were the wrong choice."

"Oh, for goodness sakes," I answered, thanking Milt for the tip on using a non-antagonistic phrase. "I am sorry you feel that way." The rudeness of his approach didn't escalate, and using the phrase for the first of many times throughout my career helped me to remain calm.

I looked at the stack of referrals on my desk that had gone unaddressed for many days, and I told myself, *I will prove him wrong. I am man enough for this job.*

By the time I left that first day, I had remembered the words of wisdom that Milt and the other successful administrator had shared with me, and I was thankful for those who trusted me. I had done my homework well.

Next Monday, and the days that followed, I spent most of my mornings trying to find who was parking in the teachers' reserved parking spaces. Usually the teachers had formed the habit of coming to school five or ten minutes late, and a parent or a visitor had taken their parking spot. By Thursday, I had made my first administrative decision. I approached the principal with my proposal, and he agreed. Each teacher received a notification in their mailbox stating the following:

Effective immediately, all reserved parking for staff in front of the school is terminated, including the principal and assistant principal. Only the nurse has top priority.

There was an outcry from the twenty teachers who had reserved spaces.

"If you arrive early, you will probably get a spot in the front," I told them. "I am the assistant principal of students, not the chief parking attendant."

On Friday of my second week, as I was locking up, I noticed a sign on the main boys' bathroom door that read *Out of order*. It was dated October 14.

"It has been out of order for over three weeks!" I mumbled to myself.

When I opened the door, the smell was awful. Each stall was filled to the brim. The toilets hadn't been cleaned, and no one was around to clean them. At that time of the day, when everybody was probably home for the weekend, I couldn't reach anyone, so I called the district office.

"I will be right down," said the assistant superintendent in charge of building and grounds.

When he arrived, he congratulated me for the new job. I thanked him and took him to the location of the bathroom. When we entered the bathroom, the smell took our breath away.

"Did you try to flush the toilets?" he asked.

"Are you kidding me? There will be fecal matter all over, and the custodians are gone for the weekend. Besides, the sign reads that they are out of order."

Without further discussion, he rolled up his pant legs and flushed each of the twelve toilets and ten urinals. I stood by expecting a flood of crap, consoled by having someone to witness it with me. Instead, to my amazement, they all flushed with no problem.

When he saw my shocked expression, he looked at me and said, "You mean you never thought of that?"

I was so embarrassed. He was kind, though.

"There is an important rule in administration. Never assume the obvious without checking first," he said as he was leaving.

I definitely needed the weekend to recoup.

30: The Gophers Are Gaining on Us

"Creativity requires the courage to let go of certainties."

-- Erich Fromm

Monday mornings were usually full of surprises. I had survived the first weeks and was recharged for whatever was next. At 9:30 a.m., a man covered with dirt walked into my office carrying a potato sack in one hand filled with something and a notepad in the other. I had no idea who he was. Without hesitation, he put his notepad down in front of me and instructed me to read his notes out loud.

"I have killed thirty-two gophers this week," I read, "but they are gaining on us. Signed, James T. Smith."

"Who is James T. Smith?" I asked.

"Me," he said, pounding his chest with his closed fist. "I am the head grounds man."

"You mean we are losing ground to the gophers?" I jokingly asked.

"This is not funny," he said with dignity. "You have to do something." He opened the potato sack to show me the most recent kill.

"What about traps?" I asked.

"Oh, no, they are out only for a few hours in the

morning before school starts. Students can be hurt," James said.

"What about poison?" I asked again.

"Oh, no, a neighbor's dog might eat it and die," he said. "In the meantime, we have about sixty-five gopher holes on the playing field, and students are getting injured daily."

"I will look into the problem," I assured him.

I called the assistant superintendent of the district in charge of buildings and grounds. He confirmed what the head grounds man for the school had said. "You cannot use poison or traps. You have to come up with a creative solution, because it cannot cost any money to the district either. I need to hear from you by next week," the assistant superintendent said.

Considering all the aforementioned limitations, I thought to myself shaking my head, *is he kidding me?*

As I was speaking about the situation with my good friend the art teacher at the school, he said, "I have an idea. I will be back in a few minutes."

He returned with a cute picture he had drawn of a gopher with a helmet and binoculars looking from a bunker. He had written on the picture the words "All Gophers Prohibited." He also made one in Spanish, just in case the gophers were bilingual: "*Los Topos Están Prohibidos.*" Tears came out of our eyes as we laughed and laughed.

"Hey, maybe we can make signs and stick them in the holes," I said still laughing.

The next day, my art teacher and friend came to my

office with six enlarged signs depicting the gopher in all his glory extolling the words, "All Gophers Prohibited," and "*Los Topos Están Prohibidos.*"

The assistant superintendent had told me that I had to be creative. I called him for a morning meeting to be held on the football field at 7:00 a.m. the following Wednesday, exactly a week after our first meeting. I invited the principal, the football coach, the athletic director, the booster president, the local recreation director, the assistant superintendent in charge of building and grounds for the district, and a parent club representative. I told them I had a solution that didn't cost any money and didn't require the use of traps or poison.

Before they arrived, I went out to the field and positioned the big signs in at least six gopher holes. The field looked like a bombed-out city with a gopher hole every few feet. My hope was for everybody to get the message that without some form of treatment that most likely was going to cost money and techniques, the problem was not going away, not to mention the severity of the situation and how unsafe the field had become.

When we all gathered, the assistant superintendent said, "What's your solution?"

I pointed to the signs. There was a long silence from all in attendance. My heart was in my throat. Had I gone too far? Maybe the joke would be on me.

Just then, someone blurted out, "That won't work. Gophers can't read in either language."

For a moment we were all silent. Then, a huge relief invaded me when everyone laughed. I seized the moment to explain my point. All attending the meeting saw firsthand the gravity of the situation. Even the assistant superintendent was surprisingly calm.

"Yes," he said, patting me on the shoulder. "Your solution didn't cost any money or involve traps or poison. We got it. You demonstrated in a creative way the urgent need to address this problem immediately for students' safety. Hey, and you met my timeline of one week!"

"The signs were a great tool to demonstrate how bad the issue is," one of the participants said. "I like that they're bilingual."

The decision to deal with the problem was in the hands of the district. Two weeks later, an extensive gopher eradication program began insuring the safety of all our students and staff.

Those first few weeks as the temporary terminal assistant principal were incredible. Parking places, bathrooms, gophers, and teachers' uneasiness with my appointment were just a few of the problems I had to resolve. I had not even had time to make a dent in the many issues surrounding student attendance and conduct, a situation that had been left unattended for a while before I took the job.

The challenges had just begun, but I never forgot the importance of including a creative sense of humor to make a point when situations seemed serious and unsolvable, a tactic that was welcomed from time to time.

31: High Noon Starring Gary Cooper as the New Temporary Assistant Principal

"The ultimate authority must rest with the individual's own reason and critical analysis."

-- Dalai Lama

The battle between the teacher's union and the district was in full force during the time of the year when this story developed, and the tension was felt throughout the entire school district. The rhetoric seemed to be getting worse. The key players of the teacher's union were staff members at the high school, the same ones for many years. The stage was set for a possible impasse in negotiations and a teacher walkout. It was my first year as temporary terminal assistant principal at the high school. I was hired in November for the school year ending in June. If I were successful, I would have a chance to be hired permanently for the coming term.

On a busy Monday, at one-thirty in the afternoon, my fellow assistant principal entered my office and told me that I was to deliver a subpoena to the head negotiator of the teacher's union immediately. He handed the document to me. My first reaction was to ask him questions.

"On whose authority am I being asked to deliver this subpoena? Why does it have to be delivered immediately? Don't you realize that if I serve the subpoena before the teacher's class is over for the day, it could have serious ramifications within the climate of the current negotiations? Could I deliver it after school?"

He told me that I had been chosen to deliver the document, that it was time sensitive, and that it had to be done right away.

At ten minutes before two, I headed toward the teacher's classroom and waited until the bell rang. After the students exited, I quietly approached the teacher. He was looking at his grade book as students arrived for the next class when I handed him the subpoena. He looked at the envelope and put it down on his desk.

"It is important, time sensitive, and you need to read the contents," I told him.

I turned and left the classroom. I wasn't sure how he was going to respond, but I expected there might be consequences from the timing of the delivery of the subpoena. At this point, I didn't have any idea of the content of the subpoena.

I returned to my office. I had just changed the atmosphere of my surroundings by rearranging the furniture to remove any barrier to open communication, as these arrangements were recommended at a seminar I had attended earlier. I had purchased a nice rug with my own money to make my office more inviting.

I was still in my office when the dismissal bell rang. Within a few minutes, the teacher stormed into my office, stood over me, and challenged me to stand up. He was threatening me and yelling, "Stand up! Stand up!"

With a soft tone of voice, I tried to calm him down. He continued yelling something like, "How dare you interrupt my class to deliver a subpoena!"

"I was directed to deliver it immediately," I told him. "I waited to deliver it between classes so I wouldn't interrupt your class while it was in session. You cannot threaten me. You need to calm down."

He stomped out of my office saying that he was done with me. Young, relatively inexperienced, and new, I was appalled by his personal threats against me. What would have happened, I wondered, if I had stood up? It wasn't so much about me but about the position I was holding. I immediately sought out the principal and told him what happened.

The principal asked, "What do you want to do about it?"

At that moment, I realized that it would be up to me how this chapter was going to unfold. I went to the superintendent of the district who also asked, "What do you want to do about it?"

I was told in a roundabout way that in union negotiations, these things happen, and I should let it go.

I needed to think about what to do next. I had a sick feeling when I went home. Why was it up to me? Why was the district not backing me up? What a stupid move to have to serve a subpoena before school was out. Now we had a real problem. If I reprimanded the teacher for his actions, that would ramp up the discourse between the union and the district, which would escalate the tension and crisis. I thought maybe the teacher would calm down and apologize the following day for his verbal threats toward me, at least out of respect for the position I held.

The following day I tried to speak to the teacher. He reiterated that he was done with me. I returned to my office and called the superintendent. Once again, he asked me, "What do you want to do about it? Have you considered all your alternatives?"

"I want an audience with the board of education in closed session to share my position," I replied.

"What are you going to say?"

"I will explain in closed session what happened," I said.

I was cautioned to be very careful. What kept swirling in my head were all the people who wanted me to let it go, to walk away from it. Something inside of me wouldn't let me do that. It became a matter of principle.

It was then that I remembered my favorite movie of all time, *High Noon*. The star was Gary Cooper. He was retiring from being sheriff when he learned that the bad guys were getting out of prison and on their way to the town by train. Everyone tells the sheriff to leave and maybe nothing will happen. He can't even get any deputies to help. His principles win out, and he stays to face the antagonists. Here was my chance to be Gary Cooper and face the challenges head on and to stand by the ethical principles I believed in.

A meeting was hastily called with the board of education. When I entered the room, I explained what had happened and what my choices were in this matter. I told them I had written a letter of reprimand for the teacher in question. The first question from a board member was, "Why have you not given it to the teacher?"

"The letter would definitely escalate the labor strife and be used against the district," I said. "This happened because of the timing of the delivery of the subpoena, which fueled the outcome, set up the teacher's union representative, and put me in a dangerous position."

I referenced the movie *High Noon* and said how Gary Cooper's character faced the same advice to let it go; the issue would die down, everyone told him. I told them that we had to draw a line in the sand about what is acceptable behavior toward a school administrator. The only levity in the meeting occurred when I mentioned that the antagonist on the train was named Miller. I told the board that I wanted to be Gary Cooper and face the issues head on.

One of the board members said that he had changed his mind and realized that I was right. He asked if there was some way around writing the letter of reprimand and deescalating the crisis.

"A meeting with the teacher, his representative, the superintendent, and a member of the board," I suggested. The board agreed, and the board member who had asked me volunteered his home as a meeting place.

I was the first to arrive for the scheduled meeting, anxious and tense, but resolved to find a solution. I knew that a resolution would require compromise. The board member greeted me and shared that the superintendent was not coming in the hopes that would help in the negotiations. It was then that I had a unique opportunity to act as a superintendent for at least an hour to help solve the problem.

About thirty minutes later, two members of the teachers' union showed up without the teacher. When asked why he was not present, they said that he was too upset to be at the meeting, and assured me that they were able to speak and act on his behalf. The two representatives were the outgoing president of the union and the new president. I knew that if there was any hope for a successful outcome, it would come from the outgoing president. He was a worthy adversary, but a very practical one. He was there to protect his teacher at all costs. The new president wanted to capitalize on the sensationalism of how I had served the subpoena as opposed to what transpired in my office.

When I described the incident, the new teacher representative said it was my word against his word, and that no one else heard what he said to me. It was then that I said another teacher had overheard him threatening me to stand up and was willing to testify if necessary. He had come to my office after the incident to see if I was all right.

The outgoing union president asked what I wanted in order to resolve the issue. All eyes were on me, once again, to come up with a solution, short of writing the letter of reprimand and putting it in the teacher's file.

My proposal included a meeting between the teacher and me with a verbal apology for his behavior toward me, and an acknowledgement of his understanding of the proper relationship that should exist between teachers and administrators. The Union would not write any articles in their publications to heighten the situation, and likewise, the district would refrain from any publications arguing the issues involved in this incident.

"No one party can benefit from this situation politically, or the deal is off," I said.

The new president was opposed to this part. It was obvious that he wanted to ramp it up more. However, that was the deal; take it or leave it. I said that both sides made mistakes from my perspective, and in a sense, this compromise didn't let either side benefit with the exception that the teacher was not being formally reprimanded for his threats toward an administrator who was acting in accordance to his duties when he was directed to serve the subpoena. Both sides were losers in this incident, and the teacher and I were collateral damage.

The teacher representatives asked for time to caucus for a few minutes. When they returned, they agreed to the terms and said the teacher would meet with me next week, and the union would arrange a time. After they left, the board member thanked me for helping to reach an agreement and for my willingness to intercede on behalf of the district.

A week later the teacher asked to see me in my office.

"Do you want me to stand up?" I said jokingly.

"No," he said.

He apologized for his behavior and thanked me for not reprimanding him with a letter in his file. He stated that he still felt it was wrong for me to deliver the subpoena during the school day. I told him that even if that were the case, his reaction was inappropriate. He acknowledged my comment by nodding yes, and we shook hands. In the coming months, the rhetoric between the union and the district took on a new level of mutual respect. This was my first taste of acting as a superintendent. Little did I know, it would not be my last. Compromising, standing for what you believe, and treating others with dignity were all skills involved in the resolution, and they were valuable lessons that stuck in my mind forever.

32: Reincarnation: Would It Happen Again?

"It's so important to understand that your good attendance ups your chances of graduating."

-- Tyra Banks

The next seven months seemed like a blur—so much to do and so little time! After resolving the gopher crisis with a creative solution and dealing with a union situation during the most delicate part of the year when negotiations were in place, it was time to address the many unresolved issues pending in my office. The stack of referrals for attendance and tardy issues was high, and I began wondering if I was ever going to catch up. I asked my secretary to give me the most recent data on attendance. Prioritizing was going to be my first approach. Some issues were in need of immediate attention.

When I studied the data, I found out that tardiness was a major issue throughout the school. The number of students coming late per day was astounding. We needed to address this issue on a school-wide basis. Second, the number of single-period absences per day was also extremely high.

At the next staff meeting, the main agenda item had to do with attendance, tardiness, and single-period absences. A shower of ideas poured forth, and the brains stormed non-stop. What would be the most appropriate course of action to address the issue? Some supported enforcement of existing school rules, and others wanted to create more effective consequences for tardiness. A few argued that the issue had gotten out of hand because of the length of time it took the administration to address the situation. Students needed to be held accountable in a timely manner.

The school rule was that if you were tardy more than five times, you had to serve detention after school. The process included teachers sending a referral to the office needing a follow-up to assign detention. It was nearly impossible to call every student to the office to assign detention. I told the teachers they needed to assign the detention, and if the student did not bring back a slip saying they had served the detention within two days, I should receive that notification to follow up with assigning Saturday school instead of school suspension. I knew that this approach would work only if the teachers' effort and mine were consistent in holding the students accountable.

"It's going to take time to work," I told the teachers. "Students are not used to being held to strict account for completion of assigned detention."

The teachers and I agreed that we had to step up to the plate and work closely together to solve this problem. It took almost four months to see a dramatic change in tardiness and single-period absences. It also included over five hundred students serving a three-hour, Saturday school assignment for not doing the assigned detention from the teachers. It became a test of resolve on our part as well to change the culture of accountability.

After three months, I received a call from the assistant superintendent inquiring about the excessive number of Saturday school referrals.

"Once we began to hold students accountable, they began to follow through with our expectations. As a result, the number of referrals for failure to serve detention has dropped dramatically," I explained. "I needed to spend the majority of my time on attendance and behavior issues."

I was able to convince the assistant superintendent that our new system was working, and I reminded him of the day he visited me the first few weeks after I was hired as assistant principal. It was 6:30 in the evening, and I was knee deep in referrals trying to catch up. As I remember it, he had asked me, "Why are you still working?"

"I am trying to get organized with this pile of referrals," I answered, showing him five stacks of papers that almost covered my whole desk.

"You need to work smarter not harder," he said. "You need to leave at five p.m. each day whenever possible."

I said to the assistant superintendent during our meeting, "It's because of your advice that I'm setting a tone of cause and effect—working smarter not harder. The number of Saturday school assignments was very high at first. Each month, the number drops as students realize that we are serious about holding them accountable for not doing detention."

He smiled as he left. I will always be grateful for his tutelage and support, as he was a bright light in the realm of administration and stood out as a key person in my personal growth.

Many stories have accumulated in my mind from the times of attendance and tardiness solutions, including the "You can't make me" one. As you can predict, not everyone liked the new emphasis on accountability. One day, an irate parent showed up and was upset about the issue of detention for his daughter for tardiness. He told me in front of her that it was his fault she was late. I asked him if he wanted to do her detention. He became irate. I told him, "Your daughter was tardy an average of three times a day and continues to miss classes as well."

He became more and more argumentative.

"You are missing the point," I told him. "Your daughter needs to focus on her education. This time I will let the detention go, but she needs to get to school on time and follow school rules."

"You are giving in," he said. Why?"

"The reason is that we are discussing her discipline and not addressing the real issue of not attending her classes regularly and on time," I answered.

Three weeks later, his daughter dropped out of school, and her problems at home contributed to her desire to quit school. This time when the father came to my office, he was asking for help in getting her back in school. Together, we managed to get her back in school and on track. From that day forward, her father became an advocate for the rules to be enforced and for parents to support the school efforts. It turned out to be a win-win situation.

There's another story that I remember as "Reincarnation, anyone?" One of the most curious and bewildering cases happened during the same month. I had called a meeting with the parent of one of my students who had been missing a great deal of school. When we met, the mother was very agitated and angry. She said, "My boy isn't doing any detention!"

Here we go again, I thought, *another parent who refuses to support school rules*. I was learning fast that we needed to bring the parents on board and improve communications for them to be aware of our new school mission. Everything was for the good of the students anyway, as we were trying to guide them and help them become more responsible. However, this mother refused to accept the consequences. As her anger grew, she said things that boggled my mind and still do to this day; things I never forgot.

"You better be careful. Did you know that the sun follows me?"

"Is that so?" I asked. It was all I could think of to say at that moment.

"Yes," she said, "and furthermore, I'm reincarnated. I have lived before!"

I thought to myself, *Is this for real?*

I managed to ask, "And in what century did you live?"

"I lived in the twelfth century," she said.

"And what did you do back then?" I was intrigued to hear more by this point.

"I was a witch and burned at the stake."

Cold chills ran down my back. This whole dialogue was getting stranger by the minute. I was biting my tongue not to tell her that almost eight hundred years had passed, and she was still a witch. Instead, I said, "Oh, for goodness sakes!"

Thank you, Flexible Milt, my old friend, your advice came in very handy. As the conference wound down, her son said he would accept the detention and try to refrain from cutting school. He told me he wanted to go to college and become a mortician. After they left my office, I was in need of fresh air. I walked outside reflecting on what had just transpired. In a million years, I never would have thought that I would meet someone who professed to be reincarnated from a previous life. Three weeks later, I met the next one—go figure!

The third story is "Reincarnation is catching." It was a great Tuesday morning. No major issues needed to be addressed, and all was calm. I was reading an article in my office when I was told that a parent wanted to see me. He entered my office, introduced himself, and told me he needed my help. I was curious as to what I could do for him. He asked that I call his son into the office.

"What happened? Your son has perfect attendance. He has no behavioral issues to my knowledge."

He said that he wanted to wait until he arrived. While we were waiting, he said, "I am sure you have never heard what he will tell you."

"The learning curve is steep," I told him, "but I have heard it all."

"I will bet you free lunch for a year if I'm wrong."

"I can't bet," I told him, "but my curiosity has been heightened by your comments."

When his son entered my office—he had just left his art class—I asked him, "How is school going for you this year?"

"Fine," he said. "My favorite class is art."

His father interrupted and said, "Tell him why art is your favorite subject."

The next words I heard gave me chills for the second time in one month.

"I'm reincarnated from the seventeenth century. I was an artisan that worked in Florence."

Holy cow, I thought. *Two in one month! Is this a landing port for the second timers?*

"Oh, for goodness sakes," I said.

We talked at some length about school and his revelations. He was a good student, but he truly believed what he was saying. After I sent him back to class, the father thanked me for being kind to his son. He broke down crying, at a loss as to what to do or say. I shared that he needed to seek professional help.

"Well, I told you that this was one you had not heard before," he said when our meeting ended.

"Well, actually, just a few weeks ago a woman told me she was reincarnated."

He shook his head in disbelief as he left my office. Once again, time for fresh air and reflecting with gratitude about the many blessings we take for granted each day.

33: Disobedience, Graffiti, and Nasty Signs in the Process of Cleaning the Swamp

"Behavior is the mirror in which everyone shows their image."

-- Johann Wolfgang von Goethe

Often when I had a moment, I read anything inspirational that would help me as I worked with students who were struggling with school. I found a small little booklet filled with poems written by middle school students in which they expressed their fears about school, teachers, and peers. It was published in 1985, but the content was as current as it is today in describing the students' fears about growing up in school. I was reading a special poem that really touched me, one that refers to truly connecting with students:

> You spoke to me of love.
> I doubted you.
> You spoke to me of caring.
> I doubted you.
> You spoke to me of my self-worth.
> I doubted you.
> You came to the hospital to visit me.
> I believed everything you said.
>
> -- Robert Ricken

From the book *Love Me When I'm Most Unlovable – the Middle School Years*

I always kept in mind that poem. It was important to connect with students in a meaningful way, not just superficially, but truly invest in them. Not long after reading this poem, I was put to the test. I had just met with a student who needed to pass physical education, or he wasn't going to graduate.

"You don't care about me," he said. "All you care about is your stupid P.E. class."

He stomped out of my office. Twenty minutes later, I went outside because I heard the sound of sirens. I saw this same student handcuffed and being taken away by the police. As I approached, the officers said they saw him writing graffiti on the brick wall. It said, "Miller is a f-----g asshole." As he went away, he was yelling, "I only wrote one word, f---, not the rest!"

After the police released the boy, I scheduled a meeting with his parents to discuss the incident. When they came in, he was quiet and respectful.

"I guess I'm not going to graduate now," he said.

I thought about the poem I had just read and said to him, "I learned long ago that I love students, not always their behavior. You need to pay for the damages you caused and return to school to graduate."

"You mean you will let me?" he asked with a new sparkle in his eyes.

"Yes, as long as you complete the requirements outlined by the school district," I said.

His parents were thankful, and he finished his

responsibilities for graduation. Upon shaking my hand while I extended his diploma, he smiled at me and said, "Thank you. You really do care. I'm sorry for what I did."

The story I call "Those Darn Tennis Shoes" is the next one to share. I was called to the gymnasium because a student was causing a huge problem. When I got there, he was arguing with the P.E. teacher. He was playing basketball in the gym with his cowboy boots on. He refused to take them off. We had just refinished resurfacing the court. He started in with me.

"What are you going to do about it, suspend me? Go ahead, I don't care."

"Let's go to my office. We need to talk," I said.

I knew him. He was a good student, hard working. I knew his family. He helped on their ranch. His behavior was totally unusual for him and out of character. When we got to my office, I said, "I'm not going to suspend you, even though I should. I want to know what is going on. This behavior is so out of character for you."

He began to cry. He was a big kid, not the type you would think would cry easily. I knew that something was causing him to explode.

"I was just told that my girlfriend might be pregnant," he said. He sobbed, and his shoulders shook with emotion.

I gave him time to gather himself and regain his composure before sending him back to class. Three days later, he thanked me for how I dealt with him. He said that he was scared and didn't know how to share this information with his parents and her parents.

"And she is not pregnant after all," he said. "That day

taught me a lot about growing up and taking responsibility for my actions."

He graduated and became a pillar of the community.

One case that comes to mind when touching the subject of graffiti is the episode that I call "Who Gets the Last Say." It was a bright sunny day when, upon arriving at school and getting out of my car, I saw the principal looking up at a twenty-by-twenty-foot sign hanging from the second floor of the school. Written in big bold letters were the words: **Baseball players have hard balls.**

The principal said, "Tear down the sign and find out who posted it."

"I will get to the bottom of it," I answered.

The next day we found a second sign replacing the old one: **Tennis players have fuzzy balls.**

Once again, the principal charged me to find out who was pranking the school. I used my connections with the students to no avail. As I drove to school the third day, I couldn't wait to see if there was another sign, and sure enough, I could see it in the distance. This time, the sign was even bigger. It read: **Golfers have dimples on their balls**.

The principal was increasingly upset. In those times, people were not video recording every happening in their surroundings, and it was not easy to catch the violators. I told him that I had investigated, without any result. The fourth day we saw the final sign, which was directed toward us: **Administrators have no balls.** At this point we laughed. The signs stopped, we went back to normal, and never found out who was behind the signs.

34: Double Standards Don't Change Anything

"Giving up smoking is the easiest thing in the world.

I know because I have done it thousands of times"

-- Mark Twain

Smoking was advertised on the radio and television back in the day. Movie stars, both male and female, held cigarettes as the dramas evolved. Young students, masters of imitation, began sneaking cigarettes at an early age, some of them keeping the buds to light them up again later. One of the many assignments that went along with the position of assistant principal was the enforcement of the no-smoking policy on campus for students.

When I began my career as an educator, upon entering the staff room, clouds of smoke billowed in every corner, as most adults couldn't live without a cigarette in their hands. Years later, when I became assistant principal, the board of education passed a resolution prohibiting staff from smoking on campus. It was hard enough to enforce the rules with the students let alone the teachers and staff!

We had an open campus, which meant that students were allowed to leave campus for lunch. However, between classes, they were expected to stay on campus. For the chain smokers, this was a huge problem. They darted across the street and escaped into the alleys adjacent to the school. I was getting daily calls from neighbors about students smoking behind their property. I went across the streets every day to catch a few students. They stayed one step ahead of me; when I went across the street, they moved to the bathrooms to satisfy the need of nicotine. I hated being the smoking police. It was frustrating. With all the other discipline issues I faced, catching the smokers was fourth or fifth on my list of things to do.

One day, I was in line at the bank when an elderly lady came up to me and said, "Are you the new assistant principal of students? I saw your picture in the newspaper."

"Yes, I am," I said. "Is there something I can do for you?"

"I was the assistant principal in the 1930s at the high school," she said. "What do you think is the toughest part of the job?"

Before I could answer she said, "I hated the smoking rules. It was the biggest waste of time chasing students off campus playing hide and seek with me."

I laughed and agreed with her. "Now the staff can't smoke on campus, either," I said.

"I still remember the smoke coming out of the teachers' staff room after each period," she said. "It was such a double standard."

I thanked her for introducing herself to me. She wished me luck. It was refreshing to hear her comments. After thirty years, the same approach to addressing smoking was in place. I knew what was needed: consistent enforcement tied to education about the dangers of smoking.

I remember having one employee who refused to comply until the district threatened disciplinary action against him. Within three years, a demand for a student smoking area on campus became an issue of major proportion.

35: Part Two of the Book on Sailing: Tack against the Wind

"You have to be fast on your feet and adaptive or else a strategy is useless."

-- Charles de Gaulle

A few days later, I was working on a stack of student referrals that looked like Mount Whitney! It was about four o'clock and my day should have been winding down. In walked the science teacher, the one who had said on the first day I started the job that I wasn't man enough for the task and the district had made a big mistake hiring me.

My first thought was, *Here we go again. What negative thing will he say now?*

"Can I talk with you in private?" he asked.

"Sure, no problem. Please close the door and sit down."

"I want to apologize for my comments regarding the first day that you took the job. I was wrong to say that to you, and I regret doing it," he said.

"I understand," I said. "Don't worry. It has been forgotten."

"You have done an amazing job cleaning up many of the issues on campus in just a few short months," he said. "However, I would be remiss if I didn't say that your spirit seems down. I haven't seen your familiar smile, the one that used to greet us all, something that I think the staff all took for granted."

His last comment stunned me. "Is it that obvious?" I asked.

"Yes. I hope you can find some joy in what you're doing. I came to say that the staff appreciates how you are managing the job."

I knew it was time for another Flexible Milt moment. I left my office and headed to my dear friend Milt's room. He usually stayed after school and tinkered in his room. It was almost 5:30 p.m., but I took a chance. Sure enough, he was there.

"Do you have a few minutes to talk?" I asked him.

"Come in," he said.

I shared with him what the science teacher had said. "In the very deepest part of myself, I know that he is right. I have been trying my best to address all the issues, but the frustrations get the best of me and are affecting my mood," I added.

He listened without interrupting, which was one of Milt's many qualities that made him so endearing: the ability to hear your whole story. "I've been waiting for this visit," he said. "You've held the position for four months and accomplished a great deal. The staff is surprised at your success, but also concerned about your being able to sustain the stamina to do the job. Do you remember the little book on sailing I gave you?"

"Yes," I said, wondering why he was bringing it up again, as it did not seem relevant to the issue at hand.

"Well, a line in the first chapter says that you should not seek storms. They will find you all by themselves."

"Sure, I get it. The job constantly brings difficult issues to address. It is the nature of the position," I replied.

"Chapter two talks about the term tacking. Do not sail into the storm, but tack back and forth against the wind. Since you took the job, you have sailed into the storm full speed ahead. You need to begin tacking if you want to survive. You need to bring a balance to what you are doing. Find time for yourself. Bring your sense of humor, the one that we all know and love, back into the picture. Remember, you need to win the war, not every battle."

"You have no idea how much I appreciate and value your words and friendship, Milt," I said, thanking him again for his time.

I resolved to remember Milt's words and reread the chapter on tacking and finding ways to sail strategically through the storms I was facing. I left work that day strangely optimistic, ready to begin the next day with recharged energy and resolve, thanks to the honest input from the science teacher and my mentor, Milt. The new approach worked and got better with time and practice. This position was always full of surprising storms, and taking them on was part of my learning curve.

36: A Penny for Your Thoughts

"When angry, count to ten before you speak.

If very angry, count to one hundred."

-- Thomas Jefferson

The year was rapidly coming to a close. It seemed to speed up when everyone—students, teachers, parents, and, yes, the assistant principal of students—was worn out. The last week brought checkout procedures. Reconciling fines from the library and lost textbooks was a must, especially for those going through graduation ceremonies. Each student needed official notification with my signature verifying that all requirements had been met and fines paid.

One graduating senior owed over seventy-five dollars in fines for lost books and library materials. When I told her she needed to pay, she told me I would have to talk to her father. I called him. He became very upset.

"What if I don't pay?"

"If you don't pay by Wednesday, your daughter will not participate in the graduation ceremony. That's a school rule."

"I will be right down," he said, and hung up the phone.

When he arrived, I could tell he was not happy, to say the least. He entered my office with a large bottle filled with pennies. "Here is the money," he said, dumping the pennies on my desk. "They're all yours. You can count them!"

He stormed out of the office. I did count them. I had to. It was exactly seventy-five dollars, the amount owed. The parent had gone to the bank to get the money, angry enough to make a point of humiliating the school and whoever was in charge of helping his daughter to be responsible. One of my secretaries was required to observe me counting the money, a school policy when any employee received any cash.

37: Potty Passes? Get Real

"If I want to be alone, some place I can write, I can read, I can pray,

I can cry, I can do whatever I want—I go to the bathroom."

-- Alicia Keys

At graduation ceremonies, I greeted the graduates as they left the stage to make sure they behaved after receiving what resembled their diplomas. They would get the official one when they turned in their cap and gown. In the past, students had tried various pranks upon leaving the stage. I wasn't prepared for what happened next.

During my first year, one of the main issues to resolve was all of the students leaving class to use the restroom. I had the shop teacher make one potty pass for each classroom. Students had to wave the potty passes when they were on campus, which helped us monitor students who were out of class for their special business. The system served as a control device for those students who practiced leaving classrooms without much thought, taking advantage of teachers.

As the first student left the graduation stage, she handed me a bright red potty pass. My first thought was that she had taken one. After her, each one of the five hundred and sixty students walking to receive their diplomas handed me a bright red potty pass upon shaking my hand. My system had worked, but their sense of humor prevailed and stayed in my mind forever as one of those unique experiences that you have only once in your lifetime. Everyone was laughing, and even I had to chuckle. The school saved money in paper and ink, as I now had a fresh supply of potty passes for next year!

After we sang the school song and the principal announced, "By the power invested in me by the school district, the class has met the requirements for graduation," everyone cheered, and the students threw their hats into the air. When the stadium was nearly empty, I sat in one of the chairs. Graduation day had been the longest day of that first year. I had given it all. In a way, I was suffering "empty nest syndrome," as students become like your children, and you live their ups and downs, wanting always the best for them, and trying to save them from paths that may take them in the wrong direction. It was a fitting end to the year. Right there, I promised myself that the next year was going to be easier. The following school year was going to find me smarter and wiser. Little did I know what the future had waiting for me.

38: Replacing Fists with Knives

"I object to violence because when it appears to do good, the good is only temporary; the evil it does is permanent."

Mahatma Gandhi

Organizing my office and getting acclimated to what was where was the first thing I did each time I began a new job. Setting up my office was important. Looking for a stapler or paper clips when you need them can take precious minutes of your busy day, and the way to resolve this is to keep them in a specific place. Placing pictures, certificates, and diplomas on the walls to give a personal touch to the office, as well as a plant here and there, was also part of the routine, as I was going through old files, creating new ones, and emptying drawers and putting things back in neatly.

Three days after beginning my job as an assistant principal of the high school, upon opening the first drawer of my desk, I was struck by the variety and sheer number of knives that had been confiscated by my predecessors. Knives of every shape, size, and color from camouflage to cartoon characters were there. It was illegal to bring knives to school and was a legitimate cause for suspension, and yet it seemed to be a common occurrence. Confiscation of knives took place both on campus and during off-campus school activities.

The first football games of the season began. I provided general supervision of the stadium where the school played our home games, in coordination with the police and teachers assigned to be part of the general supervision. We communicated using walkie-talkies. One day I received a call stating that a young person dressed in all black wearing a trench coat and a red bandana was acting strange. I radioed the police to intercept the individual in question and joined them a few minutes later.

"What are you doing?" the police asked him.

"I'm prepared to defend myself if need be," he said.

"What are you talking about?" I asked him.

"Sir, I know karate, and I have a weapon," he replied.

This last comment immediately got the attention of the police. The individual pulled out a knife about six inches in length. The police took the knife and began further questioning. Before the police escorted him from the field, I asked one more question.

"Do you have any other weapons on you?"

"Well, yes, I do," he said, looking at us and laughing.

The police immediately grabbed him, opened his trench coat, and found approximately eight more knives. They varied in length from six inches to a sword that was at least three feet long, all taped to the inside of his coat. The boy was taken into custody. The police were a little embarrassed that they hadn't checked him closer. The young man was later released to his parents. One question tormented me as I walked back to the football field: What if we hadn't checked him for more weapons?

The second incident happened within five months after the beginning of school. One day, a young man entered my office and introduced himself as the toughest kid in the junior high. For the purpose of this story, I will call him Matt.

"I'm always in trouble," he said. "I want a fresh start, and I was told that you can help me be successful."

He was a big strong kid with the build of a man.

"I had a bad reputation at my last school," he continued. "Everyone wanted to fight me, and I never turned them down."

"Let's talk," I said. "From now on, every time someone challenges you to fight, come see me. I will protect you without others knowing our deal."

"Okay," he said. "That sounds good."

The first five months went smoothly. He saw me during lunch one rainy day and told me that someone had challenged him to fight but he had laughed it off. He was creating a new reputation, and his fresh start at our school was working. I reminded him to keep his cool.

Tuesday morning of the following week, a new student enrolled. He said he wanted to meet me.

"Hi, what is your name?"

"I need your help adjusting to this new school," he told me. "You will get to know me because I'm always in trouble. I'm going to be the toughest kid you've ever had in this school."

"Really? And why is that, if I may ask?"

"Well, no one will mess with me after everybody realizes that I am the toughest," he said.

"I warn you that here we are all part of a positive family," I said.

After he left, I called his previous school and was brought up to speed. I immediately thought about Matt, and called him to my office.

"Remember, Matt," I said, "if any new student challenges you, please come to see me immediately."

About thirty minutes before dismissal, one of my students came running to my office.

"The new student challenged Matt to meet him after school off campus to fight," he said almost without breathing.

I called Matt to my office. I could tell he was agitated. "I heard about the challenge," I told him. "Let me handle it."

I kept him until dismissal and took him off campus two blocks from his job at a local hamburger joint. He thanked me for helping once again. I had returned to school but not gotten to my office yet when another student shouted, "Help! The fight is on! The fight is on!"

I called the police and ran off campus where the fight had begun. Matt had just left. One of the bystanders said the new kid had a knife and tried to scare Matt. In the scuffle, Matt grabbed the knife and cut open the bully's forearm. The police arrived, but Matt had already fled the scene. The other boy was rushed to the hospital.

Matt was on the run. He was missing for three days until I got a call. Help!" he said. "I need you."

"I will take you in to face the police," I told him.

"Only you, nobody else," he replied.

We met after school, and I took him in. The next six months were tough, but he returned to school in the fall at the local continuation school. I always wished I could have prevented the unfortunate occurrence that took place that fateful day. Some kids can't handle the pressure even when they want in the deepest of their hearts to begin afresh.

The last of the three incidents involving knives took place at a basketball game. I was on duty, and the crowd was relatively small. Sitting in the stands by the scorekeeper, I noticed a person of interest about twenty-five years of age sitting in the visitors' section. I didn't recognize him. I thought perhaps he was just one of the supporters for the visiting team. I checked again in his direction about ten minutes later and saw something strange. He got up from where he was sitting to move four or five bleacher seats closer to the floor. When he got up, he took a knife out of his pocket and put it back in his pocket. It looked like a steak knife. I headed in his direction. When I approached him, I said, "Step outside for a moment."

"I am fine right where I am," he said.

"No problem. I just want to ask you a question," I said.

He got up, and we went outside. I asked him what was in his pocket.

"You mean this?" he asked, pulling out a steak knife at least six inches in length and pointing it directly at me. The tip of the knife was about an inch from my stomach, and my back was against the brick wall.

I thought fast and said, "I like that knife better when it is in your pocket."

"Okay," he said, and put it back in his pocket.

The principal saw me and let me know that he had called the police. I tried to engage the stranger in conversation. I could tell he "wasn't all there."

"I want to go back in and watch the game," he said.

"Where is your ticket?" I asked.

"I don't need one. I live here."

"Where do you live?" I asked in disbelief.

"Upstairs," he said.

"Where upstairs? Show me."

We walked together to a corner in the attic from where he was able to see into the girls' locker room. "How long have you been living here?"

"Ah, about six weeks," he said.

"Where do you get your food?"

"The cafeteria has all kinds of food."

Just then, the police arrived and were brought up to speed. He was handcuffed. Besides the knife that got my attention, he had a tennis ball, gag, and porno books. He had been spying on the girls for over six weeks. He had found the old decorative towers used for storage and made a home there. Fortunately, no one was ever harmed.

As he left, he had the audacity to ask, "Can I get my money back for the game?"

"You snuck in free," I said. "Besides, you won't be back."

As it turned out, he was a vagrant who had prior arrests in other cities. He knew that schools were easy places to hide. As for us, we were very fortunate to have avoided serious repercussions. As we wrapped up the incident, the police advised, "When you see knives, get help first before confronting any suspect."

I thought these three incidents with knives were the last ones I would have to face. Sadly, as years passed, I had to deal with many more that also involved other weapons despite numerous efforts to make the school a safe place to study for all of the students.

39: Unresolved Issues

"The guns and the bombs, the rockets and the warships, are all symbols of human failure."

-- Lyndon B. Johnson

I mentioned a few of the many times I had to manage situations involving knives as an assistant principal. I also had to deal with dangerous incidents involving guns on campus.

School began in January as usual after the winter break. The flavor of a new year with new beginnings, new resolutions, and renewed energy was still in the environment. The event happened on a Wednesday. I hadn't had any major issues to deal with during the first two weeks, and I was feeling pretty good about it, hoping that the year was going to be smooth and free of major negative happenings.

It was not unusual for me to be in the hallways before school talking to the students, giving them high fives, chatting with them, and letting them know that I was there for them. That day I noticed that one of the students passed by me looking the other way, definitely avoiding eye contact. It seemed strange. A few minutes later, he passed me again, and, as he did, I patted him on the back.

"Smile. It is the beginning of a great day," I said.

As I patted him on his back, a cold chill came over me. I felt what I thought was a gun underneath his shirt. I told the boy to come to my office. He looked scared, but he complied. Very concerned, I kept him in front of me as I ushered him into my office. When confronted about what I felt, he said, "Yes, I have a gun on me for protection."

He surrendered the weapon without incident. I told him to sit down, as I wanted to get deeper into the situation. He told me a fascinating story. A group of students were playing a game. They were carrying BB guns and shooting at each other between classes. They had rules, one of which was that you could only shoot below the waist.

In amazement, I asked, "How many are involved?"

"About five," he said, "but more are planning to start carrying BB guns to protect themselves."

"How long has this been going on?"

"About a week," he answered.

I looked closely at his gun, and it looked like a real gun, not just a BB gun. He showed me his welts from being hit. I was amazed that innocent bystanders had not reported the game to the office.

"Everyone is afraid to snitch," he said.

The next few days were hectic. The police were involved. Parent conferences were in session, not to mention suspensions from school. This happened way before the Columbine shooting and all the other incidents that brought media attention in the whole country to the problem of gun violence in schools. We tried to move for expulsion, but after background checks, previous negative behaviors on campus were not found. These kids were mimicking a movie plot about paintball wars. It was a dangerous game, and luckily no one was seriously injured. If this happened today, the consequences would be more serious for the students involved.

The next incident occurred the following year. After school one day, the varsity tennis players said someone was shooting at them from the rooftop of the gym. I called 911 and ran to the courts. The five minutes it took me to get there seemed like an eternity. When I arrived, I saw a police officer telling the student on the roof to drop his weapon. The officer had his revolver pointed at him. For a moment, I thought the student wasn't going to comply. I yelled for him to comply. He dropped his weapon and was taken in custody.

He explained that he really didn't have any reason for his behavior. The police officer that was closest to him was ready to use his revolver had the student not surrendered his weapon.

"What are these kids thinking?" I asked the police.

A week later, the same officer was on campus after someone called 911 to report that a student was displaying bizarre behavior and walking around pointing a gun at other students. An officer had the person in sight and was asking for my assistance. I bolted out of my office to find a very dangerous situation. The officer had his gun drawn and pointed at the student, who followed the officer's demand to drop his weapon.

I heard the student shouting, "It is a starter pistol. It's a starter pistol. I'm doing a science experiment!"

The three of us walked to my office. The science teacher had selected him to go outside his classroom and shoot the starter pistol at an exact time. The teacher wanted to show the gap of time between when the trigger is pulled and when the noise is heard.

I informed the teacher that he had not gotten permission to conduct this type of experiment. Fortunately, there were no serious consequences in this case either. Considering what other school administrators have gone through involving bombs, knives, and guns, the incidents that I witnessed, as stressful as they were, couldn't be compared to the magnitude of events that evolved nationwide. Having a student die at school can be the worst nightmare school shareholders can experience. Shareholders include school administrators, teachers, parents, students, and the community.

Think about Barry Loukaitis's case in 1996. He was a fourteen-year-old student from Moses Lake, Washington, who killed one teacher and two students with a weapon he got from home. Each time an episode like this happened, we met and brainstormed cause and effect. We asked school psychologists and law enforcement to help us come up with strategies.

Conversations about prevention included implementing metal detectors and security cameras and school uniforms, not allowing long coats, rules about tucking shirts into pants to eliminate baggy clothes that made it easier for students to hide guns, banning backpacks, letting students take books home to study, banning locker use, bringing in security guards, and so on. We discussed every possibility—what, where, when, how, and why. We also discussed mental disorders, the influence of entertainment, video games that desensitize the minds of students, and the need for greater parental involvement, and yet the efforts and the progress made did not stop the killing of eighteen children at Sandy Hook Elementary School in Newtown, Connecticut, on December 14, 2012.

40: A Legacy of Inclusion, Faith, and Touching Hearts

"I think we all have empathy.

We may not have enough courage to display it."

-- Maya Angelou

The assistant superintendent in charge of human resources for the school district published a monthly bulletin called "Just a Thought." Along with the advice of Flexible Milt and the principals with whom I worked, these monthly writings were inspirational and uplifting. I had never told him how much they helped me. One day, I decided to visit him before the students arrived for the fall. When I entered his office, he was busy putting the finishing touches on his latest issue. I told him how much I enjoyed the monthly bulletins. I felt kind of funny saying it, but he seemed pleased.

"Thanks," he said. "The rumor is, how can I take the time to write these publications? Don't I have anything better to do?"

"I believe in the power of positive words," I said. "We all need them."

"How was your first year as assistant principal?" he asked me.

I liked him, so I let my guard down. I told him how difficult it had been, but I was ready to go again.

"If you ever need my help, don't hesitate to give me a call," he said. "I was a rookie assistant principal once myself. This year you will be evaluating teachers and classified staff. I will be your go-to person if you have any issues to discuss."

I thanked him and left his office with the feeling that if I needed help, he had my back.

One of the classified staff I was assigned to supervise worked as a classroom aide. He had received unsatisfactory evaluations in the past. When I began the process, I was struck by his willingness to listen to my suggestions and concerns. He had been through this before. What was most interesting was that he said all the right things during our meeting, but he went right back to his old practices. He was always late, and I had to write him up repeatedly about it.

After three months, I had a binder full of negative evaluations. I went to the district office with it and was told, "When you have two binders full, come back." It took six months, but with the help of my new mentor, we were able to remove him from the classroom.

This incident taught me how important it is to document everything and keep accurate records, a learning experience that I applied throughout my career as an administrator. To this day, I still have the many "Just a Thought" publications that I eagerly read each month when I was an administrator.

When I became a principal years later, I knew that someone somewhere might need to be inspired to keep up the good work, just as I had been back then. With that in mind, I began my own bulletin, once per month, to update teachers, staff, parents, and the community about current issues, providing input with uplifting ideas that were part of the solution. David Cottrell, in his book, *12 Choices that Lead to Your Success*, writes that it is necessary to "share your gift of experience and knowledge with others." That's your legacy.

As an assistant principal, I was very fortunate to have three wonderful counselors who worked side by side with me helping the students to be successful. Each one had a specific grade level, and they followed that class from their sophomore to their senior year. This continuity was crucial in guiding students on the right path to graduation and future job or college prospects. I had one male and two female counselors. The male was strong, forceful, and direct. I valued his advice and counsel. The two women were caring and extremely competent. With their collective help, we took on the challenges that we encountered every day. As I recall various incidents, I will include their helpful advice and how they became an integral part of the resolution of the issues.

I had been invited to speak at the local university to a group of students who were interested in the teaching profession. I had graduated from that university and was touched by the offer. After I finished speaking, I took questions. The first question came from a student who was worried about classroom control.

"Never back students into a corner," I explained. "Always find a way to de-escalate the situation."

I was feeling pretty smug when I left to a rousing round of applause. When I returned to the school, it had begun to rain. Upon entering my office, I was told that the librarian and a student were waiting. The librarian was noticeably upset.

"This boy was being disruptive in the library, and when I told him to stop, he swore at me!"

"Is that true?" I asked him.

"Yeah," he said. "I called her a bitch."

His words and his tone of voice hit me like a ton of bricks. I raised my voice and asked him to apologize to her. It escalated from there. He ran outside, and the chase was on. Now it was really raining and cold. He got away, and I couldn't find him. I returned to the office, sent the librarian back to the library, and called the boy's mother. She asked what happened, and I explained the situation to her.

"Well, it sounds as if you didn't handle it very well," she said. "I will be right down."

As I caught my breath, I remembered how smug I had been only an hour before. "Don't back students into a corner" had been my very words. The Lord was testing me and teaching me a lesson about practicing my own advice. I vowed to make it right. When his mother arrived, I was told that her son had taken a wheelchair outside in the rain. His mother and I exited my office, and there he was in all his glory doing wheelies in a puddle of water.

"Has he ever done something like this before?" I asked.

"It's all your fault!" she answered.

After he dried off, I sent him home with his mother and scheduled an appointment for the following day.

At the meeting, I apologized for raising my voice the day before, and said, "Let's begin again. What is going on? Why did you respond to the librarian in that manner?"

With the help of one of the wonderful counselors that I

mentioned, we were able to resolve the issue. The boy made amends with the librarian, and we both agreed that if we had further issues, we would both handle it better. The counselor offered her services beyond our meeting, and the parent was satisfied.

Besides documentation, leaving a legacy, and never backing students into a corner, creating a collective mentality of inclusion was part of my learning curve as assistant principal.

One of the things that became clear to me as I dealt with student attendance and behavioral issues was that the majority of students who were at most risk were those who felt left out, disenfranchised, and somehow not part of the whole. Our African American students represented about 15 percent of the total school population. I was dealing with a small group of those students who were constantly in trouble. The essence of my dialogue with them went like this:

"Why is there so much anger and distrust?"

"We don't trust the school," one of them said. "We feel there is nothing here for us. We're only accepted if we're good at sports."

"One of my cousins belonged to the Black Student Union at his school," another student said. "They have meetings and activities culminating in a trip to the state conference held in the Bay Area."

I knew that what they were saying had some truth in it. As I listened to them, I decided to create a Black Student Union on campus to begin building a network of support. I hoped it would begin a new era for the school. I looked for a member of the staff who would be the new advisor.

After exhausting the list of teachers, I decided to do it myself. Granted, the assistant principal of students was probably their last choice, but we began the journey together.

The black female participants were great and showed up at our first meetings filled with ideas. We focused on creating scholarship funds, bringing guest lecturers, and raising money for these students to attend the state conference in the Bay Area. Little by little, the boys began coming to the meetings. I made sure we had pizza and beverages to entice their attendance. Some of the hard core refused to attend, but they slowly changed.

During the first two months of the year, the first big event was the Junior/Senior Prom, and the whole school was talking about the dance. A great band had been scheduled, and everyone was going to attend even though it would be in the high school multi-purpose room. The prom was on a Saturday, and I was catching up on referrals in my office. I looked out my door, and there was one of the African American students sitting on a bench. I could tell he was crying. I stopped what I was doing and went to speak to him.

"What is wrong?" I asked.

"My mom was going to pick up my date and three other couples, but she was not able to get the limo."

"What are you going to do?"

"I'm embarrassed to tell the other couples, so I'm not going."

"You can't do that," I said. "Everyone is counting on you."

"Do you have a better idea?"

"I have a big van that could handle the whole group," I said, after thinking for a moment. "I will be your chauffeur."

"What?" he said. "The assistant principal will take us to the prom? That would be very mortifying!"

"I'll drop you off two blocks from school," I said. "I'll pick you up at the same location at the end of the dance."

He reluctantly accepted. I immediately went home and began cleaning the van. It had three rows of seats, very plush, and it looked like a classy Oakland Raiders van with silver and black side panels. As we began the journey together that night, the reaction from the participants was one of shock when they saw me at the wheel, but ultimately they were thankful that they had a ride to the dance. I dropped them off and picked them up without anyone else knowing.

When I dropped off the young man last, he paused and asked, "Why did you do it?"

"Because you needed a hand, and I was able to do it."

"It's a miracle," he said. "I'm just lucky you saw me this morning, or I would have disappointed my friends. It was fate that I was there."

"I'm glad we had a happy ending," I said.

"Yes, and thanks for dropping us off a block away. That was cool."

As I drove home, I reflected on how good I felt. From that moment on, I had six new friends. They were instrumental in the success of the newly formed club. We made a connection because they knew that I cared about them. In our first few meetings, we were able to take over basketball concessions, and the whole group got involved, even the ones who were reluctant to participate at the beginning. During the basketball season, none of these students was in trouble. They had to be free of disciplinary and attendance infractions in order to work in the concession stands. I helped out, and we all had fun.

Every year, a rally was held to highlight the clubs and organizations. This would be the first time the Black Student Union had a representative. The girls had written a script with me giving a rap wearing gold chains as they danced to music. They wore colorful costumes, and the rap went like this:

> It's Miller time and I'm down for mine,
> The name of the job is busting crime,
> If you want to be cool,
> Don't drop out,
> Chill out, fool!

We all agreed to keep it a secret. As the day approached, I hoped it would be received well. The music started, the girls and guys began dancing, and I entered. The place went nuts! Here was their assistant principal wearing gold chains and dark glasses giving a rap! It was a classic!

Afterward, the group bonded well, and we eventually attended the state conference. The importance of investing, supporting, and including students was evident. I took this concept to every school that I managed.

41: Codes of Conduct: The Slippery Slope

"Live one day at a time emphasizing ethics rather than rules."

-- Wayne Dyer

One of the toughest parts of the assistant principal's job was enforcement of the school-wide code of conduct for athletes. The consequence for drinking, smoking, or using controlled substances was removal from the team for the remainder of the season. Occasionally, student athletes would attend parties off campus or participate in activities that violated the code of conduct. After I was informed of these instances, I was required to investigate. They usually turned out to be wild goose chases. Easier to enforce were the ones where students were caught during a school activity, such as a dance, a game, or anything on campus as opposed to a party off campus.

I confess that I hated the goose chases. I would call in the alleged participants and ask if they had violated the code of conduct by drinking alcohol. If they said yes, they were suspended from the team for the remainder of the season. If they said no, they remained on the team. It was a journey into the basics of ethics. Those who had broken the code knew that if they told the truth, they would go off the team, and if they told a lie, they would remain. I became frustrated each time I had a goose chase and always wondered if there was some way to reconcile those who were truthful and the rule of removal from the team for those incidents that occurred off campus during the weekends.

One case that stands out occurred when a rumor surfaced that the girls' softball team had used their day off from practice to have a party and drink alcohol. The news of the impending inquiry was spreading fast. At 9:00 a.m., I had only interviewed two of the girls. As the second girl left, a parent entered my office and told me that she thought the process was wrong. She said that her daughter would tell me she hadn't participated even though she had. She wanted to be present when I spoke with her daughter.

I called her in and said, "I am investigating a party that supposedly took place last Friday."

"I know that the school is investigating," she said.

"Did you drink alcohol at the party?" I asked.

"No, I did not," she answered.

I thanked her and sent her back to class. After her mother had left, I felt sick to my stomach. This was a good family with strong ethical standards, and this girl was a standout student and athlete. What a dilemma for a young person to deal with, let alone a parent that I knew had a high moral compass. A few hours later, the girl asked to talk to me.

"Sure, what's up?" I asked her, showing her a chair to sit in.

"I lied to you," she said. "I did drink."

"You know that you will be removed from the team."

"Yes, I know. I can't live with myself," she said.

I told her how proud I was of her honesty. I will never forget how at such a young age, she had the courage to make such a tough decision, but the right and ethical one.

I called her mom. I wasn't looking forward to this call. Her mother said she wanted to come to the office to talk to me, and she wanted her daughter to be called back into my office. I thought she knew what had just happened. Often, students would confess to things they had done, and parents would accuse me of forcing them to talk. Actually, I never did. Students mostly told the truth.

"I wanted her to tell the truth," the mother said. "I couldn't live with it, watching her lie, even though I don't agree with the school process where saying the truth results in punishment but lying has no consequence."

"The good news is that she just came in and told me the same thing," I said. "The concept of the truth being more important is clear to her. I am proud of both of you."

She was off the team, but I never doubted about her future being built with good character and a strong parental foundation that allowed her to distinguish right from wrong.

42: Returning from Purgatory Like a Phoenix

"A failure is not always a mistake. It may simply be the best one can do under the circumstances. The real mistake is to stop trying."

-- B. F. Skinner

Being an assistant principal of students at a high school is a challenge full of all kinds of opportunities. Sometimes the desire to do what is right for students takes a direction of its own.

The principal called me to his office that early November with some interesting news. The State of California Department of Education had been trying to come up with ideas on how to get graduating seniors to not only take the state CAP test, but to take it seriously. The test was given after most seniors had already been accepted to college. It didn't affect them scholastically, nor did it appear on their transcript. It was meant to be an internal measurement for the schools to use to improve instruction and access the strengths and weaknesses of each school's programs.

As an incentive to the seniors who showed growth on their CAP test scores, a portion of the money that otherwise would have gone to each school's general fund would be used by the senior class to assist with graduation activities. Both the principal and I thought this approach was a good idea. All schools were encouraged to speak to their respective senior classes to get them fired up to do their best.

The principal set up a schedule to visit every class. During this visit, a pep talk explained the academic advantages of taking the CAP test as well as the incentive percentage to be used at the end by the graduating senior class. The students could form a committee to discuss how to best use this portion of the funds. After each visit, we both were encouraged by the seniors' responses.

Within a few weeks, early in December, the principal called me to his office. Four seniors were already there waiting for me. The spokesperson said, "Now that you both are here, we have a list of demands. Unless they are met, we will convince the seniors to throw the CAP test."

The principal and I couldn't believe what we had just heard. The principal asked them to describe their demands.

They had four demands: (1) Allow smoking on campus; (2) lower the speed bumps in the student parking lot; (3) change the current tardy policy; and (4) allocate a larger portion of any CAP money to the senior class to decide, at its discretion, how to spend it.

"No smoking on campus is a state law," I said. "However, local school boards can, if they choose, allow a designated area. You have to petition the school board. Second, the speed bumps are scheduled to be lowered within a few weeks. A tardy policy is in effect lowering the number of tardies. If you have a suggestion as to what to substitute to hold students accountable, let's hear it."

"As far as the distribution of any money is concerned,"

the principal said, "a committee made up of students, staff, and parents will meet to develop a plan. The state will not allow us to turn over money to a senior class to use as students choose without the school's official involvement."

"Do you understand what you are doing?" I asked.

"Yes," their spokesperson said. "It is simply called collective bargaining."

"To me," I said, "it sounds more like extortion. If you don't get what you want, you are going to throw the CAP test, something that is good for students and the school, and you'll pressure others to do the same."

They stood up and left the office. After they left, we sat to reflect on what had just transpired. The principal immediately called the parents of the students and scheduled conferences to discuss the situation with them. Within thirty minutes of our meeting, professionally made flyers listing the demands had been distributed all over campus. In other words, these four students had developed a premeditated plan to promote non-conformity. They encouraged students to throw the test if their demands were not met. The principal scheduled second meetings with all senior classes to remind them of what had been encouraged by the administration to support and asked the seniors again to do their best on the test.

The meetings with the parents were less than promising. They believed that the students were just collective bargaining, which, according to what one parent said, was an exercise of their first amendment right. We had hoped that they would see the absurdity of the demands and choose to support the school. The principal reassured them that lowering the speed bumps, one of the four demands, was already being addressed. He went on further to say that smoking on campus was possible if permission was requested of the board of education for this entity to establish a designated smoking area. The tardy issue wasn't even addressed at this meeting. However, the principal was clear about the inability to give the senior class a large portion of the money to use as they pleased.

"This demand will never be granted. The state guidelines are strict concerning how funds can be used."

I felt a little empty after the parents left. In all school organizations, parents are part of the team to resolve issues. At this point, the principal and I were hoping that the majority of the seniors would side with the school, since the end of their high school journey was just around the corner. However, no one from their group was willing to petition the board of education for a designated smoking spot. The seniors never even suggested a different consequence to be enacted for students' excessive tardiness. Prior to holding students accountable for tardiness, the school had registered over five hundred individual late arrivals per day. Accountability had created positive results in the sense that late arrivals were reduced dramatically to fewer than fifty. The students did not suffer any disciplinary consequence for their actions.

We would not know the outcome of the CAP test until late April. What was to come was way beyond anything we could have imagined.

The statewide CAP test results became public during spring break. The principal called me and gave me the bad news: "Our school-wide test results were extremely low. The majority of the students failed the test."

Within a few days, the school was flooded with inquiries from all over the world. The news of the students' results and the issues we had faced with them in December came to fruition. The students had been successful in ruining the test results for our school.

On Monday, the first day back from spring break, our school was flooded with reporters, and even a major television station from the Bay Area sent an investigative reporter to interview the students who had led the protest. I remember standing outside on the grassy area with the principal as the reporters talked to the spokesperson for the students.

When he explained their demands, the reporter asked, "These were the reasons you encouraged the students to throw the test?"

For the first time, the mood began to change. In the beginning, the reporters thought we were to blame. After talking with the student leaders, the worm turned. The principal explained how we approached their demands and how we visited the classrooms twice to encourage students to do their best. This approach was something every school in the state had done.

We were at a loss as to why the majority of the students were willing to go along with the small group that started with four. The news media painted a true picture of what transpired. The results backfired for the students. The school survived, and the media was not on the students' side. The principal and I hoped that the worst had passed, and that the six weeks left in the school year were going to be peaceful and uneventful. We were wrong.

One day during the second week after spring break,

cheerleader tryouts for the fall were held in the gymnasium just before the end of the day. Most students went to the gym to cheer the participants. This time, however, disruptions happened during the tryouts. One of the students threw dog biscuits at the participants, which made them cry. The student responsible for this action was the same spokesperson who had led the revolt against the CAP test. The principal suspended him for disrupting a school activity. When the student returned to school from the suspension, the principal met with his parents, and as an assistant principal, I was called to be present.

The principal started the meeting by saying to the student, "We only have six weeks left in the school year. I need some assurance that you are not going to be disruptive any further."

He thought for a moment and replied that he was not pledging allegiance to the principal. His answer was clear: He was not willing to commit to following school rules. The principal told him that without a commitment on his part to follow school rules and not be disruptive, he would have to send him to the continuation school for the remainder of the school year.

Within a few days, the school superintendent, the board of education members, the principal, and I were part of a seven-million-dollar lawsuit. The overall premise was that the first amendment rights of the student in question had been violated, because the principal's decision to remove him was motivated by the student's leadership in the CAP test revolt.

Nothing could have been further from the truth. He was simply asked not to be disruptive and to follow school rules. This is what any principal of any school would do after disruptions of this nature. What ensued was a seven-year court battle. Deposition after deposition filled my calendar for those seven years. The whole process was extremely stressful on our families, and it affected our jobs. We knew that we had never done anything to warrant this lawsuit. I knew in my heart that I had always treated students fairly. In this student's case, we had dealt with him in a number of incidents preceding his senior year during which his actions had defied school authority.

I remember first meeting him when he was a sophomore. I was walking the campus when I saw him sitting on a tree branch. He was about ten feet off the ground with his feet dangling from the limb. I introduced myself and asked him to please get down from the tree. He said he was just fine where he was.

"If you were to fall and hurt yourself," I said, "the school would be liable. To ask you to please get down from the tree is a reasonable request."

He asked me what gave me the right to make him get down. I said that as assistant principal of students, I was responsible for the health and safety of each student on the school grounds.

"If you want to sit in trees off campus, that is your choice," I said.

A crowd of students had gathered. He reiterated that he was fine and would not get down. I said to him, "I'm going to my office. If you are still in the tree by the time I get there, you will be suspended for defiance of school authority."

I walked away and stood by the library approximately one hundred fifty feet from the tree. He was smiling and still in the tree. I looked at my watch and began counting. After two minutes, I walked to my office and called his parents. While waiting for his parents, the school grounds man told me that the student had climbed down when he told him he was injuring the tree.

His parents were upset with me. They said that I should have called them to get him out of the tree instead of suspending him. I told them he had been defiant of school authority and that I had given him more than one chance to comply. I repeated to them that if he had fallen and injured himself, the school would have been liable.

"You have the right to appeal the suspension to the principal, if you choose."

This was my first but not last encounter with this young man. The fall turned to winter. It was a little brisk outside. The pine trees had been shedding like crazy. Pine needles covered the ground like a slippery carpet. One cold wintery day, I heard sirens outside my office. My first thought was that a fire had begun nearby. I went outside and saw billowing smoke coming from an area behind the science wing. I rushed to the area to find the fire department putting out a fire. The student from the tree incident and a couple of his friends had piled up a bunch of pine needles and started them on fire to roast marshmallows. Neither the fire department nor I were amused.

The fire chief said, "What you just did was very dangerous and took us away from our jobs. What if there had been a real fire, and we were here? I'll leave it to the school to handle this incident, but you would face charges for your actions if it were my decision."

I met with the parents of the group. Instead of suspension, a parent suggested an alternative discipline. He said to let the boys rake the pine needles on campus on a Saturday. I agreed. The parents were going to supervise. Ironically, during one of the depositions, their lawyer accused me of assigning unsupervised involuntary servitude for the boys. I responded that it had been agreed that the parents would supervise in lieu of suspension.

I honestly believe that the parents were glad we had found a different approach to discipline their sons, something that was good for the school community. It was the parents' idea after all. The same group of students wanted to bring their hibachi and BBQ meat during lunch. I was able to head that off, although I was told they had done it once already.

With each new incident, the issues became more unique. One rainy day, the student got my attention again. The rain had fallen hard for three consecutive days. As I was leaving my office for lunch, I saw him running as fast as he could. Then, he jumped spread eagle, landed on the soaked lawn, and skimmed along for about a hundred feet. He was soaking wet when I reached him.

"What are you doing?" I asked him.

"I'm hydroplaning. Why?"

"Well, number one, you are tearing up the lawn. Number two, you could hurt yourself. Maybe there is a piece of glass or nail in the lawn."

He thought for a minute, said okay, and left to change. *For once, he got it*, I thought. It was still raining the next day, and this time the student, with googles, kneepads, and inner tube, was running, jumping, and splashing water as he skimmed along for about a hundred feet. He informed me that the lawn would grow back and that the inner tube, kneepads, and googles had addressed my concerns for his safety.

"I understand," I said. "However, hydroplaning on campus is not okay. If you do it again, you will face suspension for defiance."

He smiled as he left.

The last in a series of disciplinary issues was the time I saw him and his friend shot putting a huge boulder as far as they could.

"What are you guys doing?" I asked.

"We're playing boulder golf."

"Well," I said, "this course is closed for the season. You need to repair the depressions in the lawn from your game." They smiled, and the round of boulder golf ended peacefully.

Going back to the last two weeks of the school year, the district first tried to mediate the issues after the lawsuit was filed by allowing the student to return to school to graduate with his class. This action did not make the lawsuit go away. The principal and I assumed that he was going to be on his best behavior now that there was a lawsuit, and things went smoothly with one crazy exception.

The last week of school, we had a quad day with various activities, including a dunk tank. Each year I volunteered to be in the tank to raise money for a worthy cause. Well, that same student decided he wanted to dunk me.

"It's not enough to be sued by this student. Now he gets to dunk me too?"

He had a bad aim and missed the target. The students were all laughing. In response, he climbed up and pushed the bar that sent me into the tank. It was a typical response from him, but I refrained from making any comments. After years of volunteering for a good cause, one student was able to sabotage a fundraiser game. From then on, dunk tanks were over for me.

After the dunk tank, I had just enough time to take a shower to go to a job interview in a nearby town right after school. Prior to the CAP test fiasco, I had a good chance for the job. With the negative publicity, I had a sick feeling as I left the campus that I didn't have a chance. All the things that were not going well at the school tormented me as I approached my destination. Students were not behaving well, particularly the seniors. Trash was everywhere. It was evident that students lacked pride in their school.

The interview was tough. I was asked about the pending litigation.

"How will your performance and effectiveness be affected by having to attend court dates? Why did all the seniors follow those few students?"

Similar questions went on and on. I told them we could only guess. It was a revolt against the state test, a test with no ability to hold them accountable. There were no consequences for throwing the test except the embarrassment they caused for our school and community, which was just beginning to surface.

The last question was a doozy: "If we visited your school right now, what would we see?"

To this day, I remember how tough it was to answer what was clear and obvious in my mind. I was ashamed of how the school looked when I left.

"Everyone is ready to leave for summer and things are very hectic now," I said. "The mood on campus is very tense."

As I drove home, I was sick to my stomach. I had failed the interview even before it began. I would not have hired me if I had been in their shoes. With the court case pending, I was not ready to commit to another employer. I vowed that things had to change next year, or else I would make a choice to go back to the classroom.

After almost seven years, we finally appeared in federal court. What happened that day was total vindication for the school district, the superintendent, the board of education, the principal, and me. The judge stated that the school district acted appropriately and that the plaintiffs had wasted a lot of time and money on this case. Their lawyer kept interrupting him, and the judge told him that if he said another word, he would be in contempt. The situation lingered for another year or two as the plaintiffs appealed all the way to the Supreme Court of the United States. Once again, we were exonerated at the highest level.

During this process, two more lawsuits surfaced, all related to students' defiance and administrators trying to enforce school rules. I found inner strength from what was transpiring with the big lawsuit.

The lawyer assigned to me said, "As long as you follow the rules and do your job ethically, you will have nothing to be afraid of from lawsuits."

His advice was true, and I was able to withstand the

suits as part of what goes with the job as a school administrator. People don't like it when they don't get their way, and they believe that school districts are the ones with deep pockets.

As the ten-year reunion of the class that led the CAP test revolt approached, I was curious to see if the school staff attended the reunion as they usually did with tenth-year celebrations, or if they boycotted it. It was customary to invite staff, and the alumni had sent invitations. I knew that probably no one would go from the school because of the effect of the test on our reputation and the embarrassment they caused to our community.

Liking closure, even in the most troubling of cases, I decided to attend. I knew good students from that class, and I hoped to reconnect with them in a positive way. When I entered, the room went silent. Then, students began applauding. It was like trying to make amends for what had transpired ten years earlier. I spoke with many students who apologized for going along with the revolt. If they had to do it over again, they wouldn't do it, they assured me. Apologies were accepted with friendly handshakes.

As I was leaving, I saw the student who had led the revolt walking toward me. He extended his hand in front of everyone. For a moment, the whole ordeal passed before my eyes, and my heart shrugged. I hesitated. The values of my upbringing were more powerful. Decency, and the absence of wanting to cause any harm to him from day one, prevailed. I accepted his handshake, and I heard the students applauding again. I can't remember the words we exchanged. I only remember that I had always treated him fairly despite the conflicting issues surrounding us. Attending that tenth-year reunion was an odd closure, but I was able to put the case behind me because forgiveness is a choice.

43: From One to Twenty-Six Hundred Hands

"As we look ahead into the next century, leaders will be those who empower others."

-- Bill Gates

For school personnel, staff, teachers, and administrators, summer break is like a cleansing. You go from a fast pace, where there is no such a thing as working from eight to five because you leave school and continue at home or in community events connected with the school, to a time of total relaxation and a disbelief that you actually can get out of bed at eight in the morning, go to the movies with the family on a Tuesday, plan a fishing trip, work in the garden, read a book just for the sake of entertainment, or watch your favorite program. That is what I was doing when I received, right before the new school year started, a flyer advertising a conference in San Francisco sponsored by law enforcement. The focus of the conference was building relationships with your constituents.

I called the principal to get his approval, and he was supportive. I was hopeful that I could get some ideas on how to make positive connections with the students in my role as assistant principal of students. The conference was going to be held in early October, and I was excited about the possibility of learning some new strategies. Time

244

passed fast, and October came. There I was, sitting at a conference that I had waited to attend with great anticipation. After two days, I was discouraged by the fact that it was really focused more on law enforcement and not schools.

On the third day, as I was walking out the back door pulling my suitcases, I saw something hanging from an umbrella. It was filled with dangling signs. Each one had a negative side and a positive side: School Pride on one side, and Pride with a slash through it on the other side. The sign on the door read "Special workshop added on Pride, guest lecturer: Gene Bedley."

An invisible force drew me into that room. I placed my suitcases in a corner and sat down ready for anything. It turned out to be the greatest workshop I had ever attended, all on building relationships in schools, just what I needed. After the workshop, I spoke at length with Gene, and he asked questions about my school and the status of the relationship between the students and the administration.

After sharing some of the issues with him, he said, "Your school needs a PRIDE project, and you're the one who needs to lead it. The pride that I am referring to stands for Personal Responsibility in Daily Effort. You need to be the cheerleader and make it happen."

How was I going to implement a program that would make a difference? I left the workshop very excited, ready to make a change. Instilling pride would forever be part of my mantra for the rest of my career.

Gene had asked me to focus on one area of change. He suggested something to do with improving the school climate. "Once you reconnect with your constituents," he said, "other things will fall into place. You'll see. The first step is to get the buy-in from the staff."

At the next staff meeting, I explained my plan and asked for their support. I told the teachers that I wanted to visit each class during the fourth period to talk about improving our school climate. It would take me three months to reach each fourth period class at our school, but the whole school community would see the fruits of their efforts over time. I wanted the teachers present to hear the talk. It was not a free prep period. Every teacher with the exception of one agreed. He said he was too busy teaching. I decided to move forward with the hope that he would change his mind.

The first class was amazing. I asked the students to close their eyes and imagine they were aliens from another planet who had just landed on our campus. I asked them to reflect on what they observed. After three minutes, I asked them to share their observations, and I wrote their points on the board:

- Trash everywhere
- Bathrooms in disrepair
- Seagull waste on the benches
- Unpleasant odors in some areas
- Paint peeling from the walls
- Black gum spots on the cement

The list went on and on.

"Who is responsible?" I asked.

"The adult beings," they replied. "This is their fault. How do we solve this?"

I didn't like what I was hearing, but they were being honest. "We need a plan," I said. "Let's address trash on campus first."

"Put trash cans where students eat," they suggested.

"How many hands are there in this school?" I asked.

We figured with teachers, students, administration, and classified staff we had around twenty-six hundred hands. The new goal was to ask students for random acts of kindness.

"Help by picking up trash," I said. "We are not trying to get publicity. This is going to be a group effort. I put a few five-dollar bills on the ground under some pieces of trash, and I saw people, staff included, walk by without stopping to pick it up. No more five-dollar bills. We do it because we care about our school. We need to take PRIDE—Personal Responsibility in Daily Effort—one day at a time."

A bright student raised her hand and said, "This is a superficial pep talk to get us to pick up trash."

"It is superficial if you do not see results," I said. "First, I will address the other issues with trash cans, graffiti, and broken bathrooms. Second, what is wrong with a pep talk? I need your hands. I need all twenty-six hundred hands."

Just then, a quiet student raised his hand and said, "I only have one hand."

I thought for a second that he was joking. He raised his other arm and he was, indeed, without a right hand.

"I lost it when I had an accident as a child," he said. "You are trying to do something good. I only have one hand, but you can count on it."

This was transformation at its best. They knew what

the problem was, but they needed a coach, a mentor, a willing person to help them to get inspired. I asked all the students to write seven things that, in their opinion, would happen to society in the future, and to date them according to when they thought these events would happen. They had five minutes to compile their list. I wrote their ideas on the board:

- War
- Earthquakes,
- Famine
- Depression
- World unrest
- Apathy in politics
- Pollution
- Inflation
- Cure of Cancer
- Medical Advances

Most of their ideas covered a span of fifty years; some were negative, some were positive. I then asked them to turn over their piece of paper to write seven things that would happen in their lives and to date them spanning the next fifty years. They shared when they were ready:

- Buying a house
- Graduation from college
- Marriage
- Retiring
- Getting a boat
- Having children
- Getting a good job

I asked them, "What is the correlation between your predictions in the world around you and its effect on you in your personal lives?"

"I guess if we have a depression, I won't have a job," one student said.

"If I don't have a job, I won't be able to buy a house," another said.

"War will affect our economy, and we will earn less money."

"I won't be able to graduate from college if I have to go to war. I may not even come back if I am killed."

"Pollution will reduce people's lifespan."

"Pollution will increase the number of diseases."

They began to realize the interconnectedness between society and how it affects us personally.

"This same test was mentioned in Alvin Toffler's book *Future Shock*," I told them. "He was concerned that most young people didn't see the connections. I am proud of you for realizing the need to be interconnected with society by getting involved, making a contribution, being part of the solution, and acting promptly to stop problems before they get bigger and uncontrollable. This is one way for us to become part of the PRIDE project," I continued, "doing the right thing to rebuild a sense of pride in our school."

A spontaneous "you have my hands" was the chant as they were dismissed.

The rest is history. The 2600 Hands program began, and with each new day, there were another thirty-five converts to the school improvement project. It wasn't very long before I found creative ways to paint bathrooms, buy more trash cans, and remove the graffiti from the walls. It was a silent revolution with more advocates each day. At the end of the three months, the one teacher who had refused to join said that he wanted me to visit his classroom because "Whatever you are doing is working."

By the end of the year, the campus had undergone a facelift. PRIDE was everywhere. We never asked for kudos. I kept my word, and so did the students. The one thing I had not counted on was the reconnection with the students in such a positive way. When they saw the improvements, they believed what I had said. It wasn't superficial because they saw tangible results.

The biggest surprise was the renewed trust the students had in the administration team and me. For the first time, students were coming to tell me who was selling drugs on campus. They wanted to be safe, too. My suspensions that year went up only in catching students who were breaking the law. It was no longer safe for them to operate on campus.

One Sunday night I received an anonymous phone call.

"One of my friends is doing cocaine. I'm frightened for him. He's lost a lot of weight. Can you help?"

He left the name of the boy and hung up. I knew who he was talking about. The boy was a good athlete. I never would have guessed. The next day I called his counselor and explained the situation. She called the boy's parents and asked them to meet with us regarding a serious matter. When the parents arrived, I called the student to come to my office. When he entered my office, I couldn't believe how much weight he had lost. He looked pale and without energy. I shared the phone call I had received the night before. The parents were shocked and upset that I would accuse their son of such a serious issue. Just then, for no apparent reason, the boy's nose began to bleed. Blood came gushing out of his nose. He could not get it to stop. I told them to take their son to the emergency room and to get some help.

He never confessed, but he dropped out of school for a few months and got help. He returned to school and graduated with his class. The parents approached me after graduation.

"You saved our son, and we will forever be grateful."

"The friend of your son who had the courage to call me is the true hero," I said. "He saved your son."

Peers have such power, if only they felt a sense of responsibility for each other, more at-risk students could be saved.

After only two years of the birth of the PRIDE Project and the 2600 Hands, the school had returned to a place of relative calm, and we were enjoying the results of a school community that had come together under the steady leadership of Roger, a wonderful principal. I will always be grateful for his strong leadership, character, and friendship. He helped me become a better administrator and allowed me to explore new ways to connect with students, to get them to engage in their own progress, and to improve the overall school environment.

44: Leaving the Harbor

"And suddenly you know:

It is time to start something new and trust the magic of

beginnings."

-- Meister Eckhart

Ships were not built to remain in the harbor. They fulfill their purpose by leaving the shore, exploring the oceans, and going to places across the sea. I got the itch to sail into new adventures. I had been a teacher, a coach, and an assistant principal of a high school for nine years, and these experiences combined had given me skills to manage both smooth and difficult situations with the school constituents. I was finishing my master's degree in curriculum and instruction with the hope of becoming a principal.

I was asked in June to go to the junior high as assistant principal. The school was in turmoil. It didn't make any sense for me to agree to a lateral transfer when things were going so well at the high school. I was dreaming of different opportunities, so my answer was, "I am happy where I am."

I realized that the district could have ordered me to go, but it didn't. A year and a half passed, and I was asked again in the month of November to go to the junior high to become the assistant principal. I was told that the new junior high principal wanted to talk to me. Out of courtesy to the assistant superintendent who was a mentor to me and a friend, I agreed to meet him.

We introduced ourselves while sitting in my van in a parking lot. He was ten years younger than I, but his demeanor was energetic and convincing, with a special gleam in his eye. He was a young Gene Bedley. Listening to him was inspirational, and from then on I knew that, in spite of all the work that had to be done to bring that school under control, he and I could do it together. He said that he was going to share everything with me— discipline, curriculum, buildings, and grounds.

The assistant superintendent encouraged me to accept the position, stating that it would show my versatility to be successful at other schools. After much thought, I agreed to take the leap of faith and left the safe harbor of the high school where I had been for over twenty years. It was hard to leave a school that I knew so well, but the challenge was calling me with a powerful voice.

The new principal and I went to the junior high school on a Friday at 5:00 p.m. The custodian didn't let us in.

"You guys start on Monday," he said. "I will see you then."

He turned around and left, and we stayed there, looking through the door in bewilderment. Monday was the first day of a positive transformation for that junior high, which became noticeable within a short period of time.

The first day at any school is hectic, but we were taking over mid-year. One of the teachers made a snarky comment: "I've seen principals and assistant principals come and go."

"Nice welcome," I said.

"You need to enforce our five hundred rules," another teacher said. "We need a line painted down the hall so only boys can walk on the left and girls on the right to avoid fights."

I mostly listened that day. I must have said "Oh, for goodness sakes" at least fifteen times.

My new secretary had put plastic ants on my desk. They looked real. She wanted me to know that she was an environmentalist who "cared for all of God's creatures."

"Oh, for goodness sakes!" I said once again minutes before 3:30 p.m. that very first day.

I sat on the parking lot curb looking at the paint peeling off the dirty walls and asked myself,

"What have I done?"

It was clear to the principal and me that we didn't need five hundred rules. What we needed to address immediately was the school climate, so we began our first week with that in mind, a climate where safety and respect from student to student, students to teachers, and teachers to students was enforced.

A teacher came to me and wanted a student suspended for using his finger to make popping noises with his mouth, which was disrupting the class, but she wasn't sure which rule he had broken.

"Do we need to make another rule?" I asked her. "How do you spell what he did?"

"This is not funny," she answered.

"We need only two basic rules: Be safe and be respectful," I said. "Repeated and intentional disruptive behavior in the classroom is disrespectful, and the offense could result in suspension."

The principal and I visited the classrooms to introduce ourselves. During our talk, we asked the students to help by being a part of the new direction of the school.

"We need heroes to help us make the school a better place. Help us, and you will see a new school."

The principal hired painters to spruce up the front of the school. He commissioned new murals painted on the hallway walls that encouraged school pride. The windows in the main office, badly stained from years of neglect, were replaced with new ones, which gave the office a fresh look. One secretary said that it was the first time in twenty years she could see outside. The changes were making a tangible and huge difference in staff morale.

The first few days that we visited classes, there were repeated stink bomb attacks between classes. No one would come forward to identify who was doing it.

I reprimanded a student the very first day for throwing an apple at a seagull during lunch. We were four hours from the ocean, but seagulls made the trip because the garbage that students left on the ground was plentiful and succulent. The asphalt had so many seagulls and other bird droppings that it looked like salt and pepper. The college student supervisors were let go that first day because they didn't make the kids pick up their garbage since "the seagulls would eat it anyway." The art teacher heard about it and drew a picture of a seagull carrying a student away, taking with it his lunch bag.

I received a note folded in half saying, "I am sorry for throwing an apple at the seagull. I'm really a good kid. I know who is doing the stink bombs. I want to be your first hero. The guy that is getting others to set off the stink bombs is Luigi. It is a way to get into his gang."

While I was reading the note, I got a call from the woodshop teacher. He informed me that someone in his class had let off a stink bomb, and no one would tell who did it. "You need to come to my class right now and solve this problem," he said. It was my third day on the job.

I looked at the class list. Sure enough, Luigi was enrolled. I took off in a flash and entered the woodshop. The teacher looked angry.

"No one will fess up!" he exclaimed.

I looked around the room and saw students laughing under their breath. I said, "Luigi, come with me."

You could hear a pin drop. As we walked down the hallway, he said, "I didn't do it."

"You have ten seconds to tell the truth, or you will no longer be a student in this school," I said.

"Where will I go?" he asked.

"Elsewhere," I said. "One, two, three, four, five, six, seven..."

He weakened at eight and admitted that, indeed, he was the one who had been setting off the stink bombs. When he opened his locker, I found over four hundred stink bombs. He was suspended and turned over to the police.

When the students heard of the incident, more than 90 percent were happy. School just might become safe again for them. When Luigi returned, he was a different student. We had turned a corner. The school environment was getting under control. The list of heroes grew, but I never forgot my first one.

I was asked to evaluate a number of staff and teachers that first year. At one of the classes that I visited, I observed that the teacher had lost her way. She was intimidated by mischievous students, which affected her ability to manage her classroom and to teach. When I entered the room, she was taking roll and not looking at any of the students. Throughout her lesson, she never made eye contact with them. Meanwhile, three students left the room and did not return, without her being aware of it. One boy went out the window, even though he knew I was watching. When she looked up, she stared at the ceiling.

When the class was over, I walked toward her and asked if she had a few minutes to talk with me. The next hour was going to be her prep period, so we had time. She asked if I liked the class.

"I am concerned," I said. "You never looked at the students, and when you did look up, you looked at the ceiling. Three boys left the room, one went out the window, and you didn't see a thing."

"Well, I get nervous, so I pick a focal point on the ceiling," she explained. She pointed to a big black dot on the ceiling. "Do you have suggestions?" she asked.

"Yes, lower you focal point to the level of your students. You need to be totally present and able to hold them accountable. I need you to understand two things: you have our support, and you are the classroom manager." It was the beginning of true accountability school-wide.

During my second year at this junior high, I had

emergency neck surgery and missed four weeks of work. I returned using a scooter to get around. I scooted around and bantered with the students. They enjoyed teasing me. By now, the majority of the staff had embraced the new school climate, and we were making changes to improve the quality and performance of our students in a safe and caring environment.

My third year began. I was called to the district office. Hal, my mentor at the district, said that he had a proposition for me. He was aware that I was completing my master's degree and would graduate in June.

"I believe that you deserve to be considered for future openings for principal," he said. "There will be many chances. You need to position yourself with a primary background just in case an opening becomes available. I will give you a crash course in elementary if you are willing."

It was hard to leave the junior high. I really enjoyed working with the principal and staff. I had learned a great deal and was truly blessed by the experience, but I needed to discover the new oceans that I had dreamed of, to test other waters and move on to reach my goal of becoming a principal.

I thanked the principal for his trust in me and his commitment to excellence at the school. In two short years, he had rejuvenated the school climate. New secretaries became part of his dynamic change, and staff collaboration was in action. To this day, he and I remain friends and talk to each other often.

My call to accept the new challenge began in haste. I would begin again!

45: First Things First: The Screamers

"Change will not come if we wait for some other person or some

other time.

We are the ones we've been waiting for. We are the change that

we seek."

-- Barack Obama

When I walked into the assistant superintendent of human resources' office, I was anxious to find out what he had in mind for me. He had told me that he would give me a crash course in elementary education. I understood that if I were to be successful at the elementary level, I would need to have elementary experience. I had taught one summer school to sixth graders. It was as close as I had been to the nuances of elementary education.

As I entered his office, he rose to welcome his new protégé. "You will do great," he said. "I'm excited for the challenges ahead. You managed well at both the secondary and middle school levels. It is time to complete the cycle. From now on, you will be exposed to all levels and types of elementary schools."

"Where do I begin?" I asked.

"I will start you at a traditional year-round school. You will be there for about three months. From there you will be part of two different schools that are also year-round.

All three are very different, and you will learn a lot in a short time. We will meet regularly to discuss your progress. I will answer your questions to the best of my ability."

I was encouraged and ready to begin elementary. I had known a few secondary administrators who had failed at the elementary level, and I knew that I had to focus on gaining the skills to succeed.

My very first day was something else. I wanted to get to the school early. When I arrived, I met the secretary to the principal. "Your office is across the hall," she said.

"As a new elementary assistant principal, who will be assigned to do my typing?" I asked.

"You do it," she said, in a voice that was short, loud, and clear.

Having one or two secretaries to dictate the letters that I was creating, to ask them to write minutes, summaries of meetings with parents and students, or to compose memos and other school business matters left me with a handicap: I typed very slowly and with only two fingers—the index finger of each hand. My new reality began to set in.

My office was located directly across from the secretary, and she was able to see me because it was surrounded by glass. I had brought with me some puppets with the thought that they would help me to connect with students, gain their trust, and let the ones having trouble know they could approach the assistant principal without fears. It was about 8:30 a.m. when the ordeal began. The principal wasn't there, so I was in charge.

An instructional aide brought a little girl to the office.

She was screaming as loud as she could. It was deafening, a screech more than a scream.

"Do you like puppets?" I asked her calmly.

She screamed louder and louder. I tried again to use a puppet to distract her, with the hope that she would refocus, but she was having nothing to do with it. She hid under the table.

"That is okay. I am here to help," I said.

She kept it up. I asked the secretary to come in. She whispered to me that this little girl had been doing this for a long time. We tried to connect with the mother and father, but there was no answer. None of the strategies that came to my mind to get her to calm down worked. The screaming had been going on for more than thirty minutes. Suddenly, she grabbed a pencil and began poking her forehead close to her eyes. I feared that if she continued doing that, she would injure her eyes. I jumped to restrain her. She had just missed her right eye. As I restrained her to keep her from hurting herself, I instructed the secretary to call 911. I was able to get the pencil out of her hands, but she tried to poke her eyes out with her fingers while trying to bite my hands.

The secretary told me that she didn't have authorization to call 911. I said in a firm voice, "You have the authorization now."

The child was relentless, still kicking me and screaming. A police officer arrived within minutes. He asked me to describe the situation. I explained it to him.

"Let her go," he said. "I'll take over."

When I let her go, she kicked him and began trying to

poke her eyes out again. An ambulance came within minutes and took the child to the hospital. She had to be taped to the gurney to keep her from harming herself or others. She couldn't have any kind of medication because no one had been able to reach her parents. Both the officer and I were drenched with sweat from the effort of restraining the child. That was how my first day at the elementary school level began.

We discovered later that the parents had just separated, and the child had been affected by their decision, but was not able to verbalize it. I told the officer that I was certified in proper techniques of restraint, but I never thought that I would need it in the elementary school environment. At the end of the day, I was exhausted. I had been pushed by a student before, but I had never been bitten and kicked.

When my friends called to find out how my first day went, they asked, "Are you bored yet?"

I told them about the despairing child episode. When I finally met the parents, they thanked me for my efforts to protect their daughter. Two days later, she walked into my office as if nothing had happened.

"Can I play with your puppets some day?" she asked.

"Sure," I said.

Two weeks later, I met my second screamer. A little boy was brought to my office screaming uncontrollably. I grabbed a puppet and handed one to him, trying to get his attention. It didn't work.

"I am going to teach you a trick," I said. "You are the only one in the whole school that can use this trick. It won't work for any other person. Take your hands and put them by your ears, and with the palms turned to the ceiling open your mouth and scream without making any noise. This trick is called Silent Rage."

He looked at me with a great deal of attention and said, "You mean, like this?" repeating the gesture that I had just taught him.

"Good job," I said. "No one will know your new secret. You count to thirty in your thoughts, and then you put your hands down and continue doing whatever you were doing before."

"Okay," he said. "It'll be my secret."

He went back to class. The day was busy, and I completely forgot to check with the teacher about how the second screamer was doing. Two days later, she came to my office and thanked me for taking care of the situation with the boy.

"He is not screaming anymore, but he has a new thing: When he gets frustrated, he makes a face, put his hands up to the ceiling, acts as if he is ready to scream, but no sound comes out of his mouth. Strangely, he gets back to work."

"It's probably just a passing thing," I replied.

I saw the student in the hall. He looked at me, and asked, "Did you tell the teacher my secret?"

"No, I didn't," I said.

"Oh, good," he said and ran away.

Four years later, a student transferred to my new school where I was the principal. He was starting fifth grade. He looked at me and asked smiling, "Do you know who I am?"

"You look familiar," I said.

"Silent Rage," he said while lifting his hands up, palms to the ceiling, and screamed without a sound.

"Oh, I hope everything worked out all right," I said.

"Thank you," he said. "I was unable to deal with problems in my family, and school was the only place where I could let my emotions surface. You helped me. I'm glad you will be my principal now."

Stories about screamers went on and on and on for the twelve-plus years that I was an administrator at the elementary school level. From the age of six, children are learning to let others know about their pains and tribulations, sometimes through silence and other times through uncontrollable loud sounds. Learning to communicate calmly with words is a process acquired through teamwork between the parents and the school. This skill is definitively not acquired overnight.

46: Conversations about Sex at Six and Head Lice Too

"How parents monitor the television and video-game habits of their children is tied to the kids' performance in school, their relationship with peers, and their weight."

-- Andrew M. Seaman, New York, Mon March 31, 2014 4:50 EDT
(*Reuters*)

When I was one month into the job, I received a note signed by the kindergarten teacher stating that Mary and Joey (fictitious names) needed to go to the assistant principal's office because they were having a conversation about sex in the classroom. When they came to my office, they were scared to death. They sat in the two chairs, little feet swinging nervously back and forth, and waited.

"What was said about sex?" I asked.

"I asked Mary if she wanted to have sex with me," Joey said. "She said no. She said that she thinks that it's yucky."

"What do you mean by having sex?" I asked.

"I heard it on television, but I wasn't sure what it meant," Joey said.

I realized now that I was not questioning high school or junior high students. I had in front of me six year olds!

"Don't talk about sex in the classroom, okay?"

"Yep," said Joey. "I think it's yucky, too."

Out of the mouths of babies!

"Did you discipline them?" the teacher asked me later.

"I told them not to discuss sex in the classroom. They heard me."

With older students, I would have used a different approach. These young ones were innocent. They were repeating what they heard—one of the dangers of television when parents are not aware of age-inappropriate programs. The first responsibility lies with the parents because they are a child's first teachers. I like how Kazuo Ishiguro put it: "When you become a parent or a teacher, you turn into a manager of this whole system. You become the person controlling the bubble of innocence around a child, regulating it."

Technology has brought a new challenge to raising children, as they not only hear remarks about sex, but they see violence and a world that could easily become a reality for them. Luckily, there is an abundance of age-appropriate TV programs and video games, but parents have to constantly monitor the media world for children to remain safe.

By the end of the second month, I was beginning to feel better about the new change. One day after recess, around 10:00 a.m., a young boy was sent to the nurse's office with suspected head lice. When the nurse confirmed that he had head lice, she called the mother to come to the school to pick him up.

"I don't have a car," said the mother. "You have my permission to deliver him."

I was the deliverer. I had a boy with active head lice in my car. I began scratching my head the minute he got in.

As we left the school, I asked him, "Do you know how to get home?"

"Sure," he said. "Turn right here."

We went straight a few more blocks, and he said, "Turn right."

I drove another block, and I heard him again: "Turn right."

Five times after this routine going around and around, I pulled over.

"Okay. Joke is over. Why do you keep telling me to turn right?"

"I thought it was funny," he said. "It took you five times to realize it." He burst out laughing.

"It is not funny. Where do you live?"

"I live down this street," he said. "Pull over, there it is."

I let him out in front of a nice big house with a beautiful, manicured lawn. As he climbed the front steps, he turned to wave goodbye. I was driving off, and something inside told me that he had lied to me.

"No way that is his house," I said to myself.

I turned around, and, sure enough, I found him skipping along the sidewalk without a worry.

I pulled my car up to the curb and got out. "Okay, now tell it to me straight. Where do you live?"

"This house," he said pointing at one fifty feet away from where we stood. He ran down the sidewalk, climbed the front steps, and jumped into the house through the front window. He turned to me and shouted, "The door doesn't work."

His mother looked out the window with a ferret wrapped around her neck. She thanked me for bringing her son home and promised that she would take care of the head lice. I couldn't wait to get back to the school to fumigate my truck. I scratched my head for the rest of the day.

There were cases where we had to send a social worker to a student's home to assist an entire family with head lice infestation. Many times, volunteer parents brought the situation up to the assistant principal's office when they noticed that a particular student had diminutive egg marks in their hair. Parents usually wore two hats: school ambassadors and their children's advocates. When they talked about the head lice issue, they were firmly protecting their own children and their whole family from getting this plague that was fast to spread and resistant to extermination.

47: Dreams Materialize: Meeting the Dreamer

"A dream doesn't become reality through magic.
It takes sweat, determination, and hard work."

-- Colin Powell

The lessons young children taught me were priceless. They were storytellers. I would find later that, even if I had a video of them taking something at a book fair without paying, they would say, as if nothing happened, "That's not me. It's someone who looks like me!" Sometimes parents would agree with them. It was amazing to witness such denial.

During the next few months, I spent two to three weeks at other year-round schools getting a flavor for their individual dynamics. After that, I met with my mentor.

"I have a new challenge for you," he said. "I have received positive feedback about you, but you have a lot more to learn about the little ones—and about the teachers too," he reiterated. "I'm moving you to our largest year-round school. It has two special programs: Spanish Immersion and Open Structure. You will spend three days a week supervising these programs as their principal. In addition, you will act as the assistant principal of students for the total school community. The other two days you will be principal of a necessary small school of approximately ninety students. It is our training ground for elementary principals."

I couldn't wait to begin. When I arrived at the large school, I was struck by its beauty. The colors were rich and vibrant. It was a brand new school with all the trimmings. When I opened the drawer of my new desk, I found a lot of yo-yo's. The secretary told me that they had been confiscated because they were dangerous. I put them in a box thinking that maybe they could be of some use later.

I wanted to come up with some incentives for the students to encourage positive behaviors like picking up trash, random acts of kindness, and so on. It seemed that this school could benefit from its own form of school pride. Old tricks adjusted for the new age group. I called around, and various businesses gave me coupons for ice cream, toys, and so on. The most unique one came from JC Penney. They heard that I was looking for things I could use as prizes.

"Yes," I said. "What do you have in mind?"

"Well," the representative told me, "We have these pig balloons on a stick. They're cute."

"How many do you have?"

"Five hundred," he said.

"How many did you start with?" I asked.

"Five hundred," he answered.

"I'll take them," I said.

When I gave them to students for random acts of kindness, they asked, "Do you have anything else?"

They were not a hit. I gave teachers a bushel of pigs, but they did not see the humor in it. I put the five hundred small pig balloons in a box next to the yo-yo's for future reference.

Spanish Immersion and Open Structure were both K-6 single-track programs. This meant they had one teacher per grade level. Spanish Immersion was fun and challenging. By the third grade, the students were nearly bilingual. It was a popular program, and I was told not to encourage future growth. The rationale was that it would cause a problem with the other elementary schools in maintaining class sizes. It was a shame as it had a strong following.

Open Structure was a world of discovery. New techniques of instruction and hands-on activities were the common method. The kindergarten room had a fort with a second floor, and students were encouraged to explore. Students used hammers and tools to create new and exciting projects. Both of the programs had parent meetings, board meetings, and site councils. It was customary for me to be out at least three to four nights a week. I was so happy to be in the role of principal/director that I didn't mind the work.

The final piece of my new assignment was my very first true job as a principal. I knew it was the laboratory for elementary principals, but I had wanted to get there, recharged and ready to begin my contribution. It was located about fifteen miles from the city in a rural setting. The school was old and in need of a facelift. The paint was peeling off the walls, and I knew that a new coat of paint would help a great deal.

When I parked my car that first morning, I saw only one other car parked there. *It must be the secretary*, I thought.

When I entered the office, the secretary informed me that there were three rules I had to learn: (1) Park in space three; (2) open the front door of the school from left to right; and (3) when you finish going to the bathroom, put the seat down.

Wow, what a nice welcome. "Here are my three rules," I said to her. "I will park in space three. I will open the door from left to right, and when you finish using the restroom, put the seat up." That was not a real smart answer. I was called to my mentor's office later that same day.

"What were you thinking?" he asked, astounded. "You have to keep your cool and remember your position. You have to be cautious with the choice of your words."

I apologized to him, and back at the school, I apologized to the secretary for my comments.

"Let's begin anew," I said, and she agreed.

The next thirty-nine days were magical. I met the classroom aide the very first day. She told me she loved art and wondered if we could have T-shirts made with the mascot on them.

"What is our mascot?" I asked.

"The nighthawk," she replied. "Here is my drawing."

It was beautiful. "Can you put this on the wall in the cafeteria?" I asked.

"Are you kidding me?" she exclaimed.

"No, I'm serious. I'll pay you," I said.

She committed to do it. She started this mini Michelangelo mural right away. Each day she spent two hours after school lying on scaffolding painting the nighthawk! It was a masterpiece when she was done.

Each day we all gathered around the flagpole and sang "God Bless America." It was patriotic and special. I met a little boy whose name may have been Andrew. He was the neatest little guy, always smiling. One day, I had all the students in the cafeteria watching President Clinton's inauguration on a big screen TV. I had given each student a box of Cracker Jacks to celebrate. Just as Bill Clinton was being sworn in, Andrew came up to me and began pulling on my pant leg.

"What, Andrew, what is it?"

"I got a Cracker Jack stuck in my nose!" he said.

"How did you do that?"

"I don't know. I guess I missed my mouth," he said.

It was all I could do not to laugh, but I kept my cool. The nurse helped with the errant Cracker Jack!

Later that day, at lunch, I noticed a group of students playing with kazoos.

"Where did you get those?" I asked them.

"It was a birthday present," said one of the girls. "It would be fun if we could learn the star spangled banner song on kazoos."

"Sure, why not?"

I immediately went out and bought ninety kazoos with the intent to teach them "The Star Spangled Banner" and, of course, the baseball hymn, "Take Me Out to the Ball Game."

It was fun practicing with the students. It built a new sense of team and togetherness. I used the ninety dollars I had in the principal's account to build self-esteem and create a positive climate.

48: Calling for Reform at All Levels

"Low standards are tactics that take pressure off teachers' unions by accepting mediocrity and failure for kids."

-- Jeb Bush

Since the school was small, we had to share cook services with another school. The students told me that they had a request when I took over as principal.

"Would it be possible to have the corn dogs defrosted properly before they are given to us as a lunch option?"

"Are you joking?" I asked.

"Every week the food is half frozen when we eat it," one student said.

"The cook is always late to our school," another student added.

I scheduled a meeting with the cook. She said that she couldn't get to our school on time. I looked into the issue and was assured by the district office that she had plenty of time to drive between schools.

"From this point on," I told her, "you need to be on time to make sure that the food is adequately defrosted, warm, and ready for the students when our lunch begins."

She continued to be late. I sent her a letter of reprimand with the progressive steps that would be taken if her tardiness continued. I was informed by the union and the district office that I could only hold her accountable to the time constraint on the days that I was actually at the school. I argued to no avail that I could depend on the secretary to keep a record of when the cook arrived. The response was that she was not an administrator and could not be responsible. In other words, I was unable to rectify the problem given my short tenure at the school. She continued to arrive late when other sites required my presence, and the food was half-frozen when served to the students. The cook wins, and the students lose.

This was my first encounter with union absurdity. In the past, as a history teacher, I had learned about the difference unions made improving working conditions for Americans. During the Great Depression, the Wagner Act made collective bargaining a system to gain what was fair in terms of wages and benefits, and the economy went through a facelift.

As years passed, administrators and managers became hesitant to address issues promptly, fearing a reaction from the union, a real headache. The union's logic in this case was foreign to me: I had to witness the cook arriving later than she was supposed to and witness her serving a frozen meal which should have been defrosted and warm, or else she was not held accountable for her lax behavior. Furthermore, she could continue such behavior under the protection of the union, because a case had to be built up for her to do the job for which she was hired to do. Who was on the students' side?

A record of misconduct must be documented by employers with specific steps to remediate the concern before actions can take place. I always felt that if an employee was not doing the job for which he or she was hired, and if the job was lacking quality or not meeting standards, the employee should be given the chance to improve or adequate replacement should be sought. The children deserve our best. Working hard, doing the best one possibly can, and excelling are values I believe in and live by to this day.

49: How Much Can Be Accomplished in Thirty-Nine Days?

"If you can't do great things, do small things in a great way."

-- Napoleon Hill

The budget reflected the number of students at the school. My health budget was seven dollars and fifty cents for the whole school year. I received a letter stating that all schools would have their health budget cut by ten percent. I sent three quarters to the district office to cover our school reduction. I didn't have enough money to even buy a box of band aids. It would be a challenge to make improvements without funds. My total school budget was under six thousand dollars a year.

I asked the superintendent to visit me at the school site. We walked around, and he was able to see that the school needed improvements, including new paint.

"The school is not due to be painted for seven years," I said. "If you provide the paint, we can do it now."

"Good idea," he said.

The custodian painted the two small buildings in two weeks. It is amazing what a coat of paint can do to a place. I kept repeating my new mantra: "Dream great dreams."

I asked if I could go to the state conference of Title One

schools because I wanted to petition the state for funding for our small school.

"Use your site council funds," said the superintendent.

"The majority of our students are from families that qualify for free lunch but are too proud to apply," I said. "We are missing out on over twenty thousand dollars in state funding."

By using our site council funds to attend the conference, I was depleting the few dollars available for other purposes, but I felt that it would be a good investment if I was successful, because it would make a huge financial impact. After much discussion, the parents finally agreed to use the site council funds for me to attend the conference. The vote was not unanimous, and some members seemed to be very upset because they felt "that it was a long shot" at best.

I had brought one of my puppets with me to the conference. I was in the elevator with my moose puppet when the state chairwoman got on. The encounter was so serendipitous that it seemed as if the Lord orchestrated it. *Here is my chance*, I told myself.

Mr. Moose went into high gear. He introduced himself and explained our plight. When we got to the bottom floor, the chairwoman smiled and said, "Nice meeting you, Mr. Moose. I'll get back to you."

I was shocked and not sure what she meant. The conference was great, and I met a lot of people with good ideas about how we could proceed with our request for support and help.

When I returned to the school, the assistant superintendent wanted to see me. He told me that a few of the parents were upset about my decision to attend the conference, and he was removing me from the school to focus on the other two programs. I would handle graduation at the small school and finish the remaining weeks of the year at the other site. I was shocked.

"They are not ready for change," he said. "The changes you made were wonderful. You painted the school, you built rapport with the students, they had the kazoo band they wanted, and you were able to plant the seed at the state conference for additional school funds. However, you have bigger fish to fry. Don't be discouraged. By the way, did you tell the K-3 teacher she couldn't teach chimpanzees even if she tried?"

"No," I answered. "What I said was, 'You have had these same children for three years, and they finish in the bottom of the state scores.' I told her that chimpanzees could score higher than her students because of her low expectations of student achievement on state tests."

"Remember, you want people to hear what you say not how you say it," he admonished.

The learning path was steep, but with every incident I became more reflective about how much my communication skills had to improve. I was pushing too hard. His advice was spot on, and I was determined to be more thoughtful in the future. When I returned to the small school on Monday, I informed the staff that I would be spending my time at the larger school for the remainder of the school year. I sensed that they were somewhat relieved.

On Wednesday, I was ready to announce the change at the site council meeting. Just before going in, I received a long distance phone call from someone asking to speak to the moose guy! I ran to the phone, and sure enough, it was the state director of Title One funding.

"I promised to call," she said. "Your school will receive special funding given the information we discovered from your meeting with me in the elevator. It will be well over twenty thousand dollars."

I was shocked and unable to speak. Finally, I was able to say, "Thank you so much. You have no idea what this means to our school."

My secretary saw how excited I was, and said, "You just got some good news. Are you staying?"

"No, but I just found out that the school will be receiving over twenty thousand dollars in Title One funding."

When I started the site council meeting, they were stunned by the announcement that my efforts on behalf of the school actually paid off. Dreams do come true if you persevere.

At the sixth grade graduation, I highlighted our accomplishments during my brief thirty-nine day tenure as their principal. The sixth graders stood up and played "Take Me Out to the Ball Game" on their kazoos. As they played, tears of joy streamed down my face. What a great gift. It was my first graduation of many future ones as a principal, but one of the sweetest. I already knew in my heart it would not be my last sixth grade graduation.

50: Swimming with More Sharks

"The harder I practice, the luckier I get."

-- Gary Player

The school year was ending. The applications to interview for various district openings had just been posted. Two elementary schools and one junior high were advertised. My mentor called me and said that I should apply for the openings. The interviews would be on the same day. He told me that I had a great chance for one of the positions.

"Do you have a preference?" he asked.

"The junior high would be my first choice, but I welcome any position where I can be a principal."

The day arrived for the interviews, and I was scheduled for all three openings. It started with one elementary school, then the junior high, and finally the second elementary school. Each school had an interview committee and a topic for a writing sample. The panel would rank the top candidates and send the first and second candidates to the superintendent for consideration.

I felt energized that day and believed that all three interviews went well. My preparation for the interviews had paid off, based on the responses from the various panels to my answers. The candidates were told that, by the end of the week, an announcement would be made of the candidates selected.

I was still working at the year-round school on a Wednesday. It was Chinese food day at the cafeteria, and the menu included chicken chow mien, fried rice, and a fortune cookie. I opened the cookie and read "Hope for the best, and expect the worst." *How odd*, I thought. Just then, I received a mysterious, anonymous phone call. The caller muffled his voice and said, "They are offering you one of the elementary schools, even though you came in first in all the interviews. The process was flawed. One of the administrators was going around telling the panels that you had already been selected number one by another, even before they had made their selection. Do not be discouraged. You will get one of the elementary schools."

He abruptly hung up. I was shocked, but for some reason I believed the caller. Within thirty minutes, I received another phone call from the district informing me that they wanted to talk to me after school and to be at the district office by four o'clock.

I thought for a moment, went to the school kitchen, and got another fortune cookie. I carefully took out the fortune and replaced it with the first one I had received that day. "Hope for the best, and expect the worst."

When I arrived at the meeting, the administrative team and the superintendent were already there. This superintendent was easy to work with. I had been the administrative representative for the administrators and had many meetings with him. He was honest, fair, and supportive, and I trusted him. I was sure that if there had been any funny business going on with the process, he would not have been aware.

When I entered the room, they were all smiles.

"It was Chinese food day at school. I got a fortune cookie."

"Oh, let us see what it says," they said jokingly.

I opened the fortune cookie and read, "Hope for the best, and expect the worst."

"No, it doesn't say that!"

"Yes, it does," I said. "Here it is."

They passed it around the table. After a few awkward moments, the superintendent said, "You have been selected to be a principal at one of the elementary schools."

"What about the junior high opening?"

"I was told that you came in second in the other interviews," the superintendent replied.

"I need to think about your offer, and I will let you know by tomorrow."

They acted surprised by my comment. I asked if I could speak to the superintendent privately. The remainder of his team left the room. With just the two of us there, I shared the phone call that I received about twenty-five minutes before I was asked to come to the district office.

"I do not know who called, but they were emphatic that the process had been compromised," I said.

The superintendent said that the rankings are simply recommendations and that the decision rested with him.

"I understand it is your decision," I said, "and you will

not have a problem with me. I accept this job that I have wanted forever. If the process was flawed, you will have a problem with the parents and teachers who were on the committees. What do I tell them when they ask me why I didn't take the job offer at the junior high or the other elementary school? I realize it is your prerogative. However, these people will feel slighted if they indeed selected me first. I will not be a part of the problem for the district."

He thanked me for accepting the job and said that he would get to the bottom of the issue with the process.

Within a few days, the members of the different committees called me and asked why I had not taken the job at their school. I told them that I had been informed that I came in second and that I had accepted the job for which the district had chosen me. They called the district office and, one by one, explained how they had been interrupted by district personnel during their deliberations while they were still ranking their top candidates, who told them that I had been selected first by another committee. The members of the committee were upset, because it was an attempt to unethically influence their ranking.

I accepted the position offered to me, and the protests died down, but that day it became clear to me that I had to be careful. I understood how powerful some representatives of the public trust were to be able to manipulate a system in front of everybody's eyes and act as if nothing had happened.

51: Dreams Transcend

"Ask and it will be given to you; seek and you will find; knock and
the door will be opened to you."

-- Matthew 7:7

The elementary school boot camp lasted six months. During this incubation period, I was exposed to all facets of the elementary school experience. My first major realization was the profound impact elementary teachers have on their students. They work with the same students all day long. The connectedness and harmony in their classrooms is almost more important than the subject matter. They teach who they are first, subject matter second. I had seen this in my travels at the junior and senior high levels for sure, but I came to the realization that the little ones are the most influenced by the impact of their first classroom teachers.

In the large schools, it was possible to move a student to another teacher in the same grade level to help both student and teacher when the need arose. At the small schools with only one teacher per grade level, if there wasn't a good fit between the teacher and a student, or between a teacher and a parent, the challenge was more difficult to resolve.

At all grade levels, the classroom teacher is critical to the success of the students, but the elementary level is the key to addressing student needs early to remediate problems before they get worse and the students fall behind.

In my past travels through the different levels, I observed all kinds of teaching styles from easygoing to very strict and demanding. I found out that most teaching styles worked as long as the students knew that the teacher cared about them.

My slogan for the elementary grades was "Learn to read by third grade, and you will be able to read to learn from then on." It meant investing in resources and focusing on helping the youngest to get the best start in their educational journey.

The elementary boot camp exposed me to the need for appropriate interventions in discipline for elementary school students. I witnessed the principal's office being used as a babysitting waiting room. I saw that as one of the first things that needed to change in the school culture. Occasionally, this approach was appropriate, but in general, it was not a deterrent for repeat offenders. I believed that in my role as principal, it was my job to provide the teachers all the tools necessary to be successful in the classroom. "Dream Great Dreams" was a theme that I used often to embody the message of hope and the language of success.

Day One as the new principal at the elementary school was electrifying. I went to what I thought was the entrance of the school and introduced myself to the secretary as the new principal.

She laughed and said, "You have the wrong school. Yours is next door."

I laughed. She could see that I was embarrassed. She

wished me well, and off I went to find the correct entrance. I had trouble finding the office as there wasn't any signage pointing the way. Summer had begun, and the school was empty, but I knew that the secretary and the attendance clerk were still working. When I opened the door, I saw the room was quite crowded. There was only about four feet between the door and the desks of the secretary and attendance clerk. Behind them was an assortment of old tables and copy machines that had seen better days. The room looked not only crowded but messy. I couldn't imagine more than three parents being in the office at the same time. My office was immediately to the left of the front door. The custodian walked in and reminded me that we had worked together before. He was ex-military and had always referred to me as "Sir." We ended up calling each other "Sir" for the duration of our time together.

"I am glad that you were the one chosen to be at this school," he said, welcoming me, and he gave me a tour of the school.

I had only six weeks to prepare for opening day. This school had an excellent reputation. Teachers in the district were always requesting to be considered for any and all openings to do a lateral transfer. Students from the sixteen other elementary schools also were applying to be accepted from grades four through six. Each grade level had one class of thirty students. The school housed the district's gifted and talented program. The remainder of the student body was a mixture of students from different economic and cultural backgrounds.

The school had many portable classrooms, a nice cafeteria, and the students' playground was beautiful.

The superintendent called me and asked to meet with him in his office. As I approached the district office, I was anxious to know the reason behind his call. I had already told him that the inconsistencies of the interview process had not been a problem for me. When I arrived, he welcomed me with a smile that had a calming effect on me. I had always liked him and trusted him. We had resolved many issues while I was the administrative middle-manager's voice.

He said he had had a chance to review the interview process under which I had been selected and had found many inconsistencies, as I had mentioned. He said many of the parents and teachers on the committees had called him complaining about their rankings, and recommendations were misrepresented. He thanked me for accepting the position offered to me by the district. I told him I understood that ultimately he had the final say as to placement of the candidates, and, based on that, I was okay with the outcome.

He mentioned that my cooperation was instrumental in the complaints subsiding throughout the process. "In the future," he said, "I will make sure that those inconsistencies are eradicated. Furthermore, I want you to have a good start at your new school. How can I help you?"

"I need roughly four thousand dollars to redo the main office," I said, taking advantage of his willingness to assist me. "The office is in shambles. I need to build a new front desk console and put a mural on the wall."

"I will provide the funds," he said. "I liked what you did at the small school when you painted it in thirty-nine days!"

He hadn't forgotten. It was obvious to me that this kind and fair professional felt bad about what transpired in the interview process and was trying to support me in the school I had accepted.

I began the process of finding a furniture contractor and a muralist. We had six weeks to complete the process. When completed, it looked great. The main thing was that we completed the work prior to the start of school. People had room to stand when entering the office. The machines were repositioned for greater access, which limited the need for the secretary to get in and out of her chair so frequently. My secretary was instrumental in creating a workspace that was efficient and aesthetically pleasing to the eye. The mural on the wall behind the two secretaries' console was awesome. It read: "Marigold – Commitment to Excellence" in large letters on a background of maroon color. It was the first thing the school community saw when entering the office.

About two weeks before school started, I was focusing on the office front door. There still wasn't any sign telling visitors where the main office was located. I wanted to paint the front door a different color. All of the doors were brown and, to my taste, ugly looking. I thought we needed something bright and cheerful. I called the maintenance and operations office and asked what colors were available. The response was one word: brown. I said what about teal or maroon like the new schools. I was told, "Brown is for old schools, and teal and maroon are for new schools."

I could not believe my ears. I immediately went to the paint store and bought a gallon of paint called midnight magic. It looked like a shade of maroon. When I returned, I asked "Sir" to paint the office door. It looked too bright. It almost took your breath away. After five coats of paint, it began to look pretty cool. It was a crimson shade of maroon. When the teachers returned to their classrooms before the new school year started, they wanted their doors painted that color, too. "Three dollars a door," I said, and all but one teacher contributed. I paid the three bucks for her, and the school had a fresh new look.

As the beginning of school approached, we were told that we could lower class sizes in grades K-3 to twenty students maximum. We were one of the first schools in the district to do this by the start of school. Many positive changes were happening even before we opened the doors.

I received a call from my old school reminding me to pick up my personal stuff. Upon arriving, the secretary said, "Make sure to take those pig balloons, yo-yo's, and puppets with you."

We both laughed.

"I'll find a use for them in my new school," I told her.

"I caution you, don't give the bushel of pigs to the secretaries or to the teachers. They will fail to see the humor in it," she said still laughing.

As I sat in my new office unpacking my yo-yo's, puppets, and pig balloons, I thought, *These will help me in campus beautification. I will find a way for students to like them. I've got it—five pig balloons for random acts of kindness, scholastic achievement, and picking up trash. I will have some rules: (1) No pig begging, and no pig rustling; (2) students have to earn them and recycle them; (3) five pig balloons, and you get to pig-out for lunch with the principal.*

Thus, the early beginnings of PIGDOM were born. PIGDOM was a place where People—little people and big people—Inspired Greatness. Now I had a vision with a catchy slogan.

Three days before the school's opening day, the teachers reported to school. During our first staff meeting, I explained the meaning of the theme for the year: "Dream great dreams today, not tomorrow." I shared with them my intention of providing the necessary support and materials for them to be successful.

"We are going to institute an environment using the language of success," I explained. "It will help all of us be successful. Anything is possible when dreams, ideas, and a clear vision are connected with an action plan to make our dreams a reality."

I asked them to prepare a list of things they envisioned for their classroom and for the new school year. "Dream big," I said.

After about an hour, they turned in their list: goldenrod-colored paper, more copy machine paper per teacher, and other mundane requests.

"Let's try again," I told them. "Dream big!"

"But there is no money," they said.

"Usually dreams bring the money," I said. "The money doesn't bring the dreams." Given a free rein, they dreamed big. The list was daunting, but I knew that if I took it one step at a time, much of their wish list was doable and achievable.

"With the help of parents, the teachers, the community, and corporate sponsors," I told them, "we will build a climate where dreams can come true." I am not sure if they believed me, but certainly, they were curious.

Here was the initial dream list:

1) Infrastructure for computer access throughout the school

2) Cable in each classroom to be able to access educational programming

3) New copy machine

4) A wheelchair

5) A portable stage for the performing arts

6) New risers for the band

7) Paint for the whole school

8) Repairing the ceiling in the cafeteria

9) A big screen TV

10) New marquee

11) New sound system for the multi-purpose room

12) Library equipped with computer lab

13) Air conditioning in all classrooms

14) Library grants

I posted the list in my office as a reminder of the task before us and began solving some of the initial wishes right away.

"I will order goldenrod paper," I said. "From then on, there will be no limit to teachers for copy paper. I will deal with those who abuse the new policy." It was common knowledge that, prior to my coming to the school, there was a big problem with some teachers using other teachers' copy paper codes. "No more codes," I said. "Let's see how it goes."

They were happy with the new method, but some were skeptical that it would work. One of the teachers made a comment that, as I recall, went like this: "It is nice to dream, but I figure that it will be ten years before I get my own computer in my classroom hooked to the Internet."

"Challenge accepted," I said with a smile.

He gave me ten years to accomplish something that, in reality, happened within a year's time, as you will read later.

The last few days before the beginning of school, teachers were getting their rooms in order, and I was busy in the office preparing for the new year. Our first newsletter to our entire school community came out explaining the theme, and the list of dreams that needed to come true was included.

During the first week of school, I visited each class and explained the PIGDOM rewards. Five pig balloons earned a lunch with the principal. Random acts of kindness, scholastic achievement, and picking up trash were ways to be recognized. No pig begging or pig rustling. They all laughed, but they understood that they had to earn the balloons.

The yard supervisor asked me after the first week what they were supposed to do after recess.

"What did you do last year?" I asked.

"We picked up trash, but there isn't any," he answered.

Wow, campus beautification was working right before our very eyes. Pride works with the help of some incentives! As I was walking back to my office, a lady asked if anyone had donated a wheelchair to the school yet.

"No, but we need one badly," I said. "Right now we use a rickety old portable chair to transport an injured student. By the time the student gets to the office, he might have a concussion, too."

She laughed and said, "I think I can get one from the hospital." An hour later, I got a phone call from the lady screaming, "I got one! I got one! I'll be there in a few minutes."

I was so excited! I went outside and waited for her. She drove up in a large truck with a big box. As they unloaded a beautiful, brand new wheelchair with all the bells and whistles, a call came from the playground on my walkie-talkie stating that a child was injured and that the rickety chair was needed. We continued putting the wheelchair together, hurried to the site of the accident, and asked the child to sit in a brand new wheelchair. We brought him to the office. I looked up to the sky and thanked the Lord for providing what we needed when we needed it. The news traveled fast: Dream No. 4 had come true at Marigold Elementary School!

The first Parent Teacher Association (PTA) meeting was very interesting. The president and officers were teachers at the school. When I talked about fundraising to accomplish some of the dreams on the list, I was told that it was the district's responsibility to address the school needs, not the PTA. I asked them to give me one hundred twenty-five dollars to have a computer center built in the library. I had found a parent who would build it if we provided the materials.

"We don't have any computers," I heard.

It was true that we didn't have any computers, but if we had a place for them, we were one step closer to being prepared for the computers that I believed we would have, and soon. The center would house six computer stations. We still didn't have access to the Internet, but that was a potential dream to come true. Finally, the PTA agreed to provide the one hundred twenty-five dollars. I learned that day to never again ask them to support funding for anything costing one hundred twenty-five dollars, and that I would have to look elsewhere for funding. In a way, it was a good lesson to learn, because it forced me to look outside, not only the district, but the community, and to explore opportunities from corporate sponsors.

52: Doing Worthwhile Things for All

"Good things happen to those who hustle,"

-- Chuck Noll

Keeping in mind some of the larger needs on our wish list, I called the local cable company and asked how we could have cable in every classroom. I was told each school in the district had one line for cable in one classroom, and it would cost over four thousand dollars to wire the whole school. After my phone conversation with the manager, I hung up somewhat dismayed. Our new theme of "Dream Great Dreams" couldn't stop with the cable issue. I had just received a magazine in the mail titled *Cable in the Classroom*, a national publication extoling the many programs geared for elementary school students. It was full of wonderful materials in science, math, and the humanities.

I wrote a letter to the executive director of the magazine and introduced myself as the Prince of PIGDOM. I explained the concept of "Dream Great Dreams" and its connection with PIGDOM. I described the school as a place where extraordinary things were happening and dreams were becoming reality.

Three weeks later, a lady walked into my office and said, "Do you know who I am?"

I looked up, and there was the director of *Cable in the*

Classroom, a person whose picture I had seen several times in the magazine, and she was standing in my office!

"You are Bobbie Kamil!"

"You must be the Prince of PIGDOM," she said.

"Yes, I am."

We both laughed and shook hands.

"I was at a conference in Sacramento and rented a car to drive here to meet you," she said. "I was very curious about what your needs might be beyond cable in the classroom. I know the owner of Chambers Cable."

"Do you know the local manager?" I asked in disbelief.

"No, I know the national owner of Chambers Cable. We will wire your entire school with cable at no cost. What else would you like?"

"We have been dreaming about being able to produce our own TV show and transmit it to every classroom once a week," I said.

"Sure," she said. "We will send you some cameras and equipment to make it easy for the students to produce their own programs."

I couldn't get over what was happening. I was in total shock.

"I have one request," she said. "Would you be willing to come to Washington, DC, to make a presentation on behalf of *Cable in the Classroom* at the National Elementary School Conference?"

I was moved by her request and accepted her invitation.

As a result of this "Dream Great Dreams" theme, everything in the school's bucket list was coming true. The students called our own TV station MGTV, which stood for Marigold TV. A big pink pig had become our logo. A curious footnote was that years later, I met one of the first MGTV students, and he informed me that he was an intern at Lucas Films in the Bay Area thanks to his early start at MGTV. What a thrill to have had that moment years later, a testimonial of the seed we planted.

I now had the challenge to prepare a speech for *Cable in the Classroom* at the National Elementary School Conference. Even though it was a year away, I was crafting the presentation and collecting pictures and events surrounding the school's new television station. PIGDOM and "Dream Great Dreams" were off to a resounding start.

I found that one success breeds another. People like to be part of something good. I knew we had very few computers, but we needed infrastructure first. I had heard that Sun Technologies was interested in helping install the infrastructure at some schools. Sun Technologies was willing to provide the infrastructure school-wide but with one condition: We needed to provide the workers to pull the cable. We were talking about something that was worth over twenty thousand dollars. I needed a six-foot trench dug to bury the cables in order to reach the portable classrooms. Support services from the district announced that they were too busy checking leaky roofs. A few parents stepped up to the plate and began digging the trench anyway. I was scolded for recruiting the parents, but in my heart, I knew that what I was doing was right for the good of all, including the students. I just couldn't pass up the gift of free infrastructure. Now we had the connectivity and the ability to hook everything together. All we needed was computers. I said build it and they will come. It would take a little time, but the dreams were coming true from the strangest places.

The technology wish list was impressive but we were missing one piece. We needed a big screen TV to project on the wall of the cafeteria. I had written to many corporate sponsors to no avail. One corporate sponsor called me to say that I should call a company named In Focus located in Oregon.

"They're a cool group," the person said on the phone. "They might help out."

We had just made little bracelets with PIGDOM on them. The kids loved wearing them. I sent a letter to In Focus and included ten bracelets. They called one morning to tell me they were sending the school a four-thousand-dollar In Focus projector. I was speechless.

"Is there anything we can do for you?" I asked.

"Yes, we need thirty more PIGDOM bracelets," the person said.

"Not a problem," I said.

It was so great to be able to make another check mark on the list of dreams coming true.

Everybody has a father, an adult, and a child inside, some psychologists say. I certainly had the three of them, and the latest surfaced in the form of talking puppets that made everybody laugh, but that made a point each time. Once day, I decided to take a yo-yo to the cafeteria and use it as a lunch activity. From that day on, I took yo-yos outside and let the students play with them. Within a few short weeks, I had a group of fifteen to twenty students getting really interested in playing with yo-yos, and they showed up every day to play. After a while, I had to create rules about where and when they could play. Soon, we formed a group of students who were practicing for the local yo-yo championship sponsored by a local toy store.

The store had recently been loaned the yo-yo collection of the Duncan family. The name Duncan was synonymous with the best in yo-yo's. In return, the local store made the commitment to host the national yo-yo contest each year. This was going to be the second year of the contest. A number of my students signed up to compete. One in particular tied in the twelve-year-old division with a young boy from Hawaii. They had a play-off, and my student won. He became a national champion. I was so proud of him.

That day he said to me, "You need to compete in the over twenty-one category."

After much thought, the child in me prevailed, and I knew I owed it to my students to compete. I tied for first place with two other contestants. One was a worker at a yo-yo company and the other a businessman from the east coast. The tiebreaker was loop-the-loops. The one with the most loops would be crowned the winner. The first player hit his baseball cap with the yo-yo after only ten loops. I knew I could do at least ten loops. The next player did 106 loops. When he exited the stage, he said to me, "Number two in the nation won't be that bad."

I asked the Lord, *Lord, I know you have more important things than this, but I need your help. It would be tough, almost impossible to make one hundred six loops. Just be with me.*

I almost lost it on the seventh loop. Time and time

again, just as it seemed I would lose it, the loop came back again and again. When I finished, I had 110 loops. I had won the championship by four loops. A little grandma came up to me after the contest.

"Your performance was much more entertaining," she said with a sweet smile.

I put my yo-yo contest performance on a DVD with the music from *Man of La Mancha*, "Dream the Impossible Dream." This dream-come-true paid big dividends. I created my own yo-yos with the inscription Kenny Wonder, The Loop Dude, a nickname the other yo-yo players gave me because, as they said, it was a wonder that I won.

When we returned to school, both the student and the principal were national champions. We enjoyed sharing this victory. Now, everyone wanted to join the club. One day a little girl came to my office and said she wanted to buy a school yo-yo but didn't have any money.

"I'm homeless," she said. "I don't have money, but I still want to get one."

"You can have one," I said.

"NO!" she said emphatically. "I want to trade for it."

Curiously, I asked, "What do you have to trade?"

"My treasure," she said. She put her hand inside the pocket of her jeans and pulled out a small red pouch with her treasure in it. It was a piece of rock that had been painted gold.

This taught me a lot about the character of this young soul. She had pride and self-respect. She didn't want a hand-out. She had something valuable to trade.

"I will put your treasure on my desk, and when you can do the first five beginner yo-yo tricks, you will have earned your treasure back."

"Thank you," she said and ran out the door clutching her new yo-yo.

Three days later, she returned to my office.

"I did it, I did it!" she shouted.

I looked up to see her with Band-Aids on her fingers as she demonstrated that she had accomplished the basic tricks. I smiled and gave her back her treasure. She thanked me and ran out the door. A few minutes later, she came back and asked if she could talk to me.

"I want you to have my treasure," she said.

"You earned both, the yo-yo and the treasure," I said.

"I know," she said. "I feel so good about earning something on my own for the first time. You give speeches, right?"

"Yes I do."

"Tell my story, because people need to know that no matter where you come from, you can make something of yourself."

I was touched by her words. I still didn't want to keep her treasure. "I will tell your story using a small colorful stone with a likeness of your treasure. However, it could never shine as brightly as yours does right now."

She accepted it and left my office with her treasure in hand and her self-esteem soaring.

A few weeks later, I went to Los Angeles to attend a conference. As I waited for my plane to disembark, I began playing with one of my custom yo-yo's. A little boy came up to me and asked if he could try.

"Well, I will teach you a few safety tricks first," I said, "and then you may have this yo-yo as a gift." After a short lesson, he thanked me and ran off. A few minutes later, a man came toward me with the little boy, a hand on his shoulder. He was upset.

"I told my children not to accept things from strangers. He wants to give you the yo-yo back."

I could tell that the boy didn't really want to give the yo-yo back, but I understood. I introduced myself to the father, gave him one of my business cards, and told him that I was an elementary school principal.

"We have a yo-yo club at our school," I said. I apologized to him for giving his son a yo-yo without his being present. He settled down and let the boy keep the yo-yo.

On Monday, the father called while I was out. His voicemail message said that he wanted to ask me a question. I immediately called him, and he thanked me for the yo-yo again.

"My son and I have been playing with it all weekend," he said. "Do you have a need for computers at your school?"

I was stunned. "Yes, we do, as a matter of fact."

"How many?" he asked.

"Quite a few," I answered as I laughed nervously.

"I am an executive for Standard Oil Refineries. We are upgrading our computers," he said. "We usually give the two-year-old computers to schools. All you need to do is come and get them."

"Yes, sir! We will be there whenever you say."

As I was thanking him, he said, "It is a small way of repaying your kindness to my son. You must be a good principal. Your school is lucky to have you."

The final piece of the technology wish was in order. There were computers for the computer lab and enough for the classrooms that requested them—another dream-come-true story, another check mark on our list. The third grade teacher was shocked. Not only did we have infrastructure, but also individual computers for the staff.

"It didn't take until the year 2007 to meet the goal," I said to him.

Anytime your thoughts are accompanied by actions, you will see results.

53: The Good, the Bad, and Resolutions

"You must be the change you wish to see in the world."

-- Mahatma Gandhi

After only a short time as the principal of Marigold, many of the dreams on our wish list came true. It was also the beginning of my thirtieth year in education, a journey of ups and downs, but most important, a journey filled with learning at all grade levels. As I crafted my presentation for the National Elementary School Conference in Washington DC, I focused on creating a message of hope, renewal, and celebration for all. I began with what I called Precepts of PIGDOM, with an outline that covered seven basic precepts:

1) Anything is possible

2) Maintain your focus and adjust your targets

3) Know the power of the language of success

4) Creativity unlocks doors

5) Inspire to motivate

6) Stretch your vision

7) Share your passion

The last point is one of the most critical to success. To begin any endeavor, we need a positive attitude, a sincerity of purpose, a belief that there is success for all, personal integrity, always see problems as opportunities, and nurture, nourish, and navigate with compassion and understanding of all that you encounter. Armed with this template, I began intermingling stories that demonstrated how each one of these precepts contributed to the success of our PIGDOM theme where people, regardless of the size of their shoes, inspired greatness, and where dreams became a reality for a better today.

I was asked by a district school psychologist if I could fill in at the regional conference of the Early Mental Health Initiative and explain how I was able to accomplish the many improvements at Marigold. I was excited, because this would be a chance to practice for my speech in Washington, DC. At the conclusion of the session, I got a resounding standing ovation. Participants came forward and asked if I would speak at their regional state conference. The evaluations and comments were gratifying: "It was awesome, entertaining, and it touched us."

I was now prepared for the national conference with so much enthusiasm. I couldn't wait to share the precepts of PIGDOM, but sometimes our plans are different from God's plans, and with only a few weeks to go before the speech, a tragedy of insurmountable pain ripped through the heart of our family. Our only son had been missing for three days in the snow. His car was found off the road. He had apparently slid on black ice and drifted into a snowbank. A postal worker saw him outside the car but failed to stop. When she returned from deliveries, she called the police because his car was still there.

I was alerted that evening while I was working at the local high school overseeing an extended day program from the local junior college. I knew in my heart that something was terribly wrong. He would have called for help under normal circumstances. I immediately had the police involved. They started checking the area but encountered a number of challenges, including the snow that began falling again, making the faded trail less readable and more difficult to follow.

The next two days were excruciatingly painful for the whole family. To lose our only son was beyond belief. We all fell to our knees when we were informed that he had not made it. This tragedy changed our world forever. At his service, the community outpouring was heartwarming. Everyone was there to help celebrate his life. The overflow crowd was able to hear the whole service thanks to the efforts of unselfish friends of our family and son.

I was in a kind of fog, still in disbelief, going through one of the darkest moments in my life. The hardest time was when everyone left. The deep sense of loss, the impotency of not being able to bring him back, the realization in the midst of all the facts that this was final just completely overwhelmed me, and the sorrow and the pain never left. Before I reached a place of acceptance, question after question passed through my mind: How did it happen? What could have I done to prevent it? Why didn't he go to the little town nearby for help?

As the day of the speech approached, I considered canceling it. I decided to follow through with it. Whether I fulfilled my commitment or not, my child was not coming back. I asked the person who helped put the PowerPoint program in the computer to install my son's photograph, and the speech was dedicated to him. It was more meaningful because, throughout the presentation, I felt his presence, as if he were there. He would have wanted me to give encouragement to others, and I strived, minute by minute, to encourage myself to get through it.

From that point on, the invitations to speak kept coming. People were interested in finding out how to duplicate the successes we were having at our school. The downside was in my own district. Upper administration told me that I was drawing too much attention to my school, and they asked me to keep a low profile. Our progress was making other schools upset because ours was shining. I was reminded of a quote: "It is amazing how much can be accomplished if no one worries about who gets credit." I really wanted the corporate sponsors to get recognition for their philanthropy, as more of them would step forward to help other schools in the community if they felt the positive peer pressure to do so.

Despite all the goals that we had accomplished at Marigold, a sad feeling followed me whenever I had free time to focus on myself because my personal life was in chaos. My marriage was failing in spite of numerous visits to marriage counselors. My personal future was uncertain, and I was surviving difficult times on a daily basis.

Hugh MacKay said it all in one sentence: "Nothing is perfect. Life is messy. Relationships are complex. Outcomes are uncertain." Advice came and went, but my inability to fix the unfixable was evident. The passing of my son was a lesson about my own limited mortality. It was time for me to start over.

At the same time, the school district was going through major changes, too. The superintendent resigned mid-year, and we became a ship without a captain. I realized that it was time to explore other avenues. Even though I knew that I had to keep my search quiet, I was sure that it was the right thing to do.

Being born and raised in Berkeley, California, I always wanted to work in the Bay Area. I began searching for the right fit. Santa Cruz was only an hour from my brother and father to the north and south in the beautiful cities of Monterey and Carmel. The weather was great, not too cold, and never hot. It was a hilly region surrounded by pine trees and beautiful views of the Pacific Ocean. Surfers waited patiently to catch the right waves, and, at any time, their black wetsuits shined with the gray, blue, and silver of the whole panorama. A number of openings for principal in the Santa Cruz area seemed promising.

I made an effort not to get distracted by my age; not many people embark on new endeavors and big changes at age fifty-five, but the internal certainty that I needed to save myself and head toward a new direction in my life helped me to pursue new leadership opportunities. The knowledge that I had gained from my experiences was a driving force that moved me to begin again—renewed, refreshed, challenged, and humbled. It had been five years since I had interviewed for the job of principal at Marigold, and over thirty years since I had interviewed outside of my current location.

I met a woman who inspired me because of the difficulties she had overcome in life. Strong and intelligent, she had the ability to sort through problems and make appropriate choices. She became my wife, and the Bay Area seemed even more attractive to me, as it was in close proximity to her job as a vocational rehabilitation counselor and a college instructor.

I updated my resume and applied to four school

districts. Luckily, I had four interviews, and each one of them was a great learning experience. In my preparation, I had a professional video of my current school highlighting the wonderful achievements we had accomplished as a team. As each interviewer went through the motions of the interview, only one of the districts was interested in seeing the video. You can guess which one I chose.

The process was very thorough. I had three interviews, the first with a panel of teachers, clerical staff, parents, and other site administrators. The second interview was with the superintendent, and the last interview was with the school board. The process took three weeks with callbacks for the second and third interviews. By the time the third interview had finished, I knew which job I wanted. As I left the last interview, my closing comment was, "If I'm selected, you will be getting two for the price of one, as my wife and I are a team."

When I received the call, I was thrilled. I was going to be part of the Santa Cruz City School District and the principal of Westlake Elementary School, a California Distinguished School. I had to wait to notify Chico Unified School District until after the board approved my appointment in July.

I left Chico in late July and traveled to my new home in Santa Cruz. When I saw my new school, I was amazed. At first, I thought it was part of the University of California, Santa Cruz, as they were located next to each other. In a tri-level property, primary grades were below, offices and library in the middle, and the intermediate grades were on the third level. What a stunning and beautiful site!

Cars came in one way and drove out the other. I thought, *Hmm ... It must be interesting before and after school, getting in and out for students and parents.*

I soon learned that parking in front of the school was one of my first challenges.

One of the first people I met when I began working was my new secretary. Let's just say that Ebby turned out to be a gift from heaven. She was the consummate professional, and she always welcomed everybody with a big smile. Her guidance and advice were helpful as I transitioned to a new reality.

The second staff member had been on the interview panel. She was a jewel. Her name was Sharon. She taught intermediate grades and had asked me during the interview if I was going to change anything. As an example of the quality of her professionalism and dedication, three months before her retirement, she asked to go to an in-service to improve instructional strategies. She said, "I think I can learn something to help my teaching." She was a life-long learner, constantly looking for ways to improve.

My new wife of three weeks and I set up our household in a small apartment located two blocks from the beach in Capitola. We walked on the beach every evening, talked, and ate in the nearby Mexican restaurants. As we met people and introduced ourselves, upon finding out which school I had selected, I usually heard a resounding, "Good luck." There are different tones of voice when you wish someone good luck. The one we heard had a touch of sarcasm.

"It's a difficult school," I heard. "Parents are very influential and have high expectations for the principal."

I met the outgoing principal. She also said, "Good luck!"

I was glad that being a principal was not my first rodeo. In one of my first letters to the parents, I spoke of the comments I had been receiving and told them that whatever we accomplished, we would do it together.

"It is a partnership," I wrote. "We will work together for common goals and outcomes."

The theme seemed to resonate with the parents. I was sure they would give me a chance to succeed. On the first day, I met the staff one by one, as I had sent out a letter asking them to stop by if they had time. It was not mandatory, but everyone stopped in except one teacher. When I met her for the first time at the district in-service training, I said, "Well, it's about time we met."

Yikes! My attempt at humor went south. She let me know in no uncertain terms how inappropriate my comments were toward her. I had been set up. Someone had said she had a great sense of humor. She wrote me a two-page letter stating that I was out of line big time. I wrote her a letter of apology. I like to think that we became friends and colleagues as the years passed.

54: Camelot in the Twenty-First Century

"Our prime purpose in this life is to help others. And if you can't help them, at least don't hurt them."

-- Dalai Lama

The thirty-first school opening for me began at a new district. Regardless of which school, the first day was always exciting, and I knew that my new school in Santa Cruz, California, would be no different. Two words described my feelings: excitement and humility. I was given a wonderful opportunity to start anew, and I looked forward to making a big contribution. I remembered reading about one of the differences between an expert and a beginner: The expert only has one way, while the beginner is usually more willing to use different ways to find the best course of action. I was an expert with beginner's eyes.

During the first days, I observed and listened. I found at Westlake Elementary School a dynamic group of teachers, a diverse student population with a percentage of students integrated into the school from outside its boundaries, an excellent arts program funded by the parents, and a school that had been declared a California Distinguished School.

Commotion began from the first day and continued each day in the parking lot. This is a pattern at every school, as many parents want to walk their child to their classroom, which creates traffic jams. I was out and about asking drivers to stay in their cars while dropping students off. Parking off campus and walking in was allowed, but it was an inconvenience, as High Street was shared with the University of Santa Cruz commuters. Parking spaces at this school were limited and usually taken by school personnel. We had a problem that needed an urgent solution. After a few days of conversations, the school partnered with the church next to our building. Our agreement was that parents were authorized to use the church parking lot while visiting the school, and church parishioners were authorized to use the school parking lot on Saturdays and Sundays. We also created a committee of volunteer parents and rotating teachers to assist with the flow of cars, minimizing the congestion during peak hours before and after school.

Another issue at the beginning of the year was class placement. It was customary for parents to request certain teachers for their children. In the first week of the school year, more than twenty parents wanted their children switched to a teacher they had requested the previous spring. The myriad of reasons were diverse, some of them were justifiable and compelling, and some were not.

"I don't want my son to be in the same classroom as Peter," one man said.

"I am a single mother, and my child needs a male figure as his teacher," another parent said.

"I don't like his teacher. My daughter had her, and I feel like she didn't make any progress," one more parent added.

I listened to their concerns with attention and respect, and every situation was evaluated with my team of teachers. People outside of the school system don't realize that each new class is structured at the end of the prior year for the current with the receiving teacher present and the goal being to have a balance in each classroom of high-, medium-, and low-achieving students, a combination of boys and girls, and other factors.

Permanent decisions about changes took place two weeks after the beginning of school, because, during the first two weeks, a parent would change his mind once he noticed his child and the new teacher were a good match. Two weeks was a reasonable wait-time to observe whether students had settled into their new class. On very few occasions, it was necessary to change students, because it was in their best interest.

I received a call from the principal who had replaced me in my old district complaining about parents trying to change the teachers that were assigned to their children.

"Hold firm," I told him. "The staff and I worked very hard for many hours to balance classes and to create successful classrooms."

Parking lot and class-placement challenges were common problems at each school that I managed. Observing, listening, and brainstorming solutions with my team of parents and teachers always worked. From time to time, new situations surfaced, such as the parent who parked his car plastered with vulgar bumper stickers in the school parking lot. One of the stickers read, "When I honk, show your tits."

"You can't park your car on school grounds," I told him. "Your stickers are offensive to the school community."

"I have the right of freedom of speech," he answered. "It is amazing how many women show me their tits when I honk."

We went back and forth regarding his rights versus other people's rights, mainly the rights of the children. Initially he agreed to park off campus, but during the rainy season, he returned to the parking lot and covered his car with a tarp that eventually blew off with the wind, leaving the situation at stage zero again. The parents called the police, and I notified the district, but his rights of expression overruled the best interests of the children.

Parking lots at schools have the reputation of being a place where parents gather to chat. Rumors and gossip begin there. I had to address situations that were untrue and that created unnecessary harm to the general school environment. It required a tremendous amount of patience and a big dose of forgiveness to deal with exaggerations, disagreements that escalated, or just flat made-up stories about a teacher or parent. Things became Administrator 101, Damage Control.

Every school has bullies, and Westlake was not an exception. A parent visited me explaining in detail that her child was being bullied on the playground and that it had been going on for a couple of years.

"I will investigate and get back to you," I told her.

Upon calling her son into my office, he told me, "Everybody gets bullied on the playground."

With additional interviews, I spotted the perpetrators and discussed the Golden Rule with them. However, the issue was bigger than what I had imagined. Coincidentally, a conference was being offered in San Jose about bullies on campus. I got together with the parent who had brought the issue to me, and we decided to go to the conference together. The first question the facilitator asked was, "Were you ever bullied in school? How many of you have memories of being bullied?"

Every hand went up.

The next question really hit home: "Do you remember the person's name who bullied you?"

Every hand went up! There was such power in that question! I clearly remembered the names of the ones who laughed at me when I stuttered, the library boys, and the ones who made fun of me when I wore the red shoes to school.

We left the conference with tools to instill a new paradigm at Westlake. I visited every class and made a presentation about the issue of bullying, specifically raising awareness about the four major types of bullying: verbal, physical, exclusionary, and cyber bullying. After my last presentation, I asked the students to vote on a name for our program since they were the sixth graders and the oldest students in the school.

"NBA," one student said. "No Bullies Allowed."

The students loved it and took pride in our school slogan "No Bullies Allowed." The parent who attended the conference with me was willing to conduct an after-school session for students who had been victims of bullying. She also trained students to observe situations during recess and to intervene when disagreements between students had the potential to become a problem. These students learned the skills to create a peaceful atmosphere at our school. We called them School Ambassadors, and, with students helping other students, the incidents of bullying were dramatically reduced. Each year, I revisited the rules and types of bullying to maintain consistency of enforcement, and I trained new Ambassadors. We became a true Bully-Free Zone!

I found a favorite spot for reflections at the end of each day before heading home: the school's third level from where I had a view of the Pacific Ocean with green pine trees surrounding me on the left and right. Complementing this place were cool breezes coupled with a mild climate. Gratitude filled my heart each day of the seven years that I spent as a principal at Westlake. My new world was blessed with a truly supportive and caring group of co-administrators. From my new superintendent to all of the district personnel, I had found a team that provided me with a newfound sense of value and support, which was very refreshing to say the least. With only six elementary schools in the district compared to the seventeen in Chico, I experienced more district involvement, as we six principals were on the same district-wide committees. The district felt like Camelot led by a kind and experienced leader.

55: Is There a Minute to Spare?

"In times of great stress or adversity, it is always best to keep busy, to plow your anger and your energy into something positive."

-- Lee Iacocca

When I interviewed for the job at Westlake, I was asked what I thought about the importance of the arts in the curriculum. "I am a strong proponent of the arts as an integral part of the core curriculum," I said. "Math, science, and technology are crucial subjects to grasp, but creativity, shapes, and colors are used to create the chassis of a new Ford model."

Little did I know that Westlake had the best art program funded by parents that I had ever seen. It provided arts instruction in music, dance, band, visual arts, and murals. An annual arts fair highlighted the year's progress in all the facets of the Arts. It started at 8:00 a.m. and culminated with the students' orchestra performance at 8:00 p.m. We had more than one hundred thousand dollars in grants and funds provided by parents to hire art teachers and to buy equipment for the program. Ken and Rachel, college and university professors, were two of the most dynamic parent-leaders I had the privilege to work at the school, as both were fully involved in the success of the arts program. We had a running joke of who was Ken One and who was Ken Two. To this day, he won't let me call him Ken One. Both of these parents became board members of the Santa Cruz City School District.

I had two different outstanding art directors, Ziggy and Dorothy, who kept the everyday operations functioning smoothly during my tenure as principal. A video was made of the various art projects completed at the end of each year. For background music to this video, I super-imposed Andrea Bocelli's "My Prayer." This video summary of results and accomplishments, with many hands authoring the creative work produced, was tangible evidence of the arts program at Westlake. Every time I showed the video to promote the program, people wiped away their tears, as it was such a powerful message of hope and celebration.

I began the "Dream Great Dreams" theme again. Within two weeks, we had new wheelchairs donated for students who had been injured on the playground. Before, children were carried up or down the hill. For the second time I began the 2600 Hands theme. It was welcomed, and it quickly became a success. Positive themes contributed to the school climate. The language of success has always worked outside, as well as inside, the classrooms. When students feel safe and cared for, they achieve more. Cognitive achievement is enhanced in a positive school environment where students want to come to school.

At Westlake, we trained our fifth and sixth grade students in conflict-resolution strategies under the direction of one of our parents. The job of these trained ambassadors was to bring conflict resolution to the primary grades during recess and lunch. These Westlake Ambassadors, wearing their bright jerseys, helped the first and second grade classes resolve small conflicts on the playground. The program was very successful at the primary level. Campus supervisors and parent volunteers assisted the intermediate levels.

I began my day outside my office, welcoming students and engaging them with a loud "good morning," a big smile, or a high five. A little boy in first grade used to look for me. He was so small that if you didn't look fast, you might miss him except for one thing. Each day he made sure that I heard his voice saluting me with a loud "Hup, Hup," his right hand touching his forehead with a fast up and down motion. It reminded me of little John F. Kennedy Jr. at his father's funeral. The difference was that his was a happy and friendly salutation. He told me that I was the general of the school. I returned his "Hup, Hup" with a salute, too. Pretty soon every student passing close to me was "hup hupping" and saluting. The whole school was doing it as we crossed each other's path. It began working well at assemblies to get students to settle down.

"Hup, Hup!" I shouted.

They stopped conversations, turned around, and returned the "Hup, Hup." They didn't want to miss it. One day, a parent called to make an appointment with me. In essence, she thought that I was being a militarist by making the students salute me.

"Oh, for goodness sake!" Remember that one?

I told her how it transpired and wrote a column in our newsletter giving credit to the small student who originated our "Hup, hups." It became our special Westlake greeting for hello and welcome. Even the conflict managers used it in their interactions with the primary students.

Another memorable event during my first year at Westlake was the beginning of major renovations to the school. We began by building a small village on the upper playground with eight portables. The primary classes moved first and then the intermediate classes moved next. It was a logistical puzzle that we navigated successfully with the help of district support staff. This was only the second district I had worked in. The difference was that, in this district, the department called support services actually provided support. They were terrific, responded when they were called, and even asked what else needed to be done. With their help, we all offered ideas to make the renovation transitions as painless as possible.

I was an advocate for the teachers, keeping on top of the various aspects of the remodeling. The district had passed a major renovation referendum for all six elementary schools and two junior high schools. It was a massive undertaking. It took us two years to complete the process that involved many meetings with the contractors and with district personnel as we navigated the myriad of big and small issues, including installing two outdoor elevators for students with physical disabilities: one for the primary classes located on the first level, and one for the intermediate classes located on the upper level. It felt like we were constantly moving students from one place to another. The staff remained in good spirits as we made the best of it.

The vibrant arts program, the conflict resolution ambassadors, the renovation meetings, and the regular management of the school kept my calendar busy, but that was not all. Out of approximately six hundred fifty students under my supervision, seventy to eighty were bused to Westlake from the beach area, referred to as

Beach Flats, where a high concentration of Hispanic families lived.

Many years ago, the district had taken this action to achieve a more ethnically and culturally balanced school population. It made our school richer to have a diverse blend of students. Each month my wife and I attended parent meetings at the Beach-Flats Community Center to discuss their issues and find ways to enrich their experience at Westlake. It was a plus that my wife, a Hispanic woman, spoke Spanish and helped facilitate the communications.

The school had gone through a transition from bilingual classes back to traditional ones before I had arrived. In my third year, our theme became "Every Child Our Future – Diversity Our Strength." We dedicated our resources to provide opportunities for each of our students to dream, to learn, and to achieve.

Three years after I began working at Westlake, the whole school community, the city, the state, and the country were shocked in disbelief and overwhelmed by sadness. I was up at 5:30 in the morning that fateful day, and in the process of getting ready to leave for school, I turned on the television. Then, I saw the news reporting that an aircraft had hit the twin towers. I had not gotten over my initial surprise when I watched a second plane hitting the towers again. September 11, 2001 marked the beginning of mourning, cries, anger, and a resolute desire for revenge for what we were convinced was unjustified and evil. I drove to the school in a complete state of shock while listening to the news on the radio. Another plane hit the Pentagon, and one crashed in a field.

I arrived at the school earlier than usual. I remember,

as if it was today, getting into the office that I shared with my secretary and the librarian, since we were in our second year of renovations, and the main office was being remodeled. I dropped my suitcase, called to cancel appointments, and began visiting classes to tell students that we were safe. I decided not to alarm the primary students but spoke straightforwardly with the intermediate classes. Many parents didn't send their children to school, and some came to pick them up as they really didn't know the extent of the terrorist attack. It was a day that I will remember for the rest of my life. A tragedy of this proportion didn't need to happen, and it was done by the hands of people who had benefited from training received in one of our aviation schools in our own country. Prayers, memorials, and other activities were organized at our school to honor the lost lives. Even though we aimed toward healing, September 11 was never the same for any of us.

56: Camelot No More

You win by working hard, making tough decisions, and building

coalitions.

-- John Engler

A lot of big changes were happening at our school and at the district level. New challenges faced our district as our beloved superintendent was retiring, and budget issues had to be resolved.

A committee comprised of the principal of each elementary school, parent representatives, and staff members was formed to discuss the closure of two of our elementary schools. A list of criteria ranked them according to facilities, size, ability to house additional students, and whatever intangibles we could muster. It was a long, tedious, and tense process full of antagonism. Finally, we decided which schools were best suited for closure: Gault and Branciforte Elementary Schools, both of which were located on the east side of Santa Cruz. We sent this recommendation to the district.

At the next board meeting, the room was filled with parents from all the schools. Each school's principal sat with them. The atmosphere was unbelievably charged with passion. We all went to the meeting thinking that the recommendation made by the committee, after many nights of consideration and discussion, would be accepted. Branciforte Elementary School had accepted the fact that they were going to be closed as an elementary school and be used for another district school program.

The day of the board meeting, a board member suggested that the closures should be balanced by geographical area: one school in the east side and the other in the west side. He added that he had driven by the one school that he felt should close, which was Bay View Elementary.

In the span of a few minutes, the die was cast in a different direction. Another school had been chosen, and the battle began again. There was a huge outcry from Bay View advocates, which compelled everybody to revisit their choice. Now the focus was being placed on either Westlake Elementary School, Natural Bridges, or Bay View—the three schools on the west side of Santa Cruz. The pressure shifted to one of them. All three schools had exemplary programs; however, the local charter school had made an offer to house and rent the facilities of whatever school was closed. They were already holding a few classes at Westlake, and we felt the possibility that our school was going to be the one.

Uncertainty floated in the air. After further turmoil, the decision was to close Branciforte Elementary School on the east side and Natural Bridges on the west side. The teachers, the clerical staff, and the students of the closed schools would be consolidated into the four remaining school sites.

The news about the Natural Bridges school closure shook the very core of the district beyond belief. Natural Bridges was one of the best schools, with a rich heritage gained over many years and plenty of space to handle additional students. Dismantling it seemed unreal. The school that the committee had initially recommended for closure had the smallest school site, but the decision was irrevocable.

Westlake and Bayview began the process of receiving personnel from Natural Bridges. Parents, teachers, and clerical staff were given a chance to request the school of their choice. The transition was difficult. The Natural Bridges school community was in mourning. Some of the teachers came to work wearing their Natural Bridges sweatshirts. I did my best to blend the two staffs and students into a cohesive group. I created a theme to fit the new situation: "Get On Board the Westlake Express." I used the train metaphor because train cars are connected and inter-dependent; they have a direction, a destination, and a purpose. Also, passengers are accustomed to trains being one of the safest means of transportation. Westlake was building a new team where the most important element was to instill a sense of security and belonging. Working together and staying together would be crucial to the wellbeing of students and meeting our objective of academic excellence and a safe environment for all. The task was not easy, but, together, we made it work.

To tell the truth, a few teachers and parents on both sides didn't want it to work, which made the process of coming together harder. Sabotage is too extreme a word to describe their reactions; it was more like ongoing resistance. However, we needed to address over and over their phrase "We didn't do it that way at our other school." These were two long years of healing, but teachers and staff were professional and always put the needs of their students first.

One of my first decisions was to completely redo the

new kindergarten portable. It had been an issue the previous year because the district had decided to go with a doublewide portable instead of a larger triple-wide. When the teachers arrived from Natural Bridges, they were able to bring with them their renovation funds to help with the transition. We had an oversight committee who voted to remove the doublewide and put a triple-wide in its place. Much to the dismay of the district, the oversight committee agreed with the teachers and approved the replacement. The train was still on track and fortunately not derailed by the first big decision in the blending process.

We slowly found ways to reach agreements as a team. Many times and in many ways I had to keep the team on track to weather various storms, which meant being available and being a good listener. The new staff was hurting and feeling out of place, and I often acted as counselor as well as principal. I needed to be calm, to stay the course, and to seek positive results. I knew that at some point I would need to leave this train station to seek other opportunities, and a new principal would have to take the school to the next level. I was at peace with that revelation as I continued managing the "Westlake Express" successfully.

57: Leaders Are More Effective with Strong Teams

"If your actions inspire others to dream more, learn more, do more, and become more, you are a leader."

-- John Quincy Adams

One tradition that my wife and I began at Westlake was to dress up for Halloween and lead the Westlake Halloween parade, which was held late in the morning at the end of academic activities. Parents, teachers, and staff dressed up as characters of history or children's literature. I announced each class as they began parading for others to see. Every year, a month prior to Halloween, students were curious and began asking me what my wife and I were going to be. The first year we were Caesar and Cleopatra, the second year we both wore Cat in the Hat costumes, the third year Woody and Jesse, the fourth year Roaring Twenties zoot suiters, the fifth year Winnie the Pooh and Tigger, the sixth year Robin Hood and his Merry Maid, and the seventh year the Musketeer and Damsel in Distress.

It was fun, and the children loved seeing us participating and leading the parade. For us, the purpose was being involved. Priority number one for me was building and maintaining a positive school environment, which is why I fully participated in school activities. My wife and I attended school art fairs, life lab events, sixth grade science camps, back-to-school nights, school carnivals, yo-yo assemblies, and so on. She took all the school pictures from prior years and organized them in albums by dates and categories, creating archives that we were proud to show at other events to promote our programs. Her involvement was a testimonial of what I stated during my interview for the position: "She and I are a team. You're getting two for the price of one."

My office had two doors: one connected to the secretary's office and the other, to the left of my desk, connected to a small, outside patio that we cemented, decorated with benches and plants, and used it for parent conferences and lunches with the student council. My pre-K teacher asked me if she could put her little dollhouse on that patio for the children to play in.

"Sure," I said. "It will be a nice place for it."

A few things began happening in that area. Littering was found. Little chairs were moved and found leaning against the wall. One morning when I arrived, I was told that the playhouse door was locked and the window had the shades drawn. It was a six-by-eight-foot dollhouse, and we couldn't get inside! We were puzzled and intrigued when we heard someone snoring loudly inside. I called the police. When they arrived, I heard the most absurd piece of information: "By law, we can't do anything as long as the shades are drawn."

The person could stay inside for as long as he or she wanted. I quickly asked for some food and water. With coffee and bagels in hand, I knocked at the door.

"Do you want some breakfast?" I asked.

The nightly guest willingly came out. He had been

sleeping in our little house for a couple of weeks, but this was the first time he had overslept. He asked if we were going to continue providing breakfast. As he was leaving, he said, "Hey, man, I'm just keeping Santa Cruz weird!"

This was an expression that I had heard before, and had seen it on bumper stickers. I guess there was some meaning behind it.

We put our own lock on the house, and the police patrolled the school surroundings for three weeks until we were sure that the night visitor had chosen a different hotel.

A principal constantly wears many hats. Each day is different. You know what you have on your calendar, but issues and challenges jump out of nowhere. A principal is a facilitator, a counselor, a manager, a problem solver, and, overall, has to be a leader to influence others. As an administrator, I wanted all the gears to be smooth and synchronized. Unfortunately, many times I had to adopt the role of disciplinarian. Luckily, my experience prior to my tenure at Westlake was a gold mine, and my credibility in this area was not disputed.

I had two kinds of parents: Those who agreed with the teachers and me about disciplinary actions and took it upon themselves to educate their children in the specific matters that needed reinforcement, and the parents who defended their children in spite of repetitive actions and evidence that showed their children breaking school rules. The few really noteworthy issues I had with students usually were a result of family problems spilling over into the school. When rule breaking involved students with special needs, they received my assistance with the school psychologist present. Navigating these situations required patience and understanding.

A student came to my office one day very upset and told me that he really wanted to go to jail. He stood defiantly in front of me and said he was going to pull the fire alarm. I told him to calm down and put myself between him and fire alarm, to keep him from pulling the alarm. He raised his fist menacingly toward me.

I said, "Don't do that."

He slugged me in the stomach, right in front of my secretary, which took me by surprise because I wasn't expecting it. As I doubled over in pain, he pulled the fire alarm. Reflecting on this episode, I am overwhelmed by empathy for all school personnel who have experienced violence and abuse in different shapes and forms from students. Some of these episodes have resulted in shootings that devastated entire communities.

This particular student was later arrested and spent more than five months in juvenile detention for other offenses. It is my understanding that after his release, he was given additional support and the necessary counseling to move forward. I want to take this opportunity to thank the skilled group of special education teachers and psychologists who worked for me, especially a school psychologist named Will, with whom I developed a friendship that has lasted for years. We exhausted all of our resources to help students with special needs.

My last year at Westlake Elementary School was very special. Our theme for the year was "Write On!" The train had reached one of the stations to tackle a new focus: the ability for all students to master the skill of writing. With teachers coaching them, they wrote story after story that they proudly read at the annual book fair.

"We didn't do it that way," was a thing of the past. We had come together to work on the tasks ahead of us, including the design for a new play structure on the intermediate playground. At the spring carnival, the play structure was ready for the unveiling. Kids with smiling faces frolicked on the swings and the new play apparatus. The students dedicated their end-of-the-year mural to me, an honor that I will never forget.

58: Celebrating Experience and Faith

"Don't aim for success if you want it.

Just do what you love and believe in, and it will come naturally."

-- David Frost

At the beginning of February, I received a very interesting phone call from Gayle, a good friend of mine who was superintendent/district administrator at a small school district. There were four school districts with the superintendent/district administrator title in Santa Cruz County. They were single school districts with their own school board. They were able to set the direction of their school at the ground level and were protected by the charters that allowed them to remain independent and not be assimilated by a larger district without their approval.

She said to me that the superintendent from one of the small school districts was retiring and that I should apply. I was flattered, expressed my appreciation for her call, and promised that I would think about it. After I got off the phone, my mind began racing. Here I was, happy with my current placement and probably with only a few years left to retirement, receiving the tempting news of another door opening for a promotion and with plenty of possibilities. After a few moments, I had to force my mind to let it go, to concentrate on the tasks of the day.

In March, I talked to my friend again, who said that the time was getting shorter for me to apply.

"Thanks for your encouragement," I said. "I'll apply. I have nothing to lose."

"If you are selected, you will love it," she said. "It offers you a chance to lead your own district."

Her words struck a chord with me. I had always been a middle manager. Here was a chance to do it my way.

I wanted to keep my decision of applying for the job very quiet in case it wasn't the right fit for me. I had survived renovations and the recent merging of staffs and students, and was looking forward to continuing my work at Westlake. A few days after applying, I received a call stating that I had been chosen to interview for the job. The interviews were happening as soon as Saturday of that week.

"My youngest daughter is getting married on Saturday. Can I interview another day?"

"Interviews are on Saturday only," she said.

"Thank you for the opportunity," I answered. "I have to decline the interview, because I need to be at my daughter's side at her wedding."

A few minutes later, I received another call:

"What time is the wedding?"

"Two p.m."

"Can you interview at seven a.m. on Saturday?"

I paused, thought for a moment, and answered yes. I was going to have enough time to interview and to go to the wedding. It was a four-and-a-half-hour drive from Santa Cruz to Chico.

The first interviewing committee was comprised of parents, teachers, and staff. The questions were predictable. I always hated the question about the mistakes I might have made in my career.

"In a career of over thirty-seven years in education, the last twenty years in administration, I am sure that I have made mistakes. However, from each misstep I have learned to be a better listener, to take time to make the right decision, and to find the lessons hidden behind the mistakes."

One of the parents implied that I had not answered the question. She was right in the sense that I didn't mention specific examples because, out of the many, none came to mind. However, I shared with them that I would not have been successful if I hadn't corrected any shortcomings along the way.

After I left that first interview, I was scheduled for an interview with the board of trustees. The board was evaluating whether I was a good fit. Meanwhile, I was sizing up the board to see if they were the right fit for me. The key to my future success hinged on the relationship between the board and me. I was impressed by the quality of professions that made up the board. They were levelheaded business people: dynamic, smart, loyal, and dedicated to the preservation of their small district at all costs. They were very proud of the school heritage and desired to maintain its status within the community.

One board member asked, "What if I disagree with something you want to do?"

"I would have to do a better job of convincing you of my position," I said. "In the end, the board has the final say. All I ask is that you hear me out before you make a final decision on the issue at hand."

As I left the interview, I felt very good. I knew I could work with them. As my wife and I drove to Chico to make it in time for the wedding, I was at peace with the interview process. When we arrived, I realized in my haste that I had not packed a belt for my suit. We rushed to a nearby Walmart to buy a belt. In that moment, my phone rang. It was the school asking if I could return for a final interview on Sunday at 4:00 p.m.

When I arrived for the final interview, I felt more relaxed. They asked me to look at the budget for the district and to make some assumptions. After looking at the bottom line, I asked, "Why are the reserves so high?"

"Thirty to forty percent is necessary as a protection for the solvency of the district," was the answer.

"I understand," I said. "I would still look for ways to bring new revenues to the district for specific purposes."

I looked at the salaries of teachers and staff. I realized that this was an area that needed improvement without affecting the healthy reserve. When I left, I knew that if I was offered the job, I would take it. After four days, I was offered the job and signed my intent to accept it with a contract that the district secretary brought to me at the Safeway Supermarket parking lot in an effort to keep the confidentiality of my decision to accept the new job until it could be stated publicly.

When I was officially approved by the board of trustees, I announced my decision to the superintendent of the Santa Cruz City School District, my staff, parents, and the students at Westlake. I had spent seven years at Westlake, a great school that I loved. In order to grow professionally as a superintendent at a school district that allowed me to continue direct contact with students, I had to make the move.

The last four months at Westlake were filled with mixed feelings. My teams were all in place, and good things were happening, but I knew that a new principal could continue and create new paths, free of the turmoil and past decisions by the district. The staff was complimentary and planned a lavish going-away party in a beautiful setting. The highlight of the evening was twofold: (1) my wife's puppet performance from the perspective of being the principal's wife, and (2) the presentation by the staff of ten Ken dolls depicting the various stages of my career.

Teacher after teacher brought the Cheerleader Ken, the Activities Director Ken, the Injured Ken, Coach Ken, Yo-Yo Teacher Ken, the Arts Ken, the Parade Leaders Ken and Maria, Suntan Ken, Principal Ken, and Older Gray Ken. With each doll, they shared an anecdote or a story. The entertainment was out of this world, with everyone enjoying the festivities and smiling and laughing as we relived the journey through the Ken dolls.

It was bittersweet to leave such a dynamic staff. This party brought special closure to the seven years I served as their principal and friend. In one of my first newsletters at Westlake, Maria and I wrote about the message behind "The Wizard of Oz." The tin man was looking for a heart, the scarecrow was looking for a brain, and the lion was looking for courage. At Westlake, we had a heart to believe that all children were able to achieve given the right opportunities, a brain to design a plan of action to meet the needs of our diverse population with different ability levels, and the courage to embrace change and new teaching practices. Just like the characters in Wizard of Oz, we realized that what we were searching for had been inside us all along. We just had to discover it and harness it.

59: Close Proximity with Mother Nature

"Life is full of beauty. Notice it.

Notice the bumblebee, the small child, and the smiling faces.

Smell the rain, and feel the wind.

Live your life to the fullest potential, and fight for your dreams."

-- Ashley Smith

So many things were running through my mind as I drove to Mountain Elementary School that first day I became superintendent/district administrator. It was a beautiful drive through the pines, and the smell of the trees was captivating. No more commute problems. I lived eight minutes from the school, which was nestled in a beautiful location three miles from the Pacific Ocean. Before my first day at the school, I was visited by environmentalists requesting me not to allow cell towers to be installed near the school. For the next four years, it was hard to get a cell phone signal because there were no cell towers nearby.

My first introduction to my new secretary had been during the interview. I was leaving the best secretary I had ever had and hoped that my new secretary would be a team player, my right hand, and efficient, as I needed her collaboration to be successful. I wasn't disappointed. Betty became a person I could count on, and in a small school setting, loyalty and confidentiality were intertwined and tantamount to our success when students' sensitive issues were handled. I knew I would have to gain her trust but was excited about the new adventure together. She was open to my vision for our future and extremely important to our collective efforts in meeting our goals.

When I asked about the programs that currently existed, I learned that each class performed a musical with sets, music, and students playing different roles. There were seven K-6 teachers, and each one had internalized that this co-curricular responsibility had to be developed each year. During my four years at Mountain, teachers excelled preparing and delivering students' quality performances. By the time students graduated, they had overcome their shyness, were able to speak in front of an audience, and at graduation, each one gave a commencement speech. With a graduating class of approximately eighteen to twenty students, it was a realistic expectation and requirement.

My first action item as a superintendent was to address a serious issue that had been left for me to resolve. I was informed that a student from the previous year was not allowed to return in the fall, due to a condition that might require special accommodations. Since she didn't live in the district, it was determined that we were unable to provide for her educational needs. I had just received a letter from her parents requesting a meeting with the board to discuss the issue. They were bringing their attorney as well. After reading all of the documents, I knew that it was not within our purview to deny services to one of our students based on a reasonable accommodation. We settled the issue by re-enrolling the student. Her parents and grandparents were appreciative of the resolution based on what was best for this student.

One of my fondest memories is of this young person giving her speech at graduation. I had chills and tears of joy. She had thrived at Mountain School. Through much great effort on her part, she persevered.

As I settled in, I met with each one of the staff to get to know them and to listen to their concerns and suggestions. I found that the sense of community had been fractured. Some felt isolated. There was a division between upper and lower grades. They had used the teacher's union to mediate grievances and to dispute teacher evaluations. They were unhappy with their compensation and wanted better health benefits.

A salary raise is a big motivator. These teachers had not had a raise in many years. I analyzed the possibilities in our budget and immediately authorized a raise that, over a period of nine months, equaled 7 percent. With that, their compensation became more in line with comparative districts.

Academically, our scores were in the 700 range on the state test, but for a small school of our size we should have been well over 800. Within four years, we established school-wide targets to improve literacy and reading, and we instituted a systemic program for math. Each year, we made significant growth culminating with a score over 900. Through collaboration and hard work, we were able to meet our targeted numbers. Our staff meetings were small but intense. Once we began working together, the connectivity to each class and its importance on the continuum of the general K-6 curriculum improved systematically.

The new leadership style soon created not only academic improvement but also social, political, and cultural changes. Staff, parents, and students embraced the positive approaches. The parents were a tremendous asset at the school. They consistently supported the arts, music, and musical performances. At previous schools, I had always tapped into parent groups as a means to help support the co-curricular programs for the benefit of all students. At Mountain Elementary, I initially ran into a problem as I came to expect their support right away rather than building rapport to achieve the same end.

This is one area that I would have done differently if I had to do it over again. With time, they realized that some of the expectations for their children could be met with their financial collaboration, as schools had limited and restricted funds. In the four years that I was superintendent, the arts were fully funded, thanks to the help and support of the parents' club.

I found in my new office a beautiful large fish tank with all kinds of fish, a gift left by the previous superintendent. My father had raised fish when I was a child, and the large angelfish reminded me of my own elementary school years. There was a ledge above the tank where I placed the Ken dolls given to me at the Westlake Elementary School farewell party. All of them were there, lined up from young Ken to gray-haired Ken. This was a conversation piece, as visitors were always curious as to why they were in my office. When school opened, and I met the parents for the first time, one of them asked if she could talk to me in private. I asked her to come into my office. She told me she was offended by the Ken dolls. She said that it was sexist that only men were portrayed as attaining success, which sent the wrong message to young girls.

"I had never thought of that," I said, "but I am willing to remove them." She paused for a few moments and said she wanted to add to my Barbie doll collection, depicting ten careers to which girls can aspire.

A few months later, I had ten Barbie dolls in my office portraying the roles of lawyers with suits, nurses in white uniforms and stethoscopes in hand, teachers with pencils carrying notebooks, doctors, astronauts, veterinarians, engineers with a hardhat, and the president! The twenty dolls lived in my office until I retired.

The first week at Mountain, I met the peacocks. There was a muster of them—ten to fifteen. They were gorgeous, but loud and messy, and loved to perch on the lunch tables to relieve themselves. It was crucial to double sanitize the student eating area. We tried to relocate them to no avail. During the fall, they were in courtship mode and attacked the parked cars as they walked near them upon seeing their reflection. In spite of that, it was hard not to like them. The school's location was secluded and had a pristine environment surrounded by nature. Three miles from the ocean, and yet it might as well have been three thousand miles. It was idyllic. I found myself mesmerized by the sounds of chickens and roosters welcoming each new morning and the presence of the peacocks with their beauty and grace. They were part of the experience at Mountain.

It was fitting that, at the last stop in my career as an educator, my new school had to have gophers too! You would think that I would have had an answer by now to eradicate them, but you would be wrong. They were still a headache. They literally destroyed the play field, so I hired a gopher eradicator who was successful at making a significant impact in reducing their number and improving the play fields at the same time. I also give credit to the local bobcat that assisted us; we could see it in the distance sitting on the fence by the baseball field, waiting to catch gophers and disappearing into the wilderness. We had specific rules for students not to go to the baseball field without adult supervision because of the bobcat sightings.

Swallows built nests on our buildings, too. They came each year by the thousands, but we were not allowed to disturb them. They were messy, and defecated by the front door of a few classrooms. It was one of the adjustments everybody had to make in order to cohabitate with nature.

Adding to our menagerie of animals were a pig and a horse. They were our neighbors, separated from our school by a chain-link fence. An apple tree was on our property. Most of the apples landed in our courtyard, but occasionally they ended up in the pasture on their side of the fence. The pig was huge and very smart. Students were allowed to pick apples from the ground to throw to the horse and pig, and almost every time, even if the apple was thrown very close to the horse for his enjoyment, that pig would run as fast as it could to steal it from the horse. It was theatrical, and we got a huge kick out of those two. In a strange way, they were part of the ambiance of the school named Mountain.

I was curious and asked about the history behind the school name, as the terrain was completely flat.

"Have you ever been to the quarry where rocks are collected to make cement and road gravel?" I was asked. "It is only a few miles up the winding road."

I had seen the trucks every day racing down the narrow road with full loads. I decided to visit it one morning prior to the beginning of my day. When I arrived, I was amazed at the variety of rocks and their sizes. A foreman walked toward me. After introducing myself to him, we chatted.

"If you need any rocks, you're welcome to take them," he said.

"Not right now, but maybe later," I said.

As I drove back to the school, "a piece of the mountain" idea came to my mind. What about if each student who graduated from Mountain took a piece of the mountain with them? After that, at every graduation ceremony, I presented each student with a piece of the mountain on a wooden plaque. My wife picked the wood already cut at a nearby lumberyard, painted the plaques with varnish, and glued an inspirational sentence on each one. Meanwhile, I went to the quarry to choose the rocks by shape and size, and took them home for my wife to clean and place on the wood with the name of each student. It was a team effort that didn't cost any money, but created a memory for students—a handmade memento to keep after departing to pursue higher dreams. Each rock was unique, just like each one of the students. The rocks represented strength and the solid education the students had received at Mountain, the foundation for their next level of learning.

60: A Stretch to the Top

"Only a man who knows what it is like to be defeated can reach down to the bottom of his soul and come up with the extra ounce of power it takes to win when the match is even."

-- Muhammad Ali

There were tragedies throughout my career that were not in the book on how to be an administrator. I had to drive a teacher to the hospital because her husband was in critical condition. When we arrived, he had just passed away.

There was a small student whose leg had been amputated because of cancer. I was unaware of that until she said to me that she was not very good with her new leg yet. Then, she rolled up the hem of her Levi's to show me her prosthetic leg. Her smile and resiliency were humbling. I had lost my own son, an accident that never left my heart, so I could only imagine the grief this little girl's parents had endured during her cancer ordeal.

One of the most traumatic incidents in my career was the loss of one of my independent-study program students at Mountain. This program was one of a kind. A class of twenty-six students, ranging from first grade to sixth grade, attended three days a week. They were like a family—the older ones helped the little ones. They were part of our school community and participated in everything, including the musicals, physical education, parades, fall festival, and the arts.

On one occasion, one of the students named Pippin planned a birthday party and invited his whole class. It was held at the beach after school one late afternoon. While the students were playing on the side of a sand dune, it collapsed and buried three of the boys. It was so sudden that by the time they were rescued, Pippin didn't survive this terrible accident. The loss was devastating to all. Profound grief took over our school. We were fortunate to have such a caring county superintendent who immediately sent his staff of school psychologists and grief counselors to help our community handle this tremendous loss. The boy's parents were simply the most wonderful and caring people. We all shared in their heartache. The school community came together in support.

At his service, the parents described their loving child in the most beautiful way. Pippin loved life and was a gentle soul. He had tried different sports including sailing at a young age. He was smart and had mature answers to situations when they arose. Honoring that, his parents made bumper stickers that read "What would Pippin do?" It was a call to action for us to never forget him and to be more like him. I kept his bumper sticker on my desk, and never forgot the message behind it: to do the right thing, because that is what Pippin would have done.

Months later, when we were forced to look for ways to save money for the school district, the possibility of closing the independent-study program seemed to be the most cost effective solution. As it played out, I found a creative way to save the program. At a meeting of the ten superintendents in our county, I asked if anyone would be willing to take on our independent study program including the funding for it. We would charge a nominal fee to use our portable classroom, but they could have the funding source. We would then come under a different formula and not have to close the program completely.

After a long silence, one of my colleagues said she would do it. She knew it was only a few thousand dollars for her district. When I asked her why she did it, she said: "It is the right thing to do."

How I admired her in that moment for her courage. Pippin's memory came to mind. I felt like he was smiling at me from heaven. The plan worked. The independent study program operated on our campus under the direction of another district. The students were not forced to leave what they had known as their school.

Another kind of tragedy was the act of school vandals destroying resources that had been hard to get and had come from hardworking citizens. On one occasion, I received a phone call from the sheriff at three o'clock in the morning informing me that our school had been vandalized. I immediately got up, dressed in a hurry, and drove to the school. When I arrived, I saw the damage. Front windows had been broken with a huge boulder, which was left at the scene. The vandals had just barely missed the large fish tank in my office with that boulder. More than ten windows had been damaged.

The sheriff shared the news that there had been a rash of vandalisms attacking businesses and schools within the county. We were very isolated, and it seemed odd that ours was targeted. My calendar for that day changed drastically as window-repair personnel had to be called to install new windows. A security camera system was ordered.

Before we could install the new gate with cameras, the vandals struck again. They broke the same windows again. We were heartbroken and couldn't understand why someone would have such a strong desire to damage our small school. We never found out who did it. The cameras and new gate kept the vandals at bay.

Being an advocate of students with special needs was close to my heart. I'd had a disability as a child. Throughout my career, I felt like a champion of special needs students. I worked closely with the staff to make their learning experience the best it could be. We invested time and energy meeting their individual needs. With supportive parents, the school psychologist, the resource teacher, and the classroom teacher we developed learning plans for success. One student once said to us, "Can you fix me now before I get too old?"

It was a challenge, but collectively we gave it our best. During my career, a few parents blamed their children's failures on the school system without realizing that they were creating roadblocks for their children's success. This was the case in a few instances at Mountain. Fortunately, our special education team was competent. Will, our school psychologist, worked well with the parents and me. We had an important vision in common: to do the best for the children and their families.

By the end of my fourth year at Mountain, I was finishing my two-year service as a representative to the small schools statewide committee. The news had been getting worse and worse for the state funding of schools. As I left the last meeting of the year, my head was full of information about dark times coming with additional budgets cuts that were going to affect school programs and personnel, including administrators. I knew it was time to consider passing the torch of my leadership. I had established, with the help of the board of trustees and staff, a fiscally solvent school budget for the coming years including a special funding source for modernization that gave the district latitude on how best to spend the money. In a time when other districts were drowning, we were on solid ground. Our test scores were soaring as we passed the 900 mark, and our working environment was positive and conducive to more growth. We had aligned the curriculum in math, language arts, and the arts, and made sure that the continuum of learning would build each year on the past year's work. I facilitated mastermind meetings where the faculty and I read and discussed books about the latest pedagogical trends, a practice that helped them to implement instructional strategies. The best practices focus was instrumental to our collective development. Our school themes for each year, "New Beginnings Create New Opportunities," "Reach for the Stars," "Step Up to Learning," and "Engaged Minds Can Move Mountains," were constructive reaffirmations that, not only provided the direction and focus for the year, but also encouragement and hope.

Upon coming home from that last meeting, I told my wife that I had reconsidered my decision to stay at the school for another year. "I'm going to retire at the end of the year."

My partner and best friend gave me the longest hug, as she knew how much I loved being part of the education system and what Mountain Elementary School meant to me. It was not an easy decision, and we held each other tight. The board of trustees was gracious and understood my decision. We had been a good team. One of the members said, "You were the right person at the right time."

I was forever grateful for their trust in allowing me to shepherd this precious academic jewel. As I reflect on the many people who had made a difference, I would be remiss in not thanking the Mountain Elementary School Board of Trustees. They were smart, inquisitive, involved, caring, and a source of continued strength throughout my tenure. With their support, I was able to bring the district forward to the desired outcomes.

61: Farewell

My last assembly at Mountain was also my last year in public education, the end of a forty-two-and-a-half-year journey working with young adults and children. That day I was presented with four rocks from the quarry. The rocks had been placed on a wooden plaque, one for each year at Mountain, and the plaque was adorned with a large peacock ornament. I was so touched and could hardly contain tears of joy to have had the unique opportunity of closing this chapter of my life at such a wonderful school.

With a certain degree of nostalgia, the last day I sat in my superintendent/district administrator chair looking out at the panorama from my office, I reflected on the principles that made me successful at schools, opened my iPad, and wrote the following inventory to share with others:

1) Organize, don't agonize.

2) Dreams come true when action plans are created and implemented as soon as possible.

3) Engage in forward thinking and thinking outside the box.

4) Reinforce the skill of listening to teachers, staff, parents, and students.

5) Create a sense of community; work hard to achieve a positive school climate that is progressive and inclusionary.

6) Promote sustainable collaboration.

7) Add value to teachers and staff through professional development to support a school-wide commitment to improved academic achievement for all students.

8) Promote the concept of teaching the whole child by pledging to maintain the co-curricular programs of art, music, and school activities.

9) Always keep in mind this question: "How will this decision affect the students?"

10) Have an open-door policy, and make yourself accessible.

I began placing my personal belongings in a box and found an old picture that had been given to me by one of my students way back when I was teaching high school. He was always drawing cartoons during his government class. One day I asked him what he was drawing. He showed me a funny-looking mountaineer climbing to the top of a mountain. He handed it to me and said, "Here, you can have it. You are always talking to us about the need for us to do well, to increase our performance, and to reach to the top." Everyone laughed. I took that piece of paper and kept it for over thirty-five years. How ironic to find it when I was leaving Mountain Elementary School. I dreamed great dreams, and the progression of my career placed me at the top of the Mountain.